HISTORY OF THE WORLD WAR

BY

FRANK H. SIMONDS

AUTHOR OF "THEY SHALL NOT PASS"—VERDUN

FULLY ILLUSTRATED

VOLUME ONE

THE ATTACK ON FRANCE

GARDEN CITY   NEW YORK
DOUBLEDAY, PAGE & COMPANY
1919

HISTORY OF THE WORLD WAR

THE SPIRIT OF FRANCE

TO MY WIFE

PREFACE

The World War, entering its thirty-fourth month, as these lines are written, has had three distinct phases, both on the military side and on the larger and more significant human side. The three military phases are supplied by the Marne campaign and its immediate consequences; the Russian campaign, with its Balkan episode and its Verdun ending; the Allied offensive in the west, which began at the Somme in July, 1916, and is still proceeding before Arras and along the old Aisne battlefield.

In the Marne campaign Germany sought a complete triumph by a swift and terrible thrust at France, the only one of her foes then in any sense prepared for war. Her thrust was parried at the Marne and permanently blocked at the Yser and at Ypres. Thereafter she had to turn east and restore the failing fortunes of Austria and protect her own imperilled marches.

In the Russian campaign Germany sought to dispose of Russia, as she had endeavoured to dispose of France in the Marne campaign. Immediate success escaped her in this field. Despite terrible defeats and long retreats, Russian resistance was not broken, although the Russian Revolution, now the main factor on the eastern front and unmistakably a consequence of Russian defeat, gives to the German campaign of 1915 a value that was not perceived at the time. What the permanent value will be remains problematical. But as she had to turn east, with her western task incomplete in 1914, Germany had, after a brief and glorious campaign on behalf of her Turkish ally, to return west in February, 1916, and seek at Verdun what she had not attained on the Marne. Her failure there cost her the initiative and condemned her to the defensive.

The campaign which opened at the Somme is still proceeding. Since they began their attack on July 1, 1916, the Allies have steadily, if only slowly, pushed the Germans back and the recent victory of Arras demonstrates that the British army has at last reached a high state of efficiency, while there are signs, far from conclusive to be sure, of a decline in German morale. At all events, the Germans remain on the defensive and the end of this third phase has not come.

Looking now to the broader horizon, it will be perceived that here, too, there are three aspects. In its inception, in the first months of battle, the conflict still seemed to men, not alone of neutral nations but of involved nations, one more war, greater and more terrible than all past wars, but a war comparable to them in origin and purpose.

But as the struggle progressed, it brought more and more clearly to the eyes of men of all nations, save those of Central Europe, the truth that the German attack was something more than a bid for world power; comparable with that of France under Napoleon or Louis XIV, of Spain under Charles V. It became clear that Germany was not attacking armies or nations alone, but also the whole fabric of our common civilization and all the precepts and doctrines of humanity, which represent the slow progress upward from barbarism.

The invasion of Belgium shocked the whole world. The crimes committed by German soldiers in Belgium and northern France, crimes not belonging to the order of excesses incident to war, but crimes ordered by commanding officers for the deliberate purpose of terrifying a helpless population and disarming men by the brutality practised upon women and children, these slowly but surely inclined the balance of neutral opinion against Germany. At first these brutal and bestial crimes only gave new heart and new determination to the nations directly assailed, but in the end they earned for Germany the condemnation of neutral nations the world over.

In its third phase there came, together with the growing anger and detestation of German violence and the clearer perception of the danger of Germanism to all civilization, the recognition that the war was, after all, one more stand of autocracy against democracy, that in its essence the German thing, already become abominable in the sight of all the non-German world, was the final expression of militarism, which had its origin in caste and Crown; that the "Superman" was only the old tyrant in a new disguise.

In this stage we have seen the Russian Revolution and the entrance of our own country into the war. The clearest definition of the war, as it is now seen everywhere save in the Central Empires, has been supplied by the President of the United States in that document which determined in fact, if not technically, American enlistment.

In succeeding volumes I shall endeavour to set forth the development of this world verdict upon German purposes and German methods. In the present volume, I have sought merely to outline the events preceding the war and the first campaigns in the struggle. Not until the first phase was completed had the real character of German menace been established, save in the minds of the French and Belgians on whose soil German armies had written their history of shame. Not until the war had entered its second phase was there apparent that spirit which was to dominate the councils and arm the spirit of the nations allied against Germany. Not until that hour was it to take on, consciously, in the minds of millions, the character of a crusade, a concerted defence of civilization against a new barbarism, which combined the science of the head with barbarism of the heart, the weapons of the Twentieth Century with the spirit of Attila.

And, conversely, when the war did take on this new character it became something different from all wars of which we have trustworthy record—a war fought not for territorial gain or battlefield success, but a war fought between two ideas, two conceptions of life, of civilization, of humanity; two faiths, of which there can be room for but one in this world, since each is utterly destructive of the other.

Tardily, perhaps, but completely in the end, we in America, far removed as we are from the European world, have perceived the issues of the war. Instinctively the mass of men and women, the plain people of the United States, like those of Britain and France, have prevailed over the wisdom of politicians and the doubts of statesmen. Late, but not too late, the nation which had Lexington and Concord in its own his tory, recognized that neutrality was impossible when a new battle for democracy was going forward. And almost at the same moment there has been heard, broken as y et and uncertainly, a new voice in Germany, repeating something of the words that now fill the world outside of the Central Empires. Whatever be the outcome of the war, at least it is certain now that even German things will never be again what they were when Prussian militarism crushed Belgium under an iron heel and German necessity thrust its bayonet through international good faith and common humanity.

My acknowledgments are due both to the French and to the British Governments and General Staffs for the courtesy which permitted me to visit their armies and their battlefields, among others the Marne, Nancy, Champagne, and the Somme, escorted by officers who explained the actions, and for the kindness and frankness with which th ey supplied all information at their disposal. To the interest of the President of France I owe my opportunity to visit Verdun and to meet General Petain during the great battle, and to Field-Marshal Sir Douglas Haig I am indebted for the chance to see the British army and to meet its Commander-in-Chief just before the battle of Arras and to look eastward from Mont St. Eloi at Vimy Ridge, soon to fall to Canadian valour. Nor should I fail to acknowledge here my gratitude to General Dubois, Governor of Verdun, who twice welcomed me to his ruined city and permitted me to visit Fort de Vaux, newly reconquered from the German Crown Prince.

On one other point I desire to make an explanation; the absence of any discussion of naval operations from my narrative is not due to any failure on my part to appreciate the greatness or the importance of the work performed by the fleets, and in an overwhelming majority of cases by the British fleet, but to the fact that it was agreed at the outset that the history of the naval operations of the war should be written for a later volume. The subject is of too great importance to be crowded in the space at my disposal in this volume.

In the years that have followed the outbreak of the war, during which I have been writing steadily about its progress, I have made too many mistakes and been too frequently in error not to appreciate the limitations of the present volume.   It represents merely an effort to interpret fairly and to an American audience the earlier incidents in the world struggle, hitherto mainly explained to Americans by commentators belonging to nations already at war who have reviewed the campaigns from the perspectives of belligerents, and have naturally paid small attention to the point of view of the citizens of a nation separated by its history, by its long neutrality, and by the expanse of the ocean from the conflict.

In so far as I have been able, I have striven to make this book an American comment upon a world war, and no one can be more conscious than am I of its limitations.

                                                        FRANK H. SIMONDS.

Upper Montclair, New Jersey,
May 1, 1917.

CONTENTS

PART I

CHAPTER III
THE TWELVE DAYS

CHAPTER IV
THE GERMAN ATTACK

CONTENTS

CHAPTER V

BELGIAN DEFENCE AND FRENCH OFFENCE

CHAPTER VI

THE BATTLE OF THE MARNE

CHAPTER VII

DEADLOCK IN THE WEST

CHAPTER VIII

THE EASTERN FIELD

CHAPTER IX

THE BATTLE OF LEMBERG

CONTENTS

CHAPTER X
WARSAW

CHAPTER XI
NEW HORIZONS AND NEW GERMAN PROBLEMS

CHAPTER XII
ON THE EAST FRONT TO THE BATTLE OF THE DUNAJEC

CHAPTER XIII

IN THE WEST, NOVEMBER, 1914, TO MAY, 1915

CHAPTER XIV

LIST OF ILLUSTRATIONS

LIST OF MAPS

PART ONE
HISTORY OF THE WORLD WAR
BY
FRANK H. SIMONDS

CHAPTER ONE

EUROPE BETWEEN 1871 AND 1904

I

THE FIRST YEARS

The full generation that lay between the signing of the Treaty of Frankfort and the crisis of Tangier was marked by no very clear and definite march of events. Between the Revolutions of 1848 and the close of the Franco-Prussian War, Europe had lived through a long series of wars, not comparable in magnitude or sacrifice to the Napoleonic and Revolutionary struggles, but sufficiently considerable to satiate the people of the various nations and reconcile the statesmen to pacific policies. Germany, during the years of Bismarck, pursued a moderate course. His greatest concern was to preserve and strengthen the great structure he had reared. If the swift rise of France from defeat led him to a minatory gesture in 1875, he heeded the warnings that came from London and Petrograd. Throughout his period of power he skilfully managed to keep the door to the Russian capital open, and while he detested the British, he never sought to challenge them upon the water.

To be sure, the Russo-Turkish War and the settlement of the Congress of Berlin led to an inevitable estrangement with Russia. Germany, having to choose between Russia and Austria, decided for the Hapsburg, and the Congress of Berlin, by destroying the Treaty of San Stefano, deprived Russia of the fruits of her Turkish triumph, and by putting the Austro-Hungarian Empire, through Bosnia and Herzegovina, on the road to Saloniki, thus made a Franco-Russian alliance inevitable. But in Bismarck's time this alliance was never a threat to German interests nor to German supremacy on the Continent, for Russia was in no mind to undertake the destruction of the Treaty of Frankfort to satisfy her French ally, while France was not willing to invite another invasion to replace the Crescent by the Cross at St. Sophia.

3

In 1881, Bismarck, by clever manipulation, thrust France into Tunis and effectively aided by Crispi, the inveterate foe of France, was able to harvest from Italian anger the entrance of the Italian Kingdom into the Austro-German Alliance, thus creating the Triple Alliance, which was too strong to be challenged by France and Russia, and, as a defensive alliance, served as the corner-stone of European peace until the middle of the first decade of the Twentieth Century.

Great Britain, moreover, inclined rather to the German than to the Franco-Russian group. Her foreign policy was still in the Beaconsfield era. She regarded Russia as her true enemy. She had joined Austria in vetoing the Treaty of San Stefano, as she had persuaded France to join her in the Crimea. Friction between Russia and Britain on the frontiers of the Indian Empire, with France all over the world where colonial enterprises were clashing, contributed to keep alive animosities born of the Crimean and Napoleonic wars. Thus, while nominally pursuing that policy, known in its day as "splendid isolation," Great Britain actually inclined toward the Germans and, while Germany under Bismarck pursued a clearly pacific course, British policy was markedly pro-German.

France, recovering materially from her terrible defeat with an alacrity that alarmed her conqueror, found herself for the time isolated in Europe. Slowly the hope of a reconquest of the "Lost Provinces" weakened in the eyes of the older generation while the newer generation found its attention and its energies consumed in the domestic strife between the Republic and its enemies, in the struggle with Boulangerism, in the battle with the Church, and in that grotesque episode which was the Dreyfus Case. It would not be fair to say that the memory of Alsace-Lorraine was banished from the French mind, but it is true that even Frenchmen believed it had disappeared in the mournful and ignoble years of the nineties. While German population increased by millions, that of France stood still, until France found herself distanced by her great rival and no longer able to match army corps with army corps on the open frontier of the Vosges. For France the years

between Frankfort and Tangier were years recalling the equally unhappy age of Louis XV. And in both periods there were not lacking
those who foretold the disappearance of France as a great nation and
spoke with ready conviction of the decadence of the French race,
forgetting how frequently in past centuries the flame of French genius
had grown dim, only to burst forth with new brilliance and dazzle the
world with its radiance. And in this time not only did the desire for
peace increase with each year in the hearts of the French people, but a
too-eager acceptance of the illusions of pacifism and internationalism
left the nation well nigh defenceless, when the crisis of Tangier brought
France within two steps of war.

In the closing quarter of the Nineteenth Century, too, the Great
Powers, with the exception of Germany and Austria, turned their eyes
beyond Europe and laboured to construct great colonial empires. France
spread her colours from Algiers to the Congo.   Tunis, the Sahara, Sene-
gal, the regions of the Upper Niger, the shores of Lake Chad, and the
vast area between the Congo-Ubangi and the Atlantic were occupied.
Madagascar was conquered.   Indo-China was expanded into a colony
greater than France in area.

Britain on her part kept pace with France in Africa, extended her
Indian Empire, expanded her commercial and political influence in
China, pushed France out of Egypt, and carried her conquests up the
Nile until Cecil Rhodes' dream of a British "all-red route" from the
Cape to Cairo was all but realized.

Russia on her side turned from the disappointments of the Dardanelles to the still unrestricted possibilities eastward to the Pacific
and southward to warm water at Port Arthur.   Siberia began to rival
the American Far West in resources and opportunity and Russia seemed
destined to achieve at the expense of the Chinese what she had missed
in the estates of the Osmanli.

Even Italy, still struggling with the terrible problems of poverty
and misery, also embarked upon the colonial enterprise, only to find
disaster in Abyssinia and military disgrace at Adowa.   Little Belgium,
through the efforts of her able if unscrupulous monarch, acquired the

vast empire of the Congo Free State and took rank with the Great Powers in possessions beyond the seas.

II. A NEW KAISER AND A NEW POLICY

In all this time Germany alone stood still. Great as Bismarck had been as the creator of the German Empire, he lacked the vision to grasp the new horizons. While he remained in power, he gave only contemptuous attention to the colonial ambitions within his own country. He welcomed the concentration of French energy upon colonial expansion because it promised the gradual extinction of the Alsace-Lorraine question. He skilfully turned every opportunity to account in bringing the French and the British into collision. Nor was he less contented to see Russia, forgetful of Constantinople and the Balkans, fixing her eyes upon Vladivostok and Port Arthur.

More than all else, perhaps, this failure of Bismarck contributed to the great catastrophe that he did not live to see. A new Germany was rising, a Germany he neither understood nor recognized. The whole fabric of German life was being made over and Germany was rapidly transforming herself into a great commercial nation, into a factory nation, into a nation whose organization, whose resources in minerals, made her a rival of Great Britain; whose merchant marine was growing by leaps and bounds and carrying the German flag into every sea and every port. This new Germany felt it unjust, immoral, that she, alone of the great nations, she, who had become in fact the most powerful nation on the European continent, should be without her colonies, without lands to which Germans could carry their language and their national faith, colonies which might serve as the markets for German manufactures and the plantations on which could be grown the raw materials needed by German industry.

And it was this Germany that William II represented when at last he came to the throne, speedily "dropped the pilot," and took from Bismarck's control the direction of the policies of an Empire which had been the Iron Chancellor's creation and for long years an instrument in his hands. In his anxiety to preserve what he had brought into being,

Bismarck had withheld Germany from the world competition in colonial expansion, he had submitted to the naval supremacy of Britain, he had smiled upon the Russian adventures in the Far East, he had uttered no protest when Great Britain had added new empires to her vast realms. And the world upon which William II looked when power at last came to him, was a world already parcelled out, with but few and unattractive patches bearing the colour of the German Empire.

In the mind of the new Emperor it was clear from the outset that the real barrier to German development, to rightful German expansion, to the acquisition of that place in the sun that soon appeared in all German patriotic phrase, was Britain. It was Britain who held the fairest spots upon the face of the earth, so far as colonial considerations were concerned. It was British sea power that dominated the trade routes. Moreover, British arms protected the sinking power of Portugal, closed Morocco because it faced Gibraltar, was presently to join with France in an agreement that should bestow upon the Republic this rich and promising colonial field of Morocco, was to conquer the Boer Republics toward which German eyes had been turned, was to lend its support to an American admiral in Manila Bay, when German thoughts turned toward the expiring colonial empire of Spain.

Unless Germany possessed a great fleet, she must be contented to accept British dictation abroad. The dictation was not aggressive, the world had endured British supremacy at sea for nearly a century without too much protest or too great discomfort. But the cardinal doctrine of British policy for centuries had been that the British fleet should be supreme and there was no inclination in London, no matter what party ruled in Westminster, to permit an equal on the blue water.

The decision of the Kaiser, summed up in the famous phrase, "Our future lies upon the sea," involved an ultimate challenge to Britain. No one can read the pages of British history from the days of the Spanish Armada to the not-less-splendid moment of Trafalgar, without recognizing this fact. Indeed the development of steam transport and the change in the character of British industry had made it inevitable that Britain would starve, unless she were able at all times to keep the seas open and insure the inward flow to her ports of the food for her dense population.

III. ENGLAND AND FRANCE DRAW NEAR

In the same fashion this challenge made it inevitable that in the end Britain should join the Franco-Russian group, as in her long history she had ever joined the weaker powers who made head against that Continental nation which at the moment crossed her path and challenged her supremacy.

Germany could believe, did believe up to the fatal moment in August, 1914, that Britain would be beguiled into staying out of that European war which was necessary to clear Germany's flanks, to dispose of a France still mindful of Alsace-Lorraine and certain to take advantage of German complications with other powers; the war that was necessary to send the Slav back behind the Niemen and the Bug, no longer a rival of Austria in the Balkans or a peril to Germany in East Prussia and Posen. But this was to mistake the genius which underlies the stupidity of the Anglo-Saxon in world affairs. For if Britain has always muddled her affairs in times of peace and in the opening hours of conflict, her instinct has saved her invariably.

In the early years of his reign William II seems to have cherished the notion that he could deal with France and Russia without war. Following the policy of Bismarck he encouraged the Russian to embark in the Japanese War. The earlier years of his reign are marked by a series of clumsy but no less sincere efforts to bridge the chasm that the Treaty of Frankfort had opened between France and Germany. But for this chasm there was but one bridge and this he could not take; Germany would not surrender Alsace-Lorraine, even at the behest of its young Kaiser, and no such idea ever entered the imperial mind.

Such hope as the Emperor may have entertained of winning France, of making her his ally against Britain, perished with the wholly unexpected termination of Anglo-French bickerings that followed Fashoda. When Kitchener, after his successful campaign to Khartum, and Colonel Marchand, after his memorable journey across Africa from the Congo to the Nile, met at the miserable little village of Fashoda, two great imperial dreams came into collision. A century and a half before France and Britain had met on the Ohio, and the whole story of Nineteenth Century Anglo-French colonial enterprise is a marvellous repetition of the American episode. In Africa as in America, too, French explorers had out-distanced British.

There was a moment in 1898 when it seemed inevitable that France and Britain were to fight one more war. But the crisis passed. France bowed. The French Foreign Minister, Hanotaux, went into retirement, as his successor Delcassé was to go after Tangier, seven years later. Kitchener prevailed and Marchand retreated. When these two soldiers met again, they met as allies on the hills of Artois, Marchand wearing the stars of a French general and Kitchener the master of Britain's military establishment.

Oddly enough Fashoda left no permanent scar. France had to decide between England and Germany. She chose to remain faithful to Alsace-Lorraine. Britain on her part, having at last perceived the solid foundation of French colonial conception, already beginning to feel almost subconsciously the challenge of German sea power, held out a hand to France. More than all else, Edward VII, when he came to the throne, animated as he was by a real affection for the French, opened the way, by his skill and tact, for that Anglo-French Entente, which was to threaten the whole edifice of German hope.

Thus, when the momentary bitterness had passed away, France and Britain proceeded to the adjustment of all their world-wide quarrels. There was a wholesale liquidation of claims and counterclaims, culminating in the famous agreement of 1904 by which France recognized British supremacy in Egypt, and Britain withdrew her half-century-old veto to French expansion in Morocco. Not since the Hundred Years War had Anglo-French relations been placed on so friendly a basis and henceforth French and British policies were to converge until a friendship expanded into a virtual alliance and a virtual alliance into an actual union in the presence of a common foe.

All of this was not the work of a moment. When the Boer War came there were not a few Frenchmen who openly expressed their hatred for Britain and their sympathy with the Africander Republics. To the very eve of the Great War there were influential Frenchmen who still nourished the ancient grudge against "perfidious Albion," as there were Britons who preserved the immemorial distrust of the "fickle Gaul." But, for all this, Fashoda was a landmark in European history, and the Anglo-French settlement that resulted carried with it the promise of the world conflict that followed the 1904 agreement by a short decade.

IV. THE CONVENTION OF 1904

The Anglo-French arrangement of 1904 was a heavy and well-nigh fatal blow to the policy of the German Emperor. With perfect accuracy he foresaw that it was the first step in the inevitable drawing together of France and Britain. Quite naturally he and the German nation as well saw in it the deliberate purpose of Britain to return to the old policy of balancing the Continental nations against one another and throwing her decisive influence on the side opposing her immediate rival. From this hour German teachers and German publicists were to speak with growing bitterness of the "iron ring" that was being forged about the Fatherland and the cult of hatred of Great Britain was to take on untold and unsuspected expansion.

In an Anglo-French understanding, limited as it was at the outset to a liquidation of lawsuits, to a settlement of wholly personal claims, Germany beheld the British nation taking its stand behind the French and giving its tremendous influence to encourage the French desire to destroy the Treaty of Frankfort and regain the "Lost Provinces."

And with this date there disappears the German policy of placating France which had long held sway in Berlin and had moved the Kaiser to innumerable gestures, which had been coldly rejected by the French or suffered to pass unnoticed. Out of this arrangement grew the German conviction that one more war with France was necessary and that there could be no realization of the dream of a German "place in the sun" until the ever-enduring French resentment was disposed of by a war, which should relegate France to the rank of a second-class nation and leave her too weak ever to cross German purposes again.   By force Germany was to try once more to separate France and Britain, without, in fact, arriving at war, but the failure of Tangier was to confirm the conviction born of the Anglo-French arrangement, and in it were the seeds of all that wrath which was to come.

CHAPTER TWO

FROM TANGIER TO ARMAGEDDON

I
TANGIER, THE FIRST GESTURE

The Moroccan Crisis of 1905 was the first clear warning of what was to come. It put forces squarely in opposition which were to meet again and again thereafter in similar conflict until there was no longer the smallest chance of preserving world peace. It was to open a new era in European history, the end of which no man can now see. It preceded the general conflict by less than ten years and it foreshadowed it with such clarity that those who come hereafter will marvel at the blindness that was subsequently displayed in many nations.

The Anglo-French Entente of 1904, while nominally a business arrangement between two nations, in fact undermined the whole structure of German policy. German challenge to British sea power was taking shape, but German policy contemplated the separation of Britain from the rest of Europe and gave its best effort to encouraging the bitterness between Paris and London and between Petrograd and London. A complete settlement between France and Britain foreshadowed a similar liquidation between Britain and Russia, which did come in due time, and beyond this it held out the menace of something more, of a possible alliance between these three Great Powers.

Was this in the minds of the British and French ministers who signed the treaty of 1904? Subliminally perhaps. Delcassé was a frank foe of Germany. British foreign policy was in Tory hands and the Government and the Crown alike felt the reality of the growing German challenge. More than any Englishman of his time Edward VII feared the German danger, and more than any man he contributed to resolving the difficulties between France and his own country. In the German mind, it was his policy that led to the Triple Entente. In the German mind, he conceived a plan to build a circle of steel about Germany, to unite Britain with France and Russia, to keep Germany from the realization of her dreams. Many years may not solve this problem, and it seems inevitable that Germans will read history one way and the rest of the world another. It does seem clear, however, that Lord Lansdowne, who held the Foreign Office, was mindful of the German challenge; it does seem patent that Delcassé saw in an understanding with Britain the possibility of a concentration of French energies toward national regeneration and defence. But underneath all lies the solid fact that the original challenge had been delivered by Germany to British sea power. Germany was free to seek her future on the sea, but Britain was bound, in the nature of things, to meet such a challenge as she best could.

At the moment it was announced, the Anglo-French agreement made no great noise in Europe. Delcassé did not communicate it directly to the German Government, a fatal blunder, as it now seems, but he informed the German Ambassador at Paris, who notified his Government, and Berlin gave no sign of disapproval, even gave an apparent assent. The agreement itself, while insuring ultimate French political supremacy in the Shereefian Empire, guaranteed the "open door" for all, and thus for German quite as much as British trade.

But Germany was only waiting. For the first time since the Treaty of Frankfort an international agreement of great importance—concerning her but slightly, to be sure—had been made without regard to her. This was a long and dismal descent from the days of the Congress of Berlin, when Bismarck, acting for Germany, had presided at the council of nations. This was the heaviest blow that had been struck at German prestige since the Empire had been proclaimed at Versailles.

In the opening weeks of 1905 Germany spoke. Russia had been defeated at Mukden, her prestige was gone and her military reputation had crumbled. France stood alone, notoriously ill-prepared for war. Not even with British help could she hope to make head against the German army, and there was yet no certainty that Britain would go to war to help France. Accordingly the Kaiser landed in Tangier and suddenly proclaimed the integrity of Morocco. He thrust a German sword

through the Anglo-French agreement and Europe came to the first
grave crisis of the century.

For days European peace seemed shattered. Germany demanded
that the question of Morocco should be reopened, that it should be submitted to a council of nations. Delcassé refused. In the end France
yielded, a weak and terrified ministry bowed. Delcassé went into exile,
a council was summoned to meet at Algeciras, and Bülow, the German
Chancellor, became a prince, in token of his sovereign's appreciation of
this "shining triumph."

II. ALGECIRAS—A GERMAN DEFEAT

But if this incident was a "crowning humiliation" for France, and
the going of Delcassé the greatest sorrow France had known since Sedan,
Germany lost at Algeciras almost all she had hoped to win. In this
conference Britain stood solidly behind the French. Russia was not
less loyal to her ally, while Italy displayed a lack of sympathy with her
German ally which roused bitterest recrimination in Berlin and was the
first authentic sign of the crumbling of the edifice of Bismarck. Germany and Austria stood alone, the Moroccan question was dealt with in
a fashion that insured new troubles, but in effect, the predominant influence of France in Morocco received the seal of approval of Europe
and the door to German participation in Moroccan estates, which the
Anglo-French agreement had closed, was not reopened.

Germany had humiliated France and angered Britain. She had
thrust her sword into the balance against European peace, but it had not
prevailed. She had not separated France from England. She had
brought the two nations more closely together. Russia, already humiliated by defeats in the East, bore with ill-concealed resentment the effort
of the Kaiser to take advantage of temporary weakness in Russian armies.
Italy turned from Germany and Austria to France and Britain to make
arrangements for the realization of her own Mediterranean ambitions.

All this the Germans clearly perceived, all this was gall and wormwood
to the Kaiser. He had hoped to separate France from Britain but he
had, in fact, brought them closer together. He had hoped to show a

mastery of a European council comparable to that of Bismarck in the Congress of Berlin but, save for Austria, he had been without friends in the council, a majority of which had been frankly hostile. It was Britain and not Germany that actually prevailed at Algeciras, and there was no mistaking the fact that Britain was even more willing than France to risk a deliberate rebuff to Germany, even if it should carry with it an appeal to arms.

Hence for Germany there was a new grievance against Britain, a new accentuation of Anglophobic sentiment, a new looking forward to "the day" which was becoming uppermost in German minds and hearts, the day when the British obstacle to German hope should be removed by a victory. But there were reasons why wise statesmanship should have perceived the facts that were now disclosed. Germany had feared that she would find herself faced by a triple alliance, she had made one gesture of war and all three were disclosed united against her. Unless she believed herself strong enough to face all three in arms, her course was marked out by Bismarck's successful policy of separating Austria and France and dealing with the former in 1866 and the latter in 1870. Instead, the German policy tended fatally to unite three possible foes and transform into allies, united against Germany, three nations widely separated up to the moment of Tangier.

For France, Tangier was a memorable incident. It marks the beginning of that new French spirit which was to blaze forth at the Marne and at Verdun and fill the world with the glory of French courage and patriotism. It was the beginning of the reconstruction of France, politically, spiritually, nationally. The French perceived the danger, the threat, the menace of German policy. They perceived that it had become a question of the future existence of France, and to such a threat France responded as she had to the menace of all Europe in the days of the Revolution.

III. AFTER TANGIER—THE NEW FRANCE

If French politicians still fettered French preparation, if French organization was still inferior to German, if France went to war in 1914 lacking in much, still there could be no comparison with 1905, when France must have fallen at the first blow. And what was all-important, the French mind was mobilized with the first call. France was saved by Tangier, although ten years were to pass before even the French would realize the fact of their deliverance.

With the British it was far different. The Tory ministry, which negotiated the Anglo-French convention, went out of power shortly. The Liberal Government that came into office turned the attention of the nation to domestic problems and in the bitterness of class war and Irish disputes the international situation passed from the minds of the British people. They forgot Germany, the Empire, the outside world; they devoted their energies and their attention to domestic differences, and they gave only impatient hearing to the few voices like that of Lord Roberts, which from time to time warned them of the danger that was Germany. Yet at the moment that they refused to recognize the outside peril the British ministers declined to renounce the policy from which flowed the danger. Faithful to the tradition of their race, they clung to the idea that Britain should be supreme at sea, and if, for a few years, they permitted British construction to fall perilously low by comparison with Germany, they changed their policy in time. And they accepted the legacy of friendship with France, they accepted the Moroccan commitment of Lansdowne, they remained steadily resolved to surrender nothing of British Empire or British influence to Germany, and only such a surrender could have conceivably appeased Germans.

In all this there was a fatal paradox. Pretending or even believing that Germany was friendly, the Liberal and Radical majority continued to follow a course which gave Germany no promise of a realization of her dreams. But against the danger that this policy brought they took no adequate step and members of the Government like Haldane continued to call Germany their "spiritual home" and make frequent visits to Berlin, after all real hope of an accommodation of Anglo-German rivalry had passed. The voice of Lord Roberts calling for adequate military preparation awakened only sneers from Liberals and Radicals.

BACKGROUND OF THE
WAR IN PICTURES

From a painting by Stanley Berkeley

NAPOLEON'S CUIRASSIERS AT WATERLOO

Waterloo (June 18, 1815) marked the overthrow of Napoleon's ambition to dominate
Europe.   Germany was the next nation to cherish the dream of world dominion

THE RISE OF GERMANY
BISMARCK

By permission of the Berlin Photographic Co.

THE BUILDING OF THE GERMAN EMPIRE

I. The Battle of Königgrätz or Sadowa was an important step in the building of the German Empire. It was the decisive battle in the Seven Weeks' War (1866), where 220,000 Prussians defeated 205,000 Austrians. This victory assured to Prussia a leading position in the German political affairs

THE BUILDING OF THE GERMAN EMPIRE

II. Napoleon Third's Capitulation at Sedan (1870) marked another important advance in the building of the German Empire. It was the first of the series of French surrenders in the Franco-Prussian War and cost the Emperor his throne. At once came the proclamation of the Third Republic in France. The Peace of Frankfort concluded the war five months later. Alsace-Lorraine was ceded by France to the German Empire, and Prussia in Germany became stronger than ever.

Prince Bismarck is seated at the table facing the defeated French Generals. Von Moltke, the victorious Prussian general, stands, with his hand on the table. He was the uncle of the Count Von Moltke who was the German Chief of Staff at the opening of the World War in 1914.

THE BUILDING OF THE GERMAN EMPIRE

III. William I, the present Kaiser's grandfather, was proclaimed German Emperor at Versailles a few weeks before the close of the Franco-Prussian War. This marked another step in the unification of Germany, under the leadership of Prussia. (It is of interest to note that the lesser German states have never acknowledged the Kings of Prussia as *Emperors of Germany*. They can be correctly spoken of only as *German Emperors*.) In the picture Bismarck stands, at the height of his success, close to the first step of the throne.

THE MAN WHO BUILT THE GERMAN EMPIRE

Prince Bismarck, the Germans' "Iron Chancellor," had a large part in the building of the German Empire and the creation of the Triple Alliance, in the days of the present Kaiser's father and grandfather. He did not realize the need for colonial expansion, otherwise Germany might have secured her "place in the Sun" while the other Powers were securing theirs. But Germany came into the colonial field too late to get her share peacefully. This was one deep-lying cause of the World War.

BISMARCK AS THE GREATEST STATESMAN IN EUROPE

The Congress of Berlin was convened in 1878 at the invitation of Bismarck to settle the affairs of the always troublesome Balkan States. Austria, France, Italy, England, Russia, Turkey and of course Germany—the chief contestants in the World War—were all represented. The most influential members of the conference were Prince Gortchakoff, Count Andrassy, Lord Beaconsfield, Lord Salisbury, M. Waddington, Count Corti, and Caratheodori, some of whom will be recognized in the picture. Bismarck was chosen President and is shown welcoming the delegates.

And the people of Britain, lulled to sleep by their rulers, their passions stirred by home problems and domestic debates, gave no heed to European matters. Thus it was that when at last the whole fabric of the British Empire was in deadly peril, the British population was totally oblivious to the truth, and Liberal journals could tell their readers that the conflict which was breaking in the first days of August, 1914, was without importance for Britain.

IV. THE END OF THE CONCERT OF EUROPE

For France, for Russia, for Germany, for Italy, Tangier is a landmark; its meaning was promptly made a part of the sum of human knowledge of millions in these countries, henceforth it gave shape to the policies and impulse to the purposes of the patriots of these nations. Frenchman, Russian, and German, alike, perceived in it the sign of an inevitable war, but the Briton saw nothing. From Tangier to the day when Belgium was invaded, British understanding of international conditions and British influence in the world declined until Germany could believe that the British had forgotten her challenge to British sea power and in July, 1914, could hope for a few brief hours that Britain would remain neutral at Armageddon.

Finally, and this is of prime importance, with the Algeciras Conference there expired the legend of a concert of Europe. Henceforth there were two groups of Great Powers and these groups naturally and inevitably tended to take opposite sides on every question of international importance that arose until their hostility paralyzed their influence and enabled the small Balkan States to unchain the tempest, by their attack upon Turkey in 1912.

After Tangier, too, it was plain that the understanding between France, Britain, and Russia marched steadily toward an alliance in fact if not in terms; an alliance which, by accident or design, found common ground in resistance to German policies. On the other hand, at Algeciras, Italy manifested patent weariness of the Triple Alliance, and her course thereafter was away from Berlin and Vienna and toward Paris and London. This course was to bring her into opposition with

Vienna over Tripoli and the Balkans and ultimately into alliance with the foes of the Central Powers.

The Tangier incident therefore early forecast a time when Italy would change sides, and this would leave Austria and Germany actually outnumbered and outweighed in European councils and abolish that real supremacy on the Continent which Bismarck had earned for Germany and preserved to the hour when he surrendered his office to the young Kaiser. With their larger ambitions wholly unrealized, Germans could foresee a time when they would be powerless to attain their visions of a Germany proportioned upon their own conception of her true stature.

And between Algeciras and Armageddon, Germany marched steadily from disappointment to disappointment, while the whole edifice of her power began to crack; not alone through the disaffection of Italy but through the perils which the rise of a Slav state in the Balkans, under Russian inspiration, brought to her one faithful ally, brought to Austria, half of whose population was Slav.

Thus, one may say accurately that the ten years that followed Tangier were but dominated by the consequences of this fatal episode. Henceforth the whole stream of European history flowed between circumscribed banks toward the inevitable cataract, which was the World War. Once it had entered these banks, the course was inescapable and the destination, however hidden from the view of those who sailed the stream, was ineluctable.

V. BOSNIA—THE SECOND GESTURE

Berlin had perceived with utter clarity that the entente between Britain and France would inevitably bring Russia and her ancient enemy into better relations. A Russian statesman had, indeed, remarked on the morrow of the Anglo-French convention, quoting from a Russian proverb: "The friends of my friend are my friends." Such a change would have the profoundest consequences in international relations, for the antagonism of Britain, which had again and again barred the Russian way to Constantinople, and British apprehensions for the safety of the northern frontiers of India menaced by Russian advance, had been pivots on which German policy had turned for years.

And in 1907, Britain and Russia signed a document which in all respects recalled the Anglo-French compact of three years before. The questions that had divided the two nations, above all the question of Persia, were solved by a mutually satisfactory partition of Persia into zones. Britain and Russia, as it were, struck hands in compromise over half a century of differences, and behind the things agreed was the suggestion that, in due course, British opposition to Russian possession at Constantinople would vanish.

Again German answer was tardy, but unmistakable. This time Austria spoke, but the words were recognized as German. The Young Turk Revolution had now come to shake the crumbling foundations of Osmanli power. Europe stood amazed while a new and professedly Liberal Party seized the reins of power in Constantinople and first tied the hands of Abdul Hamid, and, when he plotted against it, threw him into prison, stripped him of his power, and put a Sultan of their own 'choosing in his place.

For the moment there was a promise of progress, of a renewed and reformed Turkey, and in that moment the various subject races of the Turk—the Greek, the Bulgar, and the Armenian—shared in the efforts of the Young Turks while even the faithful Albanians deserted their friend the deposed Sultan. But the Young Turk cherished grandiose dreams of a restoration, not of the Turkey that remained, by internal reform, but even more strongly the dream of a restoration of the Turkey of the past by the reconquest of the lost provinces of Bulgaria, of Serbia, of Bosnia, and Herzegovina which had passed to the protection of the Hapsburgs at the Congress of Berlin.

Seizing this pretext Austria in 1908 proclaimed the annexation of Bosnia, while Ferdinand of Bulgaria proclaimed himself Czar of Bulgaria, thenceforth beyond even the nominal sovereignty of the Turk. The results of this annexation were tremendous. Austria had many claims upon Bosnia, no colonial effort in European history had been more successful on the material side. She had brought civilization, industrial development, railroads, and highways to one of the least advanced communities in the world.   But by virtue of the mandate of the Congress of Berlin her rule was unquestioned and the fiction of an occupation had become only a fiction; to translate it into a legal as well as a nominal possession was to change nothing, but to bring instant difficulties.

The Turkish protest was of no moment.   But Serbia, now become in fact the ward and protégé of Petrograd as she had been of Vienna in the days of the Obrenovitches, saw the extinction of her dream of a restored Serbia, which should include the 2,000,000 Serbs who lived in Bosnia and Herzegovina.   Russia, moved by her Serbian interests, protested vehemently against the transformation of the agreement of the Congress of Berlin into a "scrap of paper."   France and Britain supported Russia.   Italy stirred uneasily, for she had no interest in seeing Austria advance southward along the Adriatic or toward Saloniki.   In all this Austria was a rival, not an ally.

At the critical moment there came from Berlin another gesture like to that of the Kaiser at Tangier, but directed this time at Russia and not France.   Once more Germany thrust her sword into the balance, and once more the governments of Paris, London, and Petrograd had to decide between war and surrender.   And as France had been helpless in 1905, Russia, still suffering from her Japanese defeats, could not venture to risk a war with Germany.   Nor did France or Britain at this moment manifest any strong enthusiasm for carrying their championship of Russia's protest to the firing line.

Russia therefore bowed, as France had bowed, but the time was to come when Petrograd would say, when the Czar himself was to be reported as saying: "We have stood this thing long enough."   Russia accepted her humiliation in the spirit in which France had accepted hers. Henceforth the eyes of Russia turned toward Europe, toward the Balkans; the German gesture at Tangier had recalled France from Africa to Europe, the Bosnian affair recalled Slav thoughts from Asia to the Balkans.

Viewed at the moment, Bosnia was a shining success for German diplomacy. But if for the moment the Triple Alliance seemed mighty and the Triple Entente a broken reed, Bosnia, like Tangier, had consequences which were unforeseen to the German statesmen who provoked the trial of strength, consequences which abolished the profits of the play. Above all, the blow did not permanently break the connection between Russia, Britain, and France, which alone could have counted for a clear success.

On the contrary, it did weaken still further Italian attachment to the Triple Alliance, as it stimulated Italian apprehension of Austrian ambitions in the Balkans and along the Albanian shore of the Adriatic. From this was presently to flow the Italian attack upon Turkey, while the expression of opinion in Rome, consequent upon the Bosnian incident, disclosed how rapidly the Triple Alliance was weakening, so far as the Italian partner was concerned.

VI. AGADIR—THE THIRD AND LAST TIME

Before Italy stirred, however, there was one more great crisis—the last before the coming of the general war—in which the two groups of powers were ranged against each other. After Algeciras, Moroccan affairs had gone from bad to worse; anarchy had spread and extended. This anarchy had brought French troops to preserve the lives and properties of Frenchmen in Casablanca and along the Algerian frontier. In 1909 there had been a separate treaty between France and Germany, which was accepted for the moment as eliminating the question of Morocco. But there had been subsequent delay on the French part in carrying out terms, that Germany had insisted upon, for joint commercial activity in German Kamerun and French Congo.

In 1911, accordingly, Germany reasserted her liberty; Morocco, as Prince Bülow had said after Algeciras, was a bell which Germany could strike whenever she desired to call anything to French attention. In 1911 French troops had gone to Fez, called there by the revolt of the Moroccans. The expedition may or may not have been necessary. The stay of the French troops may have been prolonged. These were but incidents. The fact was that Morocco was no longer capable of

saving itself, the integrity proclaimed by the Kaiser at Tangier and reasserted at Algeciras had become an empty fiction.

In this situation and recognizing that French possession of Morocco
was now become inevitable and that "Tunisification" would shortly
close the Shereefian Empire to German desires unless Germany acted,
the Kaiser suddenly sent the notorious *Panther* to Agadir, thus
serving notice upon France and upon Europe that he purposed to share
in the division of the Moroccan estate. At the same moment Berlin
journals were filled with the promise of "*West Marokko deutsch,*" and
colored maps appeared assigning to the Kaiser the Moroccan provinces
from the mouth of the Sebu to the Wady Dra.

Once more a European war seemed inevitable. Conversations
between French and German ministers made no progress. The "sword-
rattling" at Berlin was ominous. Presently the fact began to leak out
that Germany was demanding from France "compensation" for French
possession in Morocco, compensation amounting to most if not all of
French colonial estates in Central Africa. Meantime British influence
and British official actions tended more and more to take the form of
solid support of France.

The situation was made the graver because suddenly a new spirit
manifested itself in France. The Caillaux Ministry had given evidence
of bowing before Germany, as the earlier ministry had sacrificed Delcassé in 1905. But now the French people suddenly spoke. There was
a swift and unmistakable reassertion of the old spirit of France, a firm
determination to make no further surrender, even though the alternative
should be war. Caillaux fell. A ministry made up of all the greater men
of France, headed by Raymond Poincaré and containing Delcassé, came
into power. France in 1911 had marched far from the days of 1905.

Then in London, Lloyd George, speaking for the Liberal Government at a public banquet, uttered words that could not be mistaken,
and were not. He gave the assurance to the world that the Liberal and
Radical Government controlling British destinies did not purpose to
permit British interests to be sacrificed or to allow Britain to be ignored.
The words were of little consequence, the effect of the words was amaz-

ing.   After a slight pause Germany changed her course, the Moroccan dispute was settled by the mutual cessions of territory in Central Africa by France and Germany.   By the exchange France lost a hundred thousand square miles of Congo territory, but she acquired title to Morocco and placed her title beyond the reach of further German dispute.

VII. A GERMAN DISASTER

Agadir was, then, a defeat for Germany that approximated a disaster. Here was no superficial success as at Tangier, here was no temporary accession of prestige as after Bosnia.   Germany had laid claim to a share in Morocco, having in 1905 bestowed her protection upon the Sultan.   Her people had come to believe that there was in Morocco a chance for German colonial development and a new "place in the sun." But German power had yielded to British threat and French firmness all that had been won at Algeciras, so far as Morocco was concerned, and all that had been acquired in prestige through the Bosnian episode. Germany had now acquired a few thousand square miles of Congo swamps; France, "decadent" France, had annexed an empire, and her possession had been insured by British interference.   Agadir was to the Germans as complete a disaster and national humiliation as Tangier had been to the French.

To the Kaiser was ascribed the surrender to Britain.   Never in his reign had he known such unpopular hours, and even his son joined the ranks of his critics.   There persists a legend that, at the critical moment, he summoned the financiers of Germany and asked if they were ready.   Their negative response inclined his decision to peace, so the story runs.   But if this be only legend, there is solid fact enough to show that his whole nation blamed him for his course.   Looking to the future it was plain that never again could William II safely run the risk of thwarting the will of his countrymen, even to preserve European peace, and the aftermath of Agadir was in many minds, when the crisis of late July, 1914, placed in William's hands the destinies of Europe.

After Agadir the real hope of European peace vanished; Germany turned feverishly to prepare.   France presently returned to the three-year law, to meet new German levies, and Germany responded with a *levée en masse*, not to raise recruits but to raise money to meet the needs of a war chest. Neither in France nor Russia was the future misread. After Tangier many Frenchmen and some Russians may still have preserved the hope of avoiding war. After Agadir there was no hope. Only Britain again misread the truth and lapsed back into her domestic quarrels, having by her brief intervention brought humiliation to the proudest sovereign and disappointment to the most ambitious people on the surface of the earth.

For Berlin, for Petrograd, for Paris, the question now became— "When?" Men looked to the future wonderingly, conscious that a storm was soon to break, and seeking to discover in the passing clouds some sure sign of the approach of the whirlwind. Read the French Yellow Book, published after the war began, and this state of mind is disclosed beyond all cavil—disclosed as the state of mind of those directing the fortunes of France, of Russia, and of Germany. So fixed was this belief that when the Austrian ultimatum to Serbia was uttered in July, 1914, men of all three nations simply said: "So *it* has come at last!"

The Agadir crisis was followed promptly by the Italian attack upon Turkey. Italy had found, in German activity on the west coast of Morocco, a hint that there might be a subsequent voyage of the *Panther* to the Tripolitan coast. She had found, in the German demand for "compensation" from France for French expansion in Morocco, a warrant for demanding a compensation to match Austrian annexation of Bosnia. She had found in the disorder created by the Young Turk régime, in the disarray of Turkish military force, that opportunity to which she had long looked forward. Finally, her consent to French and British bargains in the Mediterranean had been purchased by their assent to her own plan.

But the attack upon Turkey was an attack upon a nation which in Berlin was looked upon as an ally. Austrian sensibilities were instantly provoked by Italian naval operations in the Adriatic and, in fact, Italy was charged in Vienna and Berlin with being faithless to her allies and having attacked the solidarity of the alliance of the Central Powers, to which, in fact, if not in theory, Turkey adhered. Bernhardi could write in this very year that Germany ought to have attacked Italy, when Italy assailed the Turk and the complete collapse of the Triple Alliance was foreshadowed. Here was a new blow to the edifice of German influence.

After the Tripolitan War had dragged on for many more months without bringing much of glory to Italian arms, although Italian troops slowly occupied the towns of the African coast, Turkey suddenly surrendered, and the Treaty of Lausanne gave Tripoli to Italy. Turkish surrender was due to the coming of a new storm, which was in its turn to add still more to the anxiety of Austro-German statesmen, and a new peril to Austro-German—and above all to German—policy.

VIII. THE FIRST BALKAN WAR

Turkish difficulties and defeats had now raised other hopes. The Balkan States, long looking forward to the liberation of their Christian brothers beyond their own frontiers and properly alarmed by the programme of the Young Turks, seized the moment to unite in an alliance against a common foe. To the amazement of Europe, the Greek and the Bulgar put aside a hatred of a thousand years, the Bulgar and the Serb compromised their Macedonian rivalries, and all three turned to attack the Osmanli.

Until the discord between the two great groups of powers had paralyzed Europe, such an alliance would have been powerless before the mandate of the Concert of Europe. But there was no concert, and neither group cared to invite the hostility of this new alliance, so closely balanced were the Triple Alliance and the Triple Entente. One group, influenced by Russia, who had helped to form the Balkan Alliance, hoped for its success; the other, stirred by their own ambitions in the Balkans, hoped and expected Turkish victory.

But the Turk was swiftly and decisively beaten. The Bulgars defeated the main Turkish army at Lule Burgas, invested Adrianople, and reached the base of the peninsula on which Constantinople stands.

The Serb avenged Kosovo at Kumanova, took Uskup, completed his victory before Monastir, and flowed down the Vardar Valley toward Saloniki, upon which Greek and Bulgarian troops were converging. Even Greece, wiping out the disgrace of the earlier Turkish War, defeated the Turkish armies before her and seized Saloniki, the prize of the Near East, and at the same time sent her troops into Albania and conquered all northern Epirus, investing Janina as the Bulgars had invested Adrianople. Here then was an end of Turkish empire in Europe. The real contest was over in as brief a time as that in which Germany had vanquished France in 1870. The prize had been won and the only question was the division of it. Now at last Europe interfered. Repulsed at the Chatalja, the outward lines of Constantinople, the Bulgar was served with notice that he would not be permitted to hold the city, even if he took it. Then Serb, Bulgar, and Greek were bidden to come to London and put their case before the Concert of Europe at last reëstablished. To this conference the small States came, and it was to prove their ruin. Only Greece refused to discontinue her military operations, while Bulgaria declined to permit the revictualing of Adrianople.

IX. THE CONFERENCE OF LONDON

At this conference the aims of the Central Powers were at last disclosed. The Balkan Alliance had been a blow to their whole purpose. If it lasted it would bar the way to Austro-German expansion toward the East; it would erect a strong Serbia on the flank of Austria, a Serbia responsive to Russian influence and ambitious to reclaim the millions of southern Slavs remaining under Hapsburg rule. Italy looked with frank disapprobation upon Greek progress northward to Avlona and the Skumbi, and Italy and Austria agreed in opposing Slav expansion southward from the Montenegrin boundary to the new Greek frontier.

Wherefore Austria served notice that there must be a free Albania. On the surface the claim was fair. Albanians inhabited all the region from the environs of Janina to Scutari, and there was patent desire on the part of the Albanians to be free, not to be the subjects of a Greek or Slavic sovereign. But the true Austrian purpose had no concern with the wishes of the Albanians. Her desire was to break up the Balkan League. If Serbia were denied the right to reach the sea, through northern Albania, then it was inevitable that Serbia would seek compensation in the Vardar Valley. Such compensation would be at the expense of Bulgaria, for although Bulgaria and Serbia had signed a treaty partitioning Macedonia before they went to war, Serbia and not Bulgaria had conquered and held all of Macedonia and could remunerate herself as she saw fit.

The comedy of Albania long occupied the representatives of the Great Powers of Europe. Germany cleverly made Sir Edward Grey the "honest broker" of the conference and used his ignorance of the Near Eastern situation to destroy the Balkan League. He was permitted to accommodate the differences between Austria and Russia over the future boundaries between the Serb and the Albanian. There were mutual concessions made with great show of good will, although it was of more than passing consequence that the peace of Europe hung on the disposition of Ipek and Jakova, wretched Albanian villages unknown to most of the millions who would have been called to arms had the Conference of London ended in war.

Without regard to the mandate of Europe, Bulgaria burst impetuously from the conference and returned to her work, which was the capture of Adrianople. This done, she bowed to the decision of London and agreed to accept the frontier drawn from Midia to the Gulf of Enos, while Greece consented to give up northern Epirus, and Serbia and Montenegro resigned Scutari and Durazzo. But now it was necessary to settle the division of conquered territory between the three victors. Serbia and Greece had agreed. But deprived of northern Albania, through Sir Edward Grey's Albanian operation, Serbia insisted that she be permitted to hold Macedonia west of the Vardar, while Greece insisted upon keeping Saloniki, although agreeing to surrender Kavala and northern Epirus.

X. THE SECOND BALKAN WAR

Bulgaria, driven by Austrian influence, declined all compromise, insisted that she should have all that her treaty with Serbia had assured her, and maintained troops in Saloniki as a sign of her determination to possess this city also. To all appeals of Russia she remained deaf. To all dictates of caution imposed by the alliance of Serbia and Greece she turned a deaf ear. Even Roumanian warnings, combined with the demand for "compensation" about Silistria, left her obdurate. Her heart was set upon Macedonia and she refused to barter.

Finally in the closing days of June, 1913, a great Bulgarian army in Macedonia attacked the Serbs, standing behind the Bregalnitza, won a temporary advantage, but was presently forced to retreat, while a Greek advance from Saloniki and a Hellenic success at Kilkis compelled the rapid retirement of the Bulgars from all Macedonia. A Roumanian army now entered northern Bulgaria, while the Turk reoccupied Thrace and regained Adrianople. Bulgaria's ruin was complete. She had heeded Austrian advice and Austria shared in her misfortune. Austrian purpose to destroy the Balkan League had prevailed, thanks to Sir Edward Grey, but it had raised up a dangerous Serbia, it had enhanced not weakened Russian influence in the Balkans, and it had shaken the ties that had bound the Roumanian to the Austrian for a generation. The Roumanian troops which had invaded Bulgaria had openly proclaimed that they were following through Bulgaria the road which led to Transylvania and Bukowina.

The Treaty of Bukharest confirmed the Bulgarian defeat. Serbia acquired all of Macedonia and emerged from her trials a state equal in area and importance to that Sardinia which had with French help driven the Austrian out of Italy. Greece acquired all of the coast from her ancient frontier to the Mesta, including both Kavala and Saloniki. Roumania took a province from Bulgaria, and the Turk made good his claim to his Thracian districts. After two bloody wars and terrible sacrifices, Bulgaria was able to show only a small strip of land between the Rhodopians and the Ægean; Macedonia was lost, and the dream of the hegemony of the Balkans had gone temporarily to dust and ashes.

But the worst aspect of the Balkan settlement was the menace that it carried to European peace, through the inevitable rivalries of Austria and Serbia. Ever since the change of dynasties had given Petrograd and not Vienna control at Belgrad, the relations between Serbia and Austria had been bad.   Time and again Austria had bullied and mistreated her small neighbour.   The annexation of Bosnia had been as heavy a blow to the Serb as the annexation of Alsace-Lorraine by Germany had been to the Frenchman.   By refusing to permit Serbia to gain a window on the sea, Austria had renewed all Serbian resentment.

XI. BUKHAREST AND AFTER

Now, from Bukharest, Serbia emerged a considerable state; in the eyes of her own soldiers and citizens she was a real military power and the easy victories of her armies over Turk and Bulgar were taken as a promise of future success over the Austrian.   Beyond the Drina and the Save were four million Serbs and two million Croats, toward whom Serbians now looked as the Italians of the Sardinian Kingdom had looked toward their brethren of the Milanese and the Kingdom of Naples.   Nor was there any mistaking the similar stirring of race sympathy within the Hapsburg domains.

Worst of all, it was plain that Russia would henceforth regard Serbia as a ward, and never, unless under threat of war, permit Austria to strike the little Slav state.   The growth and glory of a free Serbia might shake the very foundations of the Hapsburg empire with its millions of Slavs, uneasily bearing the German and Magyar yokes, but backed by Russia, Serbia was bound to endure as a menace to Austria as far as Austrian statesmen could see.   Austria had challenged Russia in the Bosnia time; Russia had temporarily bowed, but the real answer came when Russia appeared at London, after the First Balkan War, to support the claims of the Serbs, and after Bukharest gave her protection to the new and strong Serbia, which not alone closed the Hapsburg pathway to the Ægean, but dreamed of extending the renaissance of the southern Slav to Fiume and to Triest, depriving German and Magyar alike of a window on the sea, from which they had excluded the Serb.

The Treaty of Bukharest placed Austria-Hungary in jeopardy. It had hardly been promulgated when Austria sought the permission of her Italian ally to attack Serbia. Italy, as Giolitti later confessed, declined.   But the Austrian suggestion leaves no doubt as to the Austrian purpose.   The blow that was suspended in 1913 was to fall in 1914; it could no longer be permanently prevented, after Serbia had made good her place in the sun and Austrian diplomacy had proven bankrupt in the Balkan wars.

Unhappily the question between Austria and Russia over Serbia could no longer be regarded as one concerning them alone.   Tangier, Agadir, and the intervening Bosnian episode had transformed Europe into two camps.   A dispute between two nations, each belonging to a different group, became instantly the cause for difference between the two groups.   Germany had twice challenged France and Britain, and her challenge had contributed to binding them still more closely together.   The Anglo-French friendship had expanded to include Russia, the ally of France.   And this relation between Russia, France, and Britain had barred the road to German colonial expansion at Tangier and Agadir, it had endeavoured to thwart Austrian purpose in the Balkans in the Bosnian time, and it had, in fact, appeared as a potential force at the Conference at London, if it had never been forced to declare its solidarity, because no test question was pressed to an issue.

Such, in sum, was the transformation that Europe had undergone in less than ten years.   Such had been the inexorable consequences of the Kaiser's determination to challenge British sea power and his subsequent determination to prevent Britain from drawing close to Russia and to France.   Britain had met his challenge on the water.   She had drawn close to France and to Russia until a war was to show that she stood with them absolutely.   The play of ten years had all turned against the German.   His influence in Europe had been undermined; the safety of his Austrian partner had been compromised; the loyalty of his Italian ally had been weakened and, as it turned out, destroyed; and all this had happened to a Germany, every year growing stronger in all that makes a nation strong and possessing an army unequalled in Europe, unexcelled in history.   In the minds of every German the shadow of Britain had crossed the path of rightful Teutonic expansion, and a Germany that felt she could win her rightful place in the sun by the sword felt also that, in the preceding ten years, she had not only failed to win it, but had actually lost it by reliance upon peaceful methods.

This was the Germany that spoke in July, 1914, less than a year later. The Treaty of Bukharest, in restoring peace in the Balkans, had doomed the peace of the world.

CHAPTER THREE

THE TWELVE DAYS

I

THE ASSASSINATION OF THE ARCHDUKE

The Treaty of Bukharest was signed on August 10, 1913. Such reservations as to its provisions as may have been cherished in Petrograd, Vienna, and Rome, were abolished when the Kaiser—by a gesture, memorable thereafter—conveyed to his brother-in-law, the King of Greece, his recognition that the terms of this settlement were definitive. And for ten months Europe settled back after two years of the acutest apprehension. On the surface all was calm, although the subsequent admissions of Giolitti have informed us that the ink was not dry on the document of Bukharest when Vienna began to sound Rome on the possibility of an attack upon Serbia. Rome was unresponsive and this bad moment passed.

But on June 28, 1914, the Archduke Francis Ferdinand and his morganatic wife were assassinated in the streets of Serajevo, the capital of Bosnia-Herzegovina. The crime was committed by a man of Serbian race, but a resident of Bosnia and a subject of the Emperor Francis Joseph. The deed was an abhorrent one and if no evidence that the world has yet been able to submit to any impartial jury has fixed upon the Serbian Crown or the Serbian Government any complicity in the murder, still the crime itself was manifestly the outgrowth of the agitation of the Pan-Serbs, who aimed at extending the domain of King Peter from the Drina to the Adriatic and from Cattaro to Fiume. It was a logical and unmistakable consequence of the Serbian propaganda for racial unity, which had been permitted in Belgrad and not unkindly observed from Petrograd.

There were some days when Europe waited in the keenest anxiety for a sign from Vienna. But no sign appeared and slowly, yet in the

BACKGROUND OF THE
WAR IN PICTURES

KAISER GREETS KAISER

Germany and Austria, the two faithful members of the Triple Alliance, salute each
other in the persons of their sovereigns, Wilhelm and Franz Joseph.

THE TWO KAISERS
DROPPING THE PILOT
GROWTH OF THE ENTENTE
THE CRIME OF SERAJEVO

DROPPING THE PILOT—TENNIEL'S FAMOUS CARTOON

A clash was inevitable between two such masterful natures as those of
William II and Bismarck. The ideas of the old man had been principally
confined to building and buttressing the strength, first of Prussia, then of
Germany, within her own borders. The young man, of broader vision,
looked beyond the seas and sought in other lands for Germany's place in
the sun. Bismarck was retired in 1890, two years after William's accession

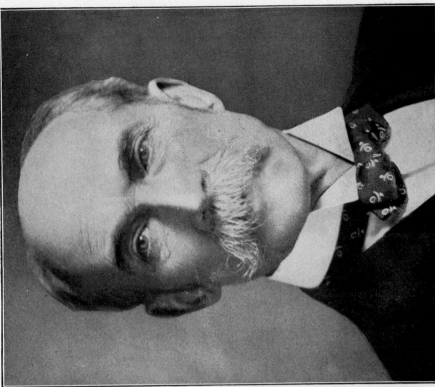

LORD LANSDOWNE

Lord Lansdowne was the British Minister for Foreign Affairs in 1904, and he is called "the father of the Anglo-French Agreement." On Black Sunday, during the fateful Twelve Days in August, 1914, he joined with Mr. Balfour in a letter to Mr. Asquith, declaring in no uncertain terms that *France must not be deserted*".

M. DELCASSÉ, FRENCH FOREIGN MINISTER IN 1904

He and Lord Lansdowne negotiated the extremely important Anglo-French Agreement without consulting Germany. "This was a long and dismal descent from the days of the Congress of Berlin, when Bismarck, acting for Germany, had presided at the council of nations. This was the heaviest blow, struck at German prestige since the Empire had been proclaimed at Versailles."

TWO STAUNCH FRIENDS AND PROMOTERS OF THE ENTENTE CORDIALE

President Fallieres of France, and King Edward VII of England—father of the present King and uncle of the Kaiser. "More than any man of his time Edward VII feared the German danger and more than any man he contributed to resolving the difficulties between France and his own country. Many Germans believed he conceived a plan to build a circle of steel about Germany"

GENERAL KITCHENER AND COLONEL MARCHAND—THE PRINCIPALS IN THE FASHODA INCIDENT

Six years before the Anglo-French Agreement, British and French plans for colonial expansion came into conflict when Kitchener and Marchand met at Fashoda on the frontier of the British and French spheres in Africa. "It seemed inevitable that France and Britain were to fight one more war. But the crisis passed." These two soldiers were to meet once again, sixteen years later, this time as allies on the Plain of Arrois.

[Photograph by Paul Thompson

CZAR NICHOLAS AND PRESIDENT POINCARE

This picture is evidence of a political friendship warmly cherished between the Powers to the east and west of Germany. Even while the diplomatic interchanges of the Twelve Days (in August, 1914) were in progress, President Poincare of France was returning from a visit to the Russian Czar.

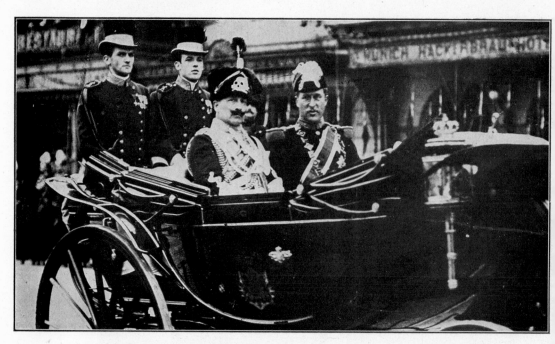

THE KAISER WITH A FORMER FRIEND—ALBERT OF BELGIUM

¶The Kaiser in former years took such delight in visiting other monarchs that he was sometimes criticized at home as a gad-about and received the nickname of *Der Reise Kaiser*—the traveling Kaiser. He has justified his wanderings in the following terms. "On my travels I design not only to make myself acquainted with foreign countries and institutions, and to foster friendly relations with neighboring rulers, but these journeys, which have often been misinterpreted, have high value in enabling me to observe home affairs from a distance and submit them to a quiet examination".

LORD ROBERTS AND LORD HALDANE

One vainly urged preparedness, the other minimized the danger and called Germany his "spiritual home," even after all hope of an accommodation of Anglo-German rivalry had passed. "The voice of Lord Roberts calling for adequate military preparation awakened only sneers from Liberals and Radicals."

Photograph by Brown Brothers   *Photograph by International News Service*

ARCHDUKE FRANCIS FERDINAND (HEIR TO THE AUSTRIAN THRONE)—
WITH HIS MORGANATIC WIFE

Both were killed by an assassin's bomb at Sarajevo, Bosnia, June 28, 1914

THE ARREST OF THE ASSASSIN

Austria asserted that his act was inspired by the Pan-Slavic propaganda in Serbia and declared war. Russia stood behind Serbia. Germany stood behind Austria. Then came Armageddon.

end completely, the crime slipped from the headlines of the newspapers and the minds of the public. On the surface, European politics seemed in the most tranquil state in the long and troubled decade that had passed. A British fleet visited Kiel; the French President set out for Petrograd; there was not a ripple on the surface of the diplomatic waters. This was, however, only the calm before the storm. On July 23d Austria sent to Serbia the most formidable ultimatum that one state had ever addressed to another.

The ultimatum itself—in addition to prescribing rules and regulations with reference to anti-Austrian propaganda and propagandists in Serbia; in addition to calling for the disbanding of patriotic societies with aims inimical to Austria and the punishment of their leaders, who were also servants of the Crown in the army and in the civil service—demanded that Austrian officials should be associated with the Serbian in the carrying out of the tasks that were set. To this ultimatum there was added a time-limit of forty-eight hours.

Here, then, on July 23d, was a new crisis, graver than the three that had preceded, because, instead of abstract questions of territory and commerce, there were now raised the concrete questions of national honour and dynastic interest which were involved in the crime of Serajevo. Ostensibly seeking to punish agitators, whose activities had led to the killing of the heir to the Austro-Hungarian thrones; ostensibly aiming to put an end to an agitation injurious to Austrian safety, the Government of Vienna had, in fact, challenged Russia, the avowed protector of Serbia.

If Russia did not now step forward to defend Serbia it was plain that the kingdom would fall under the weight of Austrian arms, or if it bowed to Austrian demands would pass actually, if not nominally, under the influence of Vienna. If Russia stood aside and permitted this to happen, then her own prestige in the Balkans and among the Slav peoples of Europe was gone. It was Bosnia over again, but Bosnia with a new and still-more-disturbing set of complexities, for in annexing Bosnia Austria had only transformed the name under which she exercised authority in Bosnia, but now she would transform the actual condition under which Serbia lived from independence to servitude.

And if Russia did step forward to protect Serbia, then she, by this act, asserted that she claimed the right to exercise an actual protection over Serbia; she claimed the right to speak for Serbia; she extended Russian influence and Russian power to the very shores of the Danube, and from Belgrad, as from the Galician frontier, threatened the integrity of the Austro-Hungarian Monarchy. If Austrian will prevailed, Serbia would become a Hapsburg appendage, but not less clear, once the issue was raised, was the fact that if Russia intervened and prevailed, Austrian safety was compromised and her prestige destroyed.

II. THE AUSTRIAN CASE

Stripped of all detail the fact was that Serbia, if not through direct governmental action at least by general popular agitation and with the benevolent blindness of the government, had plotted to undermine Austrian unity. To be sure the movement had its origin in the fact that Austria contained some million of Slavs, who were Serb by race, and perhaps desired to become subjects of King Peter. It was a situation on all fours with that which existed in Italy, before the Austrian war with France. But, whatever the moral title of a nation to its own territories and subjects, no nation can permit itself to be destroyed by outside intrigue and no nation will voluntarily surrender provinces and citizens.

When France undertook to assist in the liberation of northern Italy from Hapsburg rule, war resulted, as it was bound to result. If Russia now asserted on behalf of Serbia the same doctrine that Napoleon III had practised with regard to Sardinia, Austria would have to fight. The only difference was that Austria now raised the issue herself. She did not raise the issue until the heir to the Hapsburg throne had been murdered, although she had proposed to raise it ten months before the crime; but, having raised it, her own safety, her own integrity, her own existence as a Great Power were at stake.

And if one look squarely at the facts, there is little question that she was bound to raise the issue, because this Pan-Slav agitation was destroying the very foundations of her national existence. The right of ten million Germans and as many Magyars to rule twenty-five million Slavs may be questioned on the moral side, but the legal and international right of a nation to preserve itself cannot be questioned, save on the basis of some law higher than that recognized by nations in their common intercourse.

Austrian treatment of the Slavs within her boundaries, and her treatment of the neighbouring Slav states, had been brutal and stupid. She had gained their hatred and she had deserved it. She had sought in the Balkan wars to thwart their growth and her policy had gone bankrupt. But if her mistakes had gained her deserved hatred, and her failures had enabled the very state that hated her most to menace her existence, it was not less true that she was bound to defend her existence and her unity.

In the minds of many, Serbia has come to share the glory of Belgium and to occupy the niche of a martyr quite as completely. But the idea is fallacious. Belgium threatened no one, plotted injury to no one of her neighbours, permitted no propaganda of sedition which menaced the security and order of either France or Germany, for example, to be conducted from within her boundaries. Serbia did all these things. She did them as Sardinia carried on the *risorgimento;* she did them in the name and in the fact of patriotism; she sought to liberate and unite the mass of her race, but this liberation was predicated on the collapse of Austria.

If there had been no crime at Serajevo, it was inevitable that Austria would presently take the sword against Serbia, because only by taking the sword could she defend herself. But it was equally inevitable that Russia, bound by race and religion to the Serbs, animated as she had always been by the keenest race sympathy for her fellow Slavs, would defend Serbia, who had become her soldier on the Danube, her ally against Austria's dreams of an advance to the Ægean. Actually Serbia was only a detail in the rivalry between Romanoff and Hapsburg, which was several centuries old.

Bismarck himself had hesitated in making an alliance with Austria, because he foresaw that this meant to inherit the rivalry between the two nations in the Balkans. His influence at Vienna had sufficed to keep peace, but his support of Austria at the Congress of Berlin had made a Franco-Russian alliance inevitable. For the moment, for his own time, he had met this by expanding his alliance to include Italy, by keeping on friendly terms with Britain, and by executing a "treaty of reassurance" with Russia. But it had needed the skill of Bismarck to keep the balance true and the successors of Bismarck had neither his skill nor his resources. Italy and Austria were natural enemies and he had made them allies, Russia and Austria were natural rivals and he had kept them at peace with each other. But less than two decades after he laid down the reins, natural tendencies had overcome fortuitous circumstances.

The peril of the Balkan situation was no longer the peril of a war between Austria and Russia, or between Austria and Germany on the one hand and France and Russia on the other, with Italy a possible ally of the Central Powers. The challenge of the Kaiser to Britain had brought Britain back to the Continent. France herself would have hesitated in the early nineties to fight on the Serbian issue for her Russian ally. But the French spirit had undergone a new birth since Tangier and Agadir.

Since the war came, volumes have been published devoted simply to proving upon which of the several nations the responsibility for the conflict rests and to demonstrating that one or the other of the nations, during the fateful twelve days before the storm broke in its full fury, actually desired war, or served the cause of peace more loyally, than its neighbours.

Yet it seems probable that, in the long time hereafter, those details will be forgotten by the historian, who will perceive that the twelve days were of little meaning, that they marked a period after real hope of peace had expired, that the whole system under which Europe had lived for so long had been destroyed, and that the statesmen who laboured so frantically in the closing hours were actually as impotent as medicine men who hurl incantations and invoke charms to check the approach of a cyclone.

III. SIR EDWARD GREY

In the Albanian time Europe had permitted Sir Edward Grey to act as its agent. He had passed from one group to the other, persuading Russia to resign Scutari to the new Kingdom of Albania, wheedling Austria into consenting that Dibra should be Serbian. Austria and Italy for once were agreed, both seeking to preserve from Serb and Greek alike that Albania each hoped to inherit. Neither Russia nor Germany was in a state of readiness for war, and France was, as she continued through the critical days of 1914, willing to serve the cause of peace to her limit, provided it did not interfere with her duty as an ally of Russia.

When the Serbian crisis came, Sir Edward Grey—still under the influence of his success over Albania, still convinced that he had to deal with a question that could be adjusted as the Albanian had been—began that earnest and industrious campaign to preserve the peace of the world, which remains the admiration of the Briton—and the target of the German. From first to last he had, in this campaign, the support of the French and the Italian statesmen; he had the assent of Russia to all the propositions which he made; but never, to the closing hour, does he seem to have grasped the fact that he was in the presence of a question which could not be settled by discussion about the green table, since it involved the safety of Austria and the honour of Russia.

The whole burden of Sir Edward Grey's words, messages, explanations, discloses his conviction that to preserve the peace of Europe it was necessary to persuade Austria to withdraw her ultimatum, to suspend her action against Serbia, to consent to submit to the Concert of Europe the question between Serbia and herself, which was the question of her own integrity aggravated by the new problem raised by the murder of the Archduke.

In the very nature of things Russia was prepared to consent to any arrangement that spared Serbia, but any arrangement that spared Serbia and submitted the Austro-Serbian question to the Concert of Europe vindicated Russia's assertion of a right to protect Serbia and was bound to constitute a moral victory for Russia and a new blow to Austrian safety. Nor could Austria, remembering the experience of Germany at Algeciras, anticipate a victory in any new international gathering.

To Germany Sir Edward Grey continued to address appeals to intervene to restrain Austrian action. Conceivably it had been Germany who had moved Austria to action, to the despatch of the ultimatum, but of this there is as yet no sufficing proof. Unmistakably it lay within the power of the German Government by a word, by a gesture, to deprive Austria of the assurance German support gave. But this would have been in fact a desertion of her one faithful ally at the moment of deadly peril, and it would have foreshadowed the collapse of the Austro-German Alliance, if it had not been but the prelude to the collapse of the Dual Monarchy, already shaken by Slav intrigue within and without.

Unless Russia abandoned her championship of Serbia, or Austria consented to recall her ultimatum and leave to Europe the task of disciplining her little neighbour—a task beyond the capacity of the fragile Concert—war was bound to follow. And there never was any chance that either Austria or Russia would surrender. When Sir Edward Grey asked Germany to restrain Austria, Germany with perfect justice retorted by asking Sir Edward Grey to restrain Russia. Always the British Minister seems to have been obsessed with the immediate present, always the action of Austria in issuing the ultimatum seems to arouse his indignation and awaken his protest, but to the fatal chain of events that had made Serbia a deadly peril to Austrian existence he gave no thought.

Actually he accomplished nothing for good or for evil, actually he sought peace by suggesting temporary devices that were of no value and could be of no avail in the presence of the storm that was rising. When the storm broke he found himself without a policy, so far as his own Government was concerned, but bound by honour, if not by treaty, to stand with France and with Russia. Nor was he alone bound by honour. He had failed beyond all forgiveness, together with his as-

LORD ROBERTS OF KANDAHAR

As the last German attacks before Ypres were failing, there died within the British lines the one British soldier who had foreseen what was now happening, whose words had been greeted with sneers, whose voice had been almost silenced by the cheap and empty optimism of Liberal and Radical politicians. An old and broken man he had gone to France at the moment of the crisis, to cheer on his well-loved Indian troops. Lord Roberts died on the eve of a great victory which saved his own country from the worst he had feared for it

sociates, in not warning the British people of the danger that had for ten years been growing, but he now saw with utmost clarity that a Germany victorious over France would be a Germany which Britain could not resist and could not expect would refrain from attack.

German invasion of Belgium saved Sir Edward Grey, it saved England, because it supplied a moral issue and a moral impulse which served to enlist British effort until the nation at last perceived the material interests, the national existence, that were at stake. But if the successor of Bismarck will hereafter have to answer to his own people and in history for having involved Germany in a war against three great nations at once, the successor of Pitt and Beaconsfield will be indicted for having brought Britain to the edge of Armageddon without permitting the British people to suspect that their life and their Empire were in jeopardy.

Having entered into an arrangement with France, by which the French fleet was to guard British interests in the Mediterranean while the British fleet concentrated against the German menace in the North Sea, Sir Edward Grey could not desert France at the opening of the war, even if there were no written alliance. But if the British people had not been aroused by the invasion of Belgium it may be questioned whether Sir Edward Grey could have persuaded his Government to make good its obligations or his fellow countrymen to honour their Government's commitments.

It is difficult to find any warrant in Sir Edward's course for the storm of abuse that Germans have directed at him as a monster of bad faith, but equally difficult is the task for one, writing with such facts as are now at hand, to escape the belief that he acted with a blindness and a fatuity almost passing human comprehension. His party associates had kept Britain blind to the truth of world affairs for a decade, and when the storm arrived there was lacking any national understanding which could give force to the decisions of a Minister, at last aware of the deadly peril of his country. He knew England must stand with France to save her own life, but until Germany invaded Belgium, he was destitute of any resource by which he could reveal to his fellow countrymen the imminence and the magnitude of their peril.

Those who saw Sir Edward in the closing hours, when the World War had become inescapable, think of him as one who revealed in every word and act the emotion of a man who had seen the hope and the work of a lifetime gone suddenly to dust and ashes.   He had believed that a settlement with Germany, which would lay forever the peril of what was now to occur, was possible.   In the Bosnia time, in the Agadir crisis, at the Conference of London, he had not only striven to avoid war, but had found cause for hope that, since war had been avoided on these three occasions, the cloud that had hung over Europe so long might be finally dissipated.

His optimism had led him far afield.   It had persuaded him to sacrifice the Balkan Alliance at the Conference of London, when he accepted the Austro-German programme for Albania.   It was to cost his own country dearly in the first years of the war, which found her unprepared, because a Liberal Government, under Sir Edward's influence, had turned a deaf ear to all the warnings of those who saw Europe as it was and not through the golden haze of lofty but insubstantial dreams of world peace.   Yet complete as had been his failure, absolute as had been his misreading of the essential facts of his own time, when he occupied a post of honour and responsibility, no one could doubt the sincerity of his purposes or the tragedy, the personal tragedy, that came with the destruction of all his lifework.

IV. THE AUSTRIAN ULTIMATUM

The Austrian ultimatum was despatched to Serbia on July 23d, and it carried a time-limit of forty-eight hours.   When it was sent, the President of France, with the important members of the French Cabinet, were on the sea, returning from Russia.   The Irish crisis in Britain seemed to be about to end in civil war.   The Kaiser was in Norwegian waters.   There was no Russian ambassador in Vienna.   The Caillaux trial was dominating French attention and a French senator, speaking in his place, had just called attention to grave defects in French military organization.

In only one detail—but this a vitally important one—did chance favour the Triple Entente. The British fleet had been mobilized for its annual manœuvres shortly before the crisis came and, on a hint from Italy, received in the third week of July, demobilization was postponed. Thus British sea power was on a war footing at the crucial moment. If Germany had ever planned a raid on British shores in the first days of an Anglo-German conflict, as British naval authorities believe—such a dash as the Japanese made at Port Arthur in the opening hours of the Russo-Japanese War—the scheme was frustrated by the accidental posture of British fleets and the timely Italian hint.

On Friday, July 24th, Austria informed Russia that she did not have any intention to annex Serbian territory, and Russia replied by asking an extension of the time-limit attached to the ultimatum to Serbia. This was refused by Austria on Saturday, the day on which Russia issued her first warning note, published in the Petrograd press, an official assurance that Russia would not remain indifferent to the fate of Serbia, which, through its Crown Prince, now acting as Regent, had appealed to the Czar on the preceding day.

On this same day, Saturday, July 25th, just within the time-limit, Serbia sent a reply to Austria, which contained a surrender on most points and an agreement to submit the rest to arbitration. Austria forthwith declared the Serbian response to be unsatisfactory and withdrew her minister from Belgrad.

On Sunday, July 26th, Sir Edward Grey began his task of accommodating the world crisis. He suggested that the case between Russia and Austria be left to the mediation of the four Great Powers not directly concerned, acting through their ambassadors in Vienna and Petrograd. These nations were, of course, Great Britain, France, Italy, and Germany. Russia, having first suggested conversations directly between Vienna and Petrograd, a suggestion subsequently rejected by Austria, accepted Sir Edward's proposal but Germany rejected it on the next day.

On Monday, July 27th, when Germany had rejected his proposal, Sir Edward invited the German Government to present a formula of mediation of its own. This elicited no response from Berlin, because

Germany had already on July 25th invited France and Great Britain to restrain Russia, that is, to urge Russia to stand aside and permit Austria to punish Serbia. This proposal, described by the Germans as "localization" of the disturbance, was rejected both by France and by Great Britain.

A collapse of all preliminary efforts of Sir Edward follows the declaration of war upon Serbia, by Austria, on Tuesday, July 28th, as fighting commenced forthwith. Meantime the Kaiser, having returned from Norway on Sunday night, now addressed his first message to the Czar urging him to permit Austria to discipline Serbia. To this the Czar responded the next day by urging that the whole matter be submitted to The Hague, a suggestion never answered by the Kaiser.

Meantime the question of mobilization had become acute. Austria had been partially mobilizing against Serbia, and as early as July 25th the Russian Council had considered partial mobilization against Austria, at the same time informing the German Government that there was no hostile meaning for Germany in the approaching mobilization.

Now on the 29th, Germany for the first time began to sound Great Britain on the possibility of British neutrality if war should come. Her proposals were promptly rejected by Sir Edward Grey.

By Friday, July 30th, general Russian mobilization was proclaimed, but at the eleventh hour Sir Edward Grey suggested that the operations of Austria against Serbia should be recognized as a punitive expedition and that Austria, having reached a point within Serbian territory fixed by agreement, should permit her future course to be submitted to a conference of Powers. Austria assented to a portion of this suggestion and for the first time manifested a decided change in spirit. Russia agreed.

But on July 31st Germany addressed an ultimatum to Russia demanding that Russia desist from her mobilization within twelve hours. This was naturally ignored by Russia and on Saturday, August 1st, Germany declared war upon Russia. A general war now became inevitable and the only question that remained was as to the course of Britain and Italy.

V. GERMANY'S COURSE

In all this period it is quite clear that the British and German statesmen, alike, pursued a course aimed, ostensibly and probably honestly, at averting a general war. But Germany insisted that the war could only be averted by action of Britain and France in restraining Russia from intervening in the quarrel between Serbia and Austria, while Britain insisted that Austria should be compelled, by her German ally, to submit her dispute with Serbia to a European conference and asked Germany to restrain Austria.

Such purposes were irreconcilable from the start and failed as they were bound to fail unless one of the two great nations involved was prepared to yield everything, as France had yielded at Tangier, and Russia in the Bosnia time. Action by the German Emperor, in the sense requested by Sir Edward Grey, would have brought down upon him far more criticism at home than had beaten upon him in the Agadir time. Peace was no longer to be preserved by a compromise between the two groups of nations; the sole chance of avoiding war from July 23d onward was by the surrender of one of the groups and this, possible in 1905 and 1909, was unthinkable in 1914.

Germany's course prior to the outbreak of the war, her relation to the efforts to preserve peace made by Sir Edward Grey, has suffered naturally from the odium that justly attaches to the manner in which she acted, once the conflict had begun, both in invading Belgium and in the manner in which she conducted operations on Belgian and French soil, as well as on the high seas. This was inevitable if not entirely logical. But certainly she was as fully entitled to support Austria as was France to support Russia. France never considered demanding that Russia should abandon Serbia, and it was equally unreasonable to expect Germany to compel Austria to refrain from abolishing the Serbian menace, once Austria had so admirable an issue as the assassination of the Archduke furnished.

The fact that Germany alone was ready when the war came has contributed to creating the conviction that she alone wished it. It is unmistakable that for twenty years she had proclaimed her purpose, through her acts, to modify the *status quo;* she had challenged Britain on the sea, she had assailed France through Morocco, and backed Austria against Russia. Her teachers and soldiers had proclaimed that only through a victorious war could Germany attain her rightful place in the sun. This was strange doctrine in the Twentieth Century, but familiar doctrine in the preceding centuries that had seen the rise of France and Britain. What is essential is that it be recognized that millions of Germans held this doctrine. It was a doctrine that Europe had resisted over years when Napoleon applied it, when Louis XIV asserted it, when Charles V employed it. Europe was bound to oppose it now, but in the larger view of history it will doubtless take its place beside the other efforts of great races to revive the Roman tradition and use their superior organization and unity to dominate a continent.

That Germany actually procured the war, in the critical days of July, is as yet a mere unsupported allegation; that her whole course since the present Kaiser came to the throne had made the war inevitable, is hardly to be mistaken. That the language of her teachers and her scholars, the words of her Emperor, and the frequent utterances of her official spokesmen had ended by convincing the statesmen and several of the peoples of Europe that Germany was seeking world power—thereby bringing together nations whose unity, once achieved, threatened her interests, her legitimate interests, perhaps all her hopes and ambitions— certainly, is manifest.

But in all this the incidents of the days preceding the war are of minor consequence. We may see and believe that the war was the inevitable consequence of the new visions and pur- poses of the German people, but it is difficult not to see and to believe that the actual occasion of the outbreak was accidental and that the decision for war rather than surrender had already been reached, not by one but by all nations before Sir Edward Grey under- took to perform that task at which Mrs. Partington had failed with equal honour to herself.

VI. BRITAIN AND GERMANY

Something less than a hundred hours separate the German declaration of war upon Russia from the British declaration despatched to Germany after midnight on August 4th. In this time the real drama concerns only Britain and Germany, for Italy in due course proclaimed her neutrality while France affirmed her fidelity to her Russian ally.

In these momentous hours the whole play of German diplomacy was to keep Britain out of the conflict, for reasons too obvious to need mention. And it should be remarked that not only did Germany have good reason to believe that she would succeed, but also that she came desperately near to accomplishing her purpose, as will be disclosed when the history of what took place in London on August 2d at last sees the light of day.

Sir Edward Grey's rôle in this period is also plain. He knew that, not because of Belgium, not because of sympathy for Albert's kingdom or responsibility for its integrity, not because of unwritten but potent claims of honour binding Britain to France, must his country enter the war. Now at last he perceived that it had become a matter of life or death for his own nation and that a German victory and the destruction of France would leave Germany an enemy greater than Napoleon had been, and more menacing than any foe England had known in her long history. Unmistakably his course was to find the cause on which his nation could enter, just as Germany sought to abolish all causes.

In this situation Sir Edward's position was excessively difficult. The Cabinet in which he sat was by no means resolved to fight. Some of its members were frankly opposed to standing with France; others were, to say the least, doubtful. Strong Liberal newspapers, on which the majority party relied for support, openly proclaimed that there was no reason for British participation. The country at large had no inkling of the actual European situation and, thanks to Liberal-Radical rule for nearly a decade, had been taught to regard all discussion of the German menace as without other warrant than domestic political exigency might supply. In the critical hour Britain was asleep and Sir Edward's associates divided as to their duty and paralyzed by the lack of any popular emotion which might supply a warrant for Governmental action.

From this terrible dilemma Germany rescued Sir Edward by her decision to strike at France through Belgium. But no one can read the various documents without feeling that for him Belgium was a pretext rather than a policy. The right and the duty of Britain to defend Belgium were manifest, but it was always as essential to British interest and policy that France should be saved and only a sacrifice of British safety could have resulted, if Sir Edward, lacking the Belgian issue, had been unable to find some other on which he could bring his nation to the point of war. Nor is it less plain that the moment France was involved in the war, the commitments of the British Government in the matter of the fleets bound Britain to stand by the Republic, no matter what course Germany should take—short of guaranteeing to respect the integrity of France, her colonies and her coasts, and to refrain from attacking France.

This was clearly perceived by Lord Lansdowne, who had negotiated the Anglo-French Convention of 1904 and, on the "black Sunday," when British Liberalism stood aghast and shaken before the abyss, he joined with Mr. Balfour in a letter to Mr. Asquith affirming the belief, which was the opinion of the whole Tory party, that France could not be deserted. Conceivably this was the decisive gesture. But it was not until the invasion of Belgium became a fact that there was the suggestion of a resolved policy disclosed in the words or the actions of Sir Edward or his associates.

It remains now, rapidly to summarize the events of the closing days from August 1st, the date of the German declaration of war upon Russia, until the expiration of the time-limit of the British ultimatum addressed to Berlin.

Meantime it should be recalled that Germany, in addition to declaring war upon Russia, had demanded of France information as to what the French attitude would be; had been informed that France would follow the course dictated by her own interests; and that in due course she declared war upon the French Republic on August 3d, alleging certain acts by French aviators over German soil that were too ridiculous to obtain even passing credence.

VII. SIR EDWARD'S DILEMMA

On July 24th, following the Austrian ultimatum by twenty-four hours, Sazonof, the Russian Foreign Minister, asked the British Ambassador in Petrograd to use his influence to have Britain declare that she would stand with France and Russia. The conviction of Russian officials, held consistently by Russian and French diplomacy alike, was that the sole hope for peace was to be found in the chance that Germany would not care to fight if she knew she would have Britain in the field. This view was steadily rejected by Sir Edward Grey, who on July 25th informed the British Ambassador at Petrograd that Great Britain could give no assurance as public sentiment would not warrant a decision to participate in a war over Serbia.

This attitude endured right down to the time of the German declaration of war upon Russia. On July 30th the President of the French Republic made an appeal to the British Ambassador in Paris and on July 31st he addressed a letter directly to King George, asking for an assurance of British support. Both applications were rejected. But it is fair to say for Sir Edward that at the same time he spoke with far more explicitness to Germany, and as early as July 29th warned the German Ambassador in London that he must not mistake the pacific tone of British diplomacy for any assurance that Britain would stay out. This warning was totally ignored in Berlin, where the ruling statesmen pinned their faith to the weakness of British foreign policy and the division in the British Cabinet.

On this same day the German Government made a clear bid for British neutrality by offering to respect Dutch neutrality, to guarantee Belgian integrity and independence, provided Belgium did not stand out against Germany, and to give assurance not to annex French territory in Europe if the war turned in Germany's favour. But Germany thus tacitly declined to promise not to violate Belgian neutrality or to give any pledge not to annex French colonies after the war. This was the "shameful" proposal to quote Sir Edward Grey, which was rejected upon July 30th.

On this same day, too, the French Ambassador in London reminded the British Government of letters exchanged by France and Britain in 1912, after the Agadir crisis, which provided that, if the peace of Europe should be endangered, the two nations should proceed to a discussion of what they proposed to do. Actually this meant a discussion of combined land and sea operations. Still Sir Edward remained unresponsive and King George, on Friday, July 31st, could give only the vaguest of reassuring words to the appeal made to him directly by the President of the French Republic.

And yet on this same day, the situation began to clear, for on this day Sir Edward Grey addressed to France and to Germany an identic note asking their purposes with regard to Belgian neutrality. By the Treaty of 1839, reaffirmed by that of 1870, Britain had declared her purpose to defend the neutrality of Belgium, an engagement made also by Russia, Prussia, and Austria. France promptly agreed to respect Belgian neutrality, but the British Ambassador at Berlin was unable to get any response. The next day the German Ambassador inquired in London whether a German pledge to respect the neutrality of Belgium would insure British neutrality. Sir Edward Grey declined such a bargain at once.

But on August 1st a new problem arose. By virtue of an arrangement made long before 1914, and probably after Agadir, French fleets had taken over the British task in the Mediterranean that the British might concentrate their fleets in the North Sea. The French Atlantic coast was therefore undefended. Wherefore Sir Edward Grey was moved on this day to give to the French Ambassador a promise to ask the Cabinet, which met that afternoon, to agree that if the German fleet undertook to attack the coasts of France, the British fleet would intervene. This assurance was given by the British Cabinet and the French were informed of it on August 2d.

On August 3d Germany on her part agreed to refrain from an

THE TWELVE DAYS
(AUGUST 4-16, 1914)

KING PETER OF SERBIA

In the Twentieth Century, one does not expect to see
a king, clad in velvet and ermine, riding through the
streets of his capital on a snow-white steed, with his
golden crown upon his head. But King Peter is quite
the old-fashioned, fairy-book monarch. In December,
1914, when his troops were about to begin their successful effort to retake Belgrade, he rode along the
front of his line and harangued them, even as their chiefs
of remoter centuries were accustomed to do.

PORTRAITS OF PERSONS
THEN PROMINENT

WILLIAM II, GERMAN EMPEROR

"The Soldier and the army," he said in 1891, "not parliamentary majorities and decisions, have welded together the German Empire. My confidence is in the army." In 1900, he added, "If one wishes to decide something in this world, it is not the pen alone that will do it if unsupported by the power of the sword." And in 1906, "My first and last care is for my fighting forces on land and sea."

THE LATE EMPEROR FRANCIS JOSEPH OF AUSTRIA HUNGARY

When he came to the throne in 1848, more than one revolution was in progress in his dominions. During his reign his army was badly beaten by the Germans and there was much dissension among the many races over which he ruled. His domestic troubles were numerous and heartrending. They included the assassination of his wife and the suicide of his son. Yet he lived on through a record-breaking reign of almost seventy years, and died leaving his people engulfed in the greatest disaster of history.

THE RULERS OF THE TRIPLE ENTENTE

Nicholas, once Czar of all the Russians (*left*), the only autocrat among the Allies, was a weak ruler, much under the influence of his German wife and of wonder-working priests. But when revolution threatened he is said to have indignantly repudiated the traitorous suggestion of one of his generals, to overcome "the canaille" by letting in the Germans.

King George of England (*right*) is more fortunate. A sovereign in name only, he occupies a secure position in the hearts of his countrymen, as the focussing point and symbol of their patriotic but self-respecting loyalty.

THE RULERS OF THE TRIPLE ENTENTE

M. Raymond Poincaré, President of France, hurried back to France from Petrograd during the fatefui Twelve Days in 1914 and set to work on diplomatic correspondence with England. On July 30th, he made an appeal to the British Ambassador in Paris, and the following day addressed a letter directly to King George asking for an assurance of British support. Both applications were rejected. England refused to commit herself till she was sure that Germany was to invade Belgium, and that the Belgians meant to resist.

MR. ASQUITH, BRITISH PREMIER AND SIR EDWARD GREY, BRITISH FOREIGN MINISTER

Sir Edward Grey never grasped the inevitability of the World War. Consequently he was driven to a temporizing policy as the great catastrophe drew near. In the clear light of retrospect it is evident his position demanded that he should have warned the British people of the danger which had for ten years been steadily increasing

Mr. Asquith, like Sir Edward Grey, seems to have been simply bewildered in the crisis. They felt that they ought to stand by France, but the invasion of Belgium was needed to stir the British public to action. Only after that event was a definite settled policy disclosed by the words and acts of the Members of the Government.

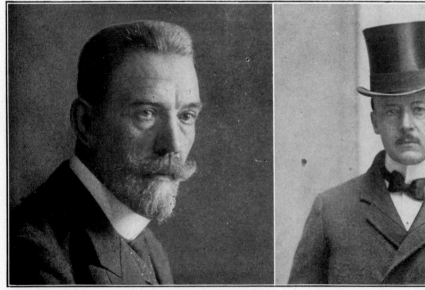

DR. VON BETHMANN-HOLLWEG—GERMAN IM-
PERIAL CHANCELLOR

For nearly forty years—he was born in 1856—the German Chancellor has held public office. He is a Brandenburger, that is to say, a Prussian of the Prussians. Before becoming Chancellor in 1909, he was the Prussian Minister of the Interior (1905), and Imperial Secretary ot State for the Interior (1907). His was the hard task of confessing to the world on August 4, 1914, that Germany was in "a state of necessity" which "knew no law," and had therefore invaded Belgium.

COUNT BERCHTOLD, AUSTRIAN PREMIER,
1914

After the assassination of the Austrian Archduke, Europe waited in the keenest anxiety for a sign from Vienna. But no sign came and the crisis seemed to have passed when, nearly a month after the crime of Sarajevo, Count Berchtold sent to Servia the most formidable ultimatum that one state had ever addressed to another. To this ultimatum was added a time-limit of forty-eight hours. One wonders what was secretly going on during these weeks of apparent inaction.

M. SAZONOF

Photograph by Paul Thompson

VON JAGOW

M. VIVIANI

DIPLOMATISTS OF THE TWELVE DAYS

M. Sazonof, the Russian Foreign Minister who appealed to England to declare she would stand by France and Russia on the day after Austria's ultimatum to Serbia. Sir Edward Grey replied then that England was not ready to go to war on Serbia's account. But the violation of Belgium greatly changed England's attitude. Gottlieb Von Jagow, the German Foreign Minister. His admission to the British Ambassador of Germany's invasion of Belgium at once provoked the British ultimatum. René Viviani, Premier of France during the Twelve Days; later, Minister of Justice, and, in 1917, head of the Allies' War Commission to the United States.

TO PROVIDE THE SINEWS OF WAR

The Finance Ministers of the Triple Entente meet to discuss ways and means. On the left is M. Bark, representing Russia; in the centre, M. Ribot, representing France —in 1917 he became French Premier; on the right, Lloyd-George, then England's Chancellor of the Exchequer and later, Prime Minister.

attack upon France by sea, if Britain would remain neutral, but declined to give any commitment as to Belgium. This occasioned no surprise because on the previous day Germany had informed the Belgian Government of its intention, provoked by alleged French activities, to enter Belgian territory and to advance up the Meuse Valley to attack France.

On this same day Belgium addressed an appeal to Britain for diplomatic support and Sir Edward Grey told the Belgian Minister that a German invasion would mean war with Great Britain. France offered Belgium five army corps, which were declined. But the British assurance sent to Belgium arrived only on the morning of the 4th of August, when the German invasion of Belgium had begun.

VIII. BELGIUM DECIDES TO FIGHT

On Monday, August 3d, Belgium reached its heroic decision to defend its own neutrality and responded to the brutal German ultimatum with a declaration of purpose, contained in moderate language, which will remain memorable. In declaring that she purposed to defend her soil against German violation she asserted that she had at all times been equally prepared to defend herself against France or Britain and thus demolished the whole German edifice of allegation, that France was planning to attack Germany through Belgium.

Sir Edward Grey was getting on firm ground now. An invasion of Belgium, unless Belgium were willing to defend herself, might still have left his Cabinet cold, but once Belgium had made up her mind to fight he was assured that there would be little more hanging back in England.

August 4th is the last day. King Albert, now in the presence of actual invasion, appealed to Great Britain, Russia, and France to help him defend his country. Great Britain sent an ultimatum to Germany, which expired at midnight, demanding that satisfactory assurances be furnished of German determination to respect Belgian neutrality.

Notable on this last day, also, was the speech of the German Chancellor in which he told his countrymen and the world that Germany was in "a state of necessity" which "knew no law," and had therefore invaded Belgium. It is in this speech, too, that he made the frank admission that the invasion of Belgium was in violation of the rules of international law.   He went further and openly conceded that what was being done was "a wrong that we will try to make good again as soon as our military ends have been reached.   When one is threatened as we are, and all is at stake, he can only think of how he can hack his way through."

When the public indignation of the world had become manifest, the German Government endeavoured to find post-mortem warrant for its course in Belgium by the "discovery" of documents in Brussels alleged to disclose a conspiracy of Belgium with Britain and France. Such devices were as futile as the efforts to find excuse for a declaration of war upon France in imaginary aeroplane raids by French craft dropping bombs over German cities.   Whatever effect they may have had upon German opinion, these fictions have long been dismissed by neutral publics, which have accepted as final the blunt, brutal, but at least honest words of the German Chancellor spoken at the moment when the decision had been made.

Not less memorable is the incident that marked the final interview between the British Ambassador and the German Chancellor.   To Sir Edward Goschen, calling to take his leave of the Chancellor, Bethmann-Hollweg made his famous inquiry as to the purpose of Great Britain to make war upon Germany merely for the sake of "a scrap of paper." The "scrap of paper" was the British guarantee of the integrity of Belgium, contained in the Treaty of 1839 and reaffirmed in the document of 1870. The full extent of German surprise, apprehension, and anger, provoked by the decision of Great Britain, was revealed in this interview for the first time.

Meantime, as Von Jagow had already told the British Ambassador, the invasion of Belgium had become an accomplished fact and there could be no drawing back for Germany.   Accordingly, with expiration of the time-limit of the British ultimatum at midnight on August 4th, Great Britain declared war upon Germany. Thus the triple Entente in the presence of the fact of war became a triple alliance at the precise moment when the Triple Alliance was facing the defection of Italy, who promptly announced that the terms of her alliance with Austria and Germany, which were for action in a defensive war only, did not require her to participate in a war which she considered aggressive on their part, and that she therefore proclaimed her neutrality. This prompt declaration of Italian neutrality was of incalculable military advantage to France, since it automatically released for service on the German frontier several army corps stationed along the Alps.

August 4, 1914, therefore, marks the complete ruin of the whole edifice that Bismarck had erected; his alliance had collapsed; the union of all the rivals of Germany, which he had feared and in his life time prevented, had come to pass. All of this, too, German statesmen might have perceived would inevitably occur, had they been guided by British tradition rather than contemporary British policy. Such, across the centuries, had been the unfailing answer of Britain to a challenge to her supremacy at sea.

CHAPTER FOUR

THE GERMAN ATTACK

I

THE TWO STRATEGICAL CONCEPTIONS

From the morrow of the Franco-Prussian War the German General Staff, like the French, had been engaged in formulating the plans by which they would act in the next war. With the lapse of years it had come to be accepted as inevitable that the superior organization and the largely increased population of Germany, together with her central position, would enable her to take the offensive at the outset of operations. The alliance of France with Russia and of Germany with Austria and Italy had broadened the scope of the plans without changing the essential fact that Germany would have the initiative. And as Italy yearly moved farther away from her partners, her assistance was presently eliminated as a factor both by Germany and her enemies.

Having the offensive, the German problem was to decide whether to attack France, leaving to Austria, reinforced by a few German covering troops in East Prussia and Posen, the task of containing Russia until France was disposed of, or to detain France at the strongly fortified and easily defensible Alsace-Lorraine frontier, and level the main blow at Russia. The decision was made for the attack upon France. Since it failed, and perhaps before, the alternative has been strongly advocated, but it is easy to understand and accept the reasons that controlled the decision for France.

These reasons were various. As to Russia it was recognized that her mobilization would be slow, it was known that in organization and equipment her troops were inferior to the German. But it was equally notorious that Russian strategy did not include an immediate offensive; that the Russian plans for mobilization were to be carried out behind the Bug and far east of Warsaw; that Russian strategy, in fact, rested upon

78

the conception, enduring from the Napoleonic Era, of a retreat, without decisive engagement, into the vast regions to the east, where Napoleon's army had perished, where roads were few, transport difficult, and the machinery of the German army would work at the least advantage. Finally, this meant not a quick decision but a long delay; it meant also, in a war opening in August, that Germany would meet winter on the road to Moscow or Petrograd.

Speed, too, was the very essence of German strategy. Napoleon had been defeated in the Waterloo campaign in less than a week after he took the field. Six weeks had sufficed to dispose of Austria in 1866, and the decisive battles of the Franco-Prussian War were not divided by a longer span from the date of mobilization. German finance, the whole nature of Germany's economic fabric, was not adjusted to a long war. What was to be sought was a quick decision. This might also serve to keep Britain out of the war as a French defeat might lead Russia to abandon the struggle, when Paris had fallen.

A quick decision could only be obtained in the west, but such a decision there might be expected to settle the war. At all events, the French army beaten and flung back behind the Loire, Paris and northern France conquered, the Germans could send their best troops east and rely upon reserves to meet the French efforts, while the costs of the war would already be saddled upon a France which would no longer be able to avoid paying the huge indemnity Germany had reckoned on in her calculations before the war.

All German calculations had arrived at the same point that France could be crushed within six weeks after the war broke out, that in this time Russian activities would not become too serious for Austria to deal with alone, or aided by a few German corps in the north. But the success or failure of the German strategy would be measured by the success or failure of the German army in bringing France to a decisive battle early in the second month of the war, destroying the French field armies in that battle and, thanks to the German heavy artillery, taking Paris and all the barrier fortresses from Luxemburg to Switzerland.

Unhappily for Germany, the question of Belgium was involved by reason of the manner in which French strategy, in the years following the great French disaster of the Franco-Prussian War, had undertaken to guard against the blow German strategy was preparing.

II. THE BELGIAN PROBLEM

Recognizing the growing superiority of Germany in numbers, France had sought to meet this by the erection on her eastern frontier of a splendid system of forts, based upon the four great fortresses of Verdun, Toul, Épinal, and Belfort and buttressed by many other detached forts connecting the larger strongholds. Actually a wall of steel—with but one gap, southwest of Nancy—opposed itself to German advance across the whole extent of Franco-German frontier.

Given German superiority in heavy artillery, these forts were likely to fall, but defended by the whole field army of France, they would in all probability hold out far beyond the six weeks' period and knowing as we now know, that trench war was bound to come, there is no escape from the conclusion that the decision of the German General Staff against attempting to force this barrier, given their time limitation, was wise.

There was, then, only the road through Belgium, since the Swiss route was unsuitable for use by great masses of men and Switzerland had an army far more formidable than the Belgian. The decision, therefore, was for the Belgian route and it was made many years before the war. The proof of this is found in the strategic railroads built to the Belgian frontier and signalled by military writers as early as 1909. Well-built double-track lines led through the comparative wilderness of the eastern Ardennes and ended exactly on the Belgian frontier. They had no commercial value and served no peaceful purpose. But they did enable Germany to mobilize vast masses, far more rapidly than any one suspected would be the case, squarely on the Belgian frontier.

Once across the Ardennes, the road by the Meuse and Sambre valleys led straight into the plains of northern France. This road was not barred by any French forts. The sole obstacles were the Belgian fortresses of Liége and Namur, both out of date, both unprovided with modern equipment, and both lacking in subsidiary defences. Germany reckoned, wisely, as the event showed, that these would prove no considerable obstacle and would fall to her great howitzers with a minimum of delay.   As for the Belgian army, German High Command could hope that it would not intervene.   But if it did, it was too small and too poorly organized to offer serious resistance.   The event proved this to be true.

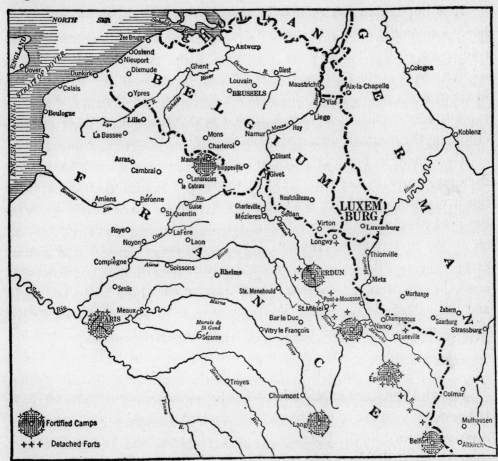

WHY THE GERMANS WENT THROUGH BELGIUM
"A wall of steel, with but one gap, southwest of Nancy, opposed itself to German advance across the whole extent of Franco-German frontier"

With the political aspects, as well as the moral problems, involved in the invasion of Belgium, German High Command did not concern itself. It could hope again, that Britain, like Belgium, would not interfere with the march of Teutonic hosts against France by the Belgian road. It could believe that, even if Britain entered the war, she would not send her scanty army to the Continent in time to intervene (another calculation almost justified by the event). But it was satisfied that even if this should take place, it still possessed a margin of superiority in numbers and material, which would insure the victory, even at the very worst.

It is impossible not to believe that German High Command over-bore German diplomacy in the matter of Belgian neutrality, and that the soldier imposed his will upon the statesman. The conviction of the soldier was that, using Belgium as a highway, he could destroy France in the time at his disposal and that no other method would avail. He came so near to absolute success that it is impossible to criticize his decision, on the military side.

Here then, in brief, is the whole German strategical conception for the first thrust of the war. It was broken at the Battle of the Marne, but it was not until after the battles of Flanders had made the western deadlock absolute that it was finally abandoned. It supplies the clue to all of the first phase of the war. In this conception all was foreseen except the possibility of a French retreat without a decisive battle, until the conditions of contest should have turned against the Germans and the balance of numbers, rightly reckoned certain to be heavily with the invader at the outset, should be partially restored.

III. FRENCH STRATEGY

French High Command had based its course upon the lessons of 1870. It knew the purpose of Germany to risk all on a single throw and seek a decisive victory in the opening weeks. It knew that Germany might come through Belgium, but it could never be certain of this and it was compelled to base its initial concentration upon the more probable objective of German attack, which remained the eastern frontier. But it had made its plans to meet the Belgian thrust. What it could not foresee was the number of troops Germany would send through Belgium, the rapidity with which Belgian forts would fall, and the extraordinary mobility of German troops, due to the unexpected use of motor transport.

It was understood between France and Russia that if the German blow was directed at France, Russian troops would enter East Prussia in the third week of the war, as they did. It was believed that this would compel the Germans to return east and weaken their armies in France before the decisive battle. The terrible defeat of the Russians at Tannenberg partially wrecked this hope, but the Russian victories in Galicia ultimately compelled the Germans to give over their efforts in the west and go to the rescue of their Austrian ally.

It was the hope of the French, by taking the offensive in Lorraine and Alsace, as well as in the Ardennes, if the Germans came through Belgium, to win such successes as to imperil the German armies in the north and force them to return to the Rhine to defend their own country. This hope expired in the heavy defeats of the French at Morhange and Neufchâteau in the first three weeks of the war. It was the hope of the French, if they were beaten in these opening contests, to stand on their own frontiers, before Nancy, behind the Meuse from Verdun to Charleville and thence to Lille and break the fury of the German assault on lines long foreseen. This hope was realized absolutely before Nancy, momentarily behind the Meuse, but fell when the Germans succeeded in sending unexpected masses far west and overwhelming the British. It was the further hope of the French, if all these plans failed, that it would be possible to make a successful stand behind the Aisne, the Oise, and the Somme. But the collapse of the British and the unforeseen rapidity of Kluck's advance defeated this hope also.

But beneath all these conceptions lay the fundamental purpose not to risk the fate of the whole French field force until the chances of victory were unmistakable. There was to be no repetition of the blunders of 1870, the defeat of French armies in detail, the isolation of Bazaine, the sacrifice of MacMahon to political and dynastic considerations. French High Command was even prepared to evacuate Paris, if necessary, but it did not mean to risk a decisive battle, while the odds were against it. This was the conception that dominated the whole French campaign and led to the supreme victory of the Marne, which wrecked the whole German strategy and obtained a tactical triumph on the battlefield as well.

Thus, while the various French armies suffered local defeats, none was ever routed, none was ever captured, and all retained their form from the beginning to the end of the campaign.   This purpose, and not the local reverses suffered by the French in the opening days of the war, explains the great retreat, which at the moment seemed to the world the promise of French ruin and long deluded the German commanders into believing that they had achieved the purpose for which they were acting.   But for the Russian disaster at Tannenberg, the whole French fundamental conception might have prevailed, and after the Marne the Germans might have been compelled to go back to their own frontier, because of the Russian pressure in East Prussia and along the lower Vistula.

The second phase of the war came with the German attack upon Russia in May, 1915.   At this time Germany definitely adopted the plan of crushing Russia, while holding France and Britain in the west. She was able to do this because, with all her successes, Russia had not quite succeeded in performing her part of the Franco-Russian plan; she had not been able to invade East Prussia and make good her hold there. But to understand the first months of the war, it is simply necessary to see the rival plans working out, to observe Germany endeavouring to crush France while holding back Russia, with Austrian aid; France seeking to avoid disaster and strike back at the favourable moment; Russia trying to take advantage of the despatch of German troops to the west and sweep through East Prussia to the Vistula, while defeating Austrian troops in Galicia and Volhynia.

Having been defeated at the Marne, Germany was able, by reason of her heavy artillery and machine guns, instruments that she had expected to win for her the decisive battle, to take a defensive position in France and hold it, but she never was able again to win any considerable ground on the offensive, even in her tremendous Verdun drive in 1916, and she was unable to prevent her western foes from ultimately passing to the offensive.   All her conceptions for forty years had been of a swift, tremendous thrust, a colossal battle, and a victory that should settle the fate of France for the period of the war, probably forever. When the decision at the Marne was made absolute in Flanders, the whole character of the war and the nature of the outcome were changed. That is the reason why, in the minds of military writers, the Battle of the Marne remains the most important incident in the first two years of the war.

Tannenberg was only less important than the Marne, since it brought about the ruin of the original Franco-Russian conception, gave Germany the necessary time to make good her hold in France and to make her final effort in Flanders. Russian pressure in the east ultimately became effective, precisely as French and Russian General Staffs had expected, but it became effective in November, instead of September, in Galicia, not in East Prussia. When it became effective Germany had to abandon her western campaign, turn her attention to the east, undertake a number of more or less limited efforts, and at last organize her great drive against Russia, which began in late April, 1915.

If Joffre had been defeated at the Marne the whole German plan would have succeeded precisely as Germany had calculated. If Hindenburg had been defeated at Tannenberg, the whole German plan would have collapsed as French and Russian strategy had expected. But Tannenberg was relatively a small affair, and Russia's losses, although large, were insignificant compared with her main strength. Hence she was able to keep on with Galicia and ultimately to force Germany to abandon the west. On the other hand, the whole German plan was defeated at the Marne because the bulk of German military strength was used there.

CHAPTER FIVE

BELGIAN DEFENCE AND FRENCH OFFENCE

I
LIÉGE

In the event of an attack coming from Germany, the main reliance of Belgian defence was the fortress of Liége, situated some twenty miles west of the German frontier, commanding the crossings of the Meuse River and the railroad coming from the Rhine at Cologne to Brussels and Antwerp, the great trunk line from Germany.

Liége was surrounded by twelve isolated forts, the work of the celebrated Brialmont. It had ranked in its day as one of the finest of European fortresses, but it had been allowed to fall into disrepair and no effort had been made, as in the case of the French fortresses of Verdun and Belfort, to strengthen its works as the improvement in heavy artillery became pronounced. These forts were isolated and they were neither connected by any field works nor had there been any care taken to keep their field of fire free by forbidding the construction of buildings.

The forts had permanent garrisons of trained artillerymen, but the city itself was without any sufficient garrison and it had been calculated that it would take 75,000 men to defend its wide circle. Still it was the general expectation of Europe that Liége, however insufficient as a permanent barrier to German advance, would serve as a sufficient obstacle to permit the arrival of French and British troops to the west of the town and their junction with the Belgian field army. This army, actually in process of reconstruction, had been organized and trained with the idea that it would take its position west of Liége, behind the Geete River, its right resting on Namur, its left upon the Diemer at Diest. Here it was expected that it would be able, thanks to the resistance of Liége, to hold a solid front and prevent the overflow of German masses into the plain east of Louvain until aid came.

Belgian mobilization was ordered on August 1st; it was completed by August 6th. Something more than one hundred thousand men, the field army of the nation, were then concentrated behind the Geete. The King took command, establishing his headquarters at Louvain.

Meantime, there had been very striking developments. On August 4th, twelve regiments of German cavalry had crossed the frontier from the direction of Aix-la-Chapelle; moved rapidly west to the Meuse, which they reached at Visé, just south of the Dutch frontier and north of Liége; forced the crossing of the river, driving in a weak Belgian force, which recoiled upon Liége; and thus gained the west bank of the Meuse.

On August 5th the Tenth German Army Corps under Emmich reached the front of the eastern forts of Liége, demanded permission to pass unopposed and, this permission being refused, undertook to take the town by assault, seeking to penetrate between the forts.

At this time the whole 3d Division of the Belgian field army, and two brigades of the 4th, occupied the ground between the forts and, supported by their fire, successfully repulsed the German attacks through the days of August 5th and 6th. On this latter day, however, the arrival of masses of German troops, which began to cross the river above and below, threatened to cut off the retreat of the field forces and General Leman, the commander of Liége, ordered these to retire upon the main Belgian army concentrated behind the Geete. This retreat was successfully conducted.

On August 7th the German infantry penetrated between the forts, occupied the city and the citadel, but were unable to take the forts. These maintained their fire until German and Austrian heavy guns were brought up, but under this attack they crumbled almost instantaneously. The last fort fell, accepting the Belgian official report, on August 16th, but the German reports place it much earlier. Actually, as an obstacle to German advance, Liége lost its importance by August 10th and the city itself was in German hands on the 7th.

As German mobilization and concentration were hardly completed before August 12th, and the great advance did not begin until several days later, it may be fairly said that Liége, despite the common belief at the time, actually did not delay the Germans materially. It gave a great moral impulse to French and British peoples, it earned a place in history through the devotion of its defenders. It was, however, taken with no great loss, in spite of contemporary reports. But it was not taken by a *coup-de-main* as the Germans had hoped.

II. BELGIAN "BATTLES"

Meantime the Belgian field army, having completed its concentration, was standing behind the Geete between Diest and Namur, that is between the Meuse and the Diemer. Against it there now began to beat the first waves of German advance, the screen of cavalry, which preceded the advance of the infantry. On August 12th there was a very sharp skirmish at Haelen, in which German cavalry were handsomely repulsed. This "battle" filled the press of the world at the time, and, with the grotesque reports of the resistance at Liége, then current, gave a totally inaccurate impression of what was happening.

From August 12th to August 18th this skirmishing continued, the Belgian army keeping its position. Its expectation was that the French and British troops would arrive in time to make possible the defence of Belgium on the line of the Geete, or at the least on the lines of the Dyle, famous in the wars of Louis XIV, one flank resting on Antwerp, the centre covering Brussels, and the line continued through Namur and prolonged by French troops behind the Meuse to the forts of Givet in France. On August 15th the first German attack upon the line of the Meuse south of Namur at Dinant had been repulsed by French troops, which had just entered the town.

On the morning of August 18th, however, the King of the Belgians at last realized that the French and British would not arrive in time. At that moment he was faced by six German corps—three advancing from the Meuse, having crossed north of Liége; three from the south, which had forced the passage of the river at Huy. These were the advance corps of the armies of Kluck and Bülow respectively. Behind them five more corps were known to be advancing. To face more than 500,000 Germans (eleven corps), the Belgians had about 100,000, the value of two big corps.   At this moment the British were just detraining near Maubeuge, and the French army, which was to act with the Belgians, was just south of Philippeville, on the edge of French territory.

It was useless to wait longer.   Belgian resistance had been prolonged to the last moment and, unless the army was now to be uselessly sacrificed, a retreat was inevitable.   Accordingly, on the morning of August 18th, King Albert ordered a retirement upon the fortified camp of Antwerp, which had been constructed with the idea of serving as a place of asylum for the entire field army of Belgium in just such an emergency as had now arrived.   The retreat was made good on August 19th, and on August 20th, the entire army, less a division detached to Namur, was inside the Antwerp defences.

Meantime, the German army, now beginning to display that mobility which was due to an enormous train of motor transport, moved rapidly forward, occupied Louvain on August 19th, entered Brussels on August 20th, and then, turning half left, started for France.   This was the army of Kluck.   On the same day that Louvain was occupied the advance guards of Bülow appeared before Namur, which was defended by a weak division of Belgians, who, four days later, were to receive as a reinforcement two battalions of French troops.   These arrived just in time to retire, thus doing precisely what Winston Churchill's British detachments were to do in the case of Antwerp, less than two months later.

Namur, like Antwerp and Liége, was defended by a circle of detached forts, which were, however, in much worse condition than those of either of the other fortress towns.   Against these forts the Germans now brought up the heavy artillery which had demolished the forts of Liége. The bombardment began on August 21st, the day after Brussels fell; by the next day most of the forts were in ruins.   The following day the situation was hopeless and almost all the forts had been silenced.   Accordingly the garrison, some 12,000 Belgians, together with the French who had come so tardily, slipped out, just avoiding envelopment, and retreated south.   August 23d, then, saw the occupation of Namur, which had been the corner-stone of the whole Anglo-French strategy in the Belgian campaign.   Two days later the last fort fell, but by this time the war had gone south into France.

The fall of Liége was far more prompt than Allied commanders had expected, but it did not gravely injure their plans.   It did prevent a junction between the Anglo-French and the Belgian armies, if such a junction was ever contemplated.   But this is not certain, for there were grave dangers apparent in any campaign in eastern Belgium.   The collapse of Namur, under two days' bombardment on the other hand, was not only unexpected, but turned out to be a real disaster, which was the prelude to many that were now to follow.

III. THE MORAL VALUE

Such, briefly, is the story of the Belgian campaign, which lasted from August 4th to August 18th, the date when the Belgian army retired from the pathway of German advance.   Belgian resistance continued at Namur for five more days.   Actually the Belgian army was only able to hold back the cavalry screen of German advance for the days before the infantry had concentrated and began its great drive.   When this began, the Belgian army had no choice but to get out of the way.

There were no engagements of any size during the whole period; there was no battle, and the forts of Liége and Namur fell as the Germans had calculated they would fall.   In so far as they had reckoned on Belgian submission the Germans had been disappointed, but otherwise their plans had worked exactly as they expected them to work; they had brushed the Belgian army out of the way in a minimum of time and with inconsiderable losses.   Having now contained the Belgian field army in Antwerp, they turned south for the drive at Paris, August 20th, the date of the occupation of Brussels, marking the turn of Kluck.

The surprises of this brief Belgian campaign were supplied by the efficacy of German heavy artillery and the number of troops the Germans had been able to mobilize and send through Belgium.   Miscalculation on the first point had wrecked any Allied plan to join the Belgian field army on the Geete or the Dyle.   Miscalculation as to the

BELGIUM "THE COCKPIT OF EUROPE" IN PICTURES

ALBERT OF BELGIUM (BORN 1875, ACCEDED
TO THRONE, 1909

The fighting king of "the Cockpit of Europe" is so old-fashioned that he led his army in person and asked no better fate than to share the hardships and dangers of his soldiers. His democratic attitude toward his soldiers he himself has attributed in part to his observation of the late James J. Hill's attitude toward his railroad employees—for King Albert, before his accession to the throne, paid a long visit to the United States, spending a large part of the time studying American railroading as Mr. Hill's guest.

BELGIAN CAVALRY

ONE SHOT FROM A GERMAN 42-CENTIMETRE GUN PUT THIS BELGIAN FORT OUT OF COMMISSION

Students of German strategy assert that the Germans long ago decided to strike quickly at France through Belgium when "The Day" should come. The French frontier was strongly fortified. Switzerland was a difficult country and strongly defended. There remained—Belgium, dangerously peaceful and prosperous, like the United States. Her little army and her forts were easily reducible by the terrible German guns.

BELGIAN BATTERY ON THE MARCH

WAR ENTHUSIASTS IN BRUSSELS

Shouting, flag-waving crowds in the cities of Belgium enthusiastically voiced their approval of the Government's decision to resist the violation of Belgian territory. And the little Belgian army, in full realization that the day of fairy-tales was past, set itself to play the rôle of Jack, against the German Giant.

BELGIAN SOLDIERS AT REST DURING A LULL IN THE FIGHTING

Germans under Emmich arrived before Liége on August 5, 1914. For two days of almost incessant fighting General Lehman with the third Division of the Belgian army maintained his defence of the city. Then fresh masses of German troops arrived and to save his exhausted soldiers Lehman retired upon the main Belgian army concentrated behind the Geete. The Germans occupied the city on the 7th, but the nearby forts held out against them for several days.

A typical Belgian soldier

General Lehman, defender of Liége

Awaiting the Uhlans

THE INVASION OF BELGIUM, EPITOMIZED IN PICTURES

The German hordes invaded the land which was open, flat, sea-girt, seeming to invite the invader.

The little Belgian army stood its ground as long as possible, resisting to the limit of its strength.

But it was all of no avail and the Germans marched into Brussels, the capital city, on August 20th, seventeen days after crossing the border.

RUINED TOWN HALL AT YPRES

About the sleepy little Flemish town of Ypres for more than a month raged one of the most intricate, confused, and indescribable conflicts in all the history of the war; fought by men of more races, religions, colours, and nationalities than any battlefield in western Europe had known since the onrush of the soldiers of Islam was halted on the field of Tours. Asia, Africa, and even America and Australia shared in the glory and the slaughter.

BELGIUM UNDER GERMAN RULE

I. General Von Bissing, military governor of Belgium, is here shown in consultation with his staff. He is the man with the heavy moustache who stands with the knuckles of both hands resting on the map, upon which the attention of all is concentrated. (He died at his post in Belgium in March, 1917).

BELGIUM UNDER GERMAN RULE

II. Even the civil governors of Belgium, here shown, have a decidedly military appearance. Nearly all are in uniform, booted and spurred. His Excellency Von Sandt, head of the Commission, is at the end of the table leaning slightly forward, with eyes cast down.

second factor was shortly to lead to heavy defeats at Mons and Charle-roi.   Nor were German numbers in Belgium to be measured solely by the ten corps of Bülow and Kluck (an eleventh was detached to watch the Belgians in Antwerp).   Still a third army, composed of three Saxon corps under Hausen, coming west through the Ardennes and aiming at the Meuse crossings south of Namur, notably at Dinant, was to surprise the Allies completely and further contribute to the destruc-tion of all their plans.   By August 21st hardly less than 700,000 German troops had crossed Belgium and were approaching the French frontier. In addition there were the army of the Grand Duke of Würtemberg, five corps strong, which was in the Belgian Ardennes north of Sedan, and the army of the Crown Prince, also containing five corps that had passed through Luxemburg and was just breaking into France about Longwy.   Twenty-three corps were then employed by the Germans— aside from two cavalry corps, a corps left in Belgium, and twenty-one were to come on the battlefield of the Marne.   Eight additional corps were presently identified in Alsace-Lorraine.

Even the briefest military summary of the Belgian episode cannot, however, completely ignore the moral value.   The Belgians had failed, as did the Spartans at Thermopylæ.   A dwarf had met a giant, and, as invariably happens outside of fairy tales, the dwarf had been beaten. Yet the decision of Belgium to resist, transformed the character of the whole war in the minds of the nations which were now fighting Ger-many; it contributed materially to influencing Italian sentiment; it gave form and colour to the world conflict, and it had an influence which cannot be measured either by the paltry numbers or the insig-nificant skirmishes, the very names of which were forgotten in a few days by a world that was to see a Battle of the Marne within a fort-night after Namur fell.

Had Belgium failed to resist German invasion, the whole significance of the German decision to disregard the Treaty of 1839 would have been lost.   As it was, Belgium became in a very real sense the issue of the war, and popular sympathy in neutral countries all over the world was lost to Germany at the outset of the conflict.   This would have been of minor consequence had Germany been able to win that decisive victory which alone could justify the invasion of Belgium even in her own eyes. But when the decision of the Marne turned against her and the war became not a short and swift triumph but a long and terrible agony, the Belgian incident was a heavy and a permanent handicap.

No one who was alive in the August days, when Belgian resistance began, and dwelt outside of German or Austrian frontiers, will ever forget the instant and enduring impression that Belgian heroism created, and nowhere more than in America was the Belgian incident destructive of German hopes of sympathy and even of more practical assistance in her tremendous struggle. But for Belgium it is not difficult to believe that American neutrality would have taken a very different character, and it is far from improbable that the Allies would have failed to find in America that source of munitions which was to contribute so much to save them from disaster in the first two years of the war.

IV. FRENCH BEGINNINGS—MÜHLHAUSEN

Of a necessity, French mobilization was based upon the assumption that Germany would attack from Alsace-Lorraine. Modifications to follow the disclosure of a purpose to use Belgium had long been prepared. But it was not only a question whether the Germans would pass through Belgium at all; there was also the question as to whether they would make the main or even a considerable attack from this direction. There could be no way of knowing about this in advance. Accordingly the French had always assigned five army corps to act between the Meuse and the Sambre and relied upon the British expeditionary army to supply the balance needed to hold the line in this region should the Germans come this way. Presumably they also relied upon the Belgian army.

French mobilization proceeded with extreme regularity. The great masses of men were equipped and concentrated within the time set. There was nothing of the disorder and confusion of 1870, although a lack of guns and of equipment was presently signalled, when it came to reserves. The French mobilization was slower than the German, of which it fell far short in the numbers it prepared for the first shock, but it was an eminently successful operation.

Meantime, while mobilization was proceeding, the French undertook their first thrust.   A large garrison had been maintained in peace times in the fortress of Belfort, commanding the gap between the Vosges and Switzerland.   This garrison, reinforced by the first troops mobilized, stepped out and over the frontier on August 7th, the day the Germans penetrated Liége.   The next day it had reached Altkirch and defeated a German force.   On August 9th it entered Mühlhausen, next to Strassburg the largest city of Alsace-Lorraine.   This success thrilled France and was accepted as proof of the approaching deliverance of the "Lost Provinces."

But on the night of August 9th a surprise attack by the Germans turned the French out of Mühlhausen, which was retaken after desperate street fighting.   In this first operation French commanders began to display faults which were to prove expensive a little later.   New forces had now to be sent to Alsace; General Pau took command, succeeding the general that had failed.   By August 19th the French were back in Mühlhausen, while other detachments were overflowing from all the Vosges crests and approaching the Rhine.   Unhappily for the French this campaign was to come to a sudden end, because of the first real disaster not far away.

V. MORHANGE—THE FIRST DISASTER

In all the military discussion which preceded the present war it was fully recognized that the first great clash between the French and German troops, in the next struggle, would come east of Nancy and along the frontier which had been created by the Treaty of Frankfort.   No forts, on either side of the line, barred this natural gateway between the valleys of the Rhine and the Moselle.   Nancy itself was but eleven miles from the frontier.   North of this gateway the forts of Metz and Thionville in Germany, the Verdun-Toul barrier in France, closed the way; south, the Vosges and the forts of Épinal forbade any general operation, as far as the Belfort gap.   But here in a fairly open country it was believed that the first, and perhaps the decisive, battle of the war would be fought.

French mobilization and concentration were here completed behind the Moselle and the Meurthe, while the covering troops occupied their regular post upon the considerable mass of hills, known as the Grand-Couronne of Nancy, just across the Meurthe, and extending north almost to Pont-à-Mousson. Despite a few early skirmishes at the frontier, the Germans seem to have made no especial effort even to disturb the French concentration.

But about August 12th there came the first official announcement of French operations. These seemed to push steadily forward; by August 13th there was a French success across the German frontier. In the week that followed, the movement swelled into something approaching a real invasion. By August 19th, the day Mühlhausen was reoccupied, the French had passed the line of the Metz-Strassburg railroad and were in Saarburg, Dieuze, and Delme, fifteen or twenty miles from the frontier. This was the high-water mark.

On August 20th the French army at last came in contact with the main German force, the army of the Crown Prince of Bavaria, while a second German army, that of Heeringen, was signalled west of Strassburg and north of the Donon Mountain. These two armies faced respectively the armies of Castelnau and Dubail. They seem to have waited for the French attack upon positions carefully selected and prepared.

The battle which followed, named Morhange by the French and Metz by the Germans, is noteworthy, apart from its local value, as revealing the type of engagement in all the first days of the war. The French, advancing to attack, displaying much impetuosity and some lack of discipline, came suddenly under the fire of the heavy German artillery—field artillery, not the sort of gun that had already levelled the forts of Liége.

This heavy artillery outranged the French field gun, the famous "75," and, unsupported by any artillery, the French infantry were beaten upon by a storm of shells, fired from a distance and by an unseen

foe.   They were also held up by barbwire entanglements and trenches.
After a brief engagement a French corps—the Fifteenth, of Marseilles
—broke and fled.   Its rout compromised the whole army although the
Twentieth Corps—the famous Iron Corps, commanded by Foch, who
here won his first laurels—now, and in the subsequent retreat, performed
miracles.   At the same time the Germans passed to the attack.   The
end of the invasion of Lorraine had come.

In the next days the French retirement was rapid; some thousands of
prisoners, some guns, and several flags were left in the German possession.   By August 23d the Germans were well within French territory,
they had occupied Lunéville, pressed beyond to Gerbéviller, were at the
edge of the Grand-Couronne, hardly eight miles from Nancy.   They had
now got about as far into French territory as the French had been in
German territory at the Battle of Morhange.   But this was another
high-water mark.

With great rapidity the French troops, which had retaken Mühlhausen, were drawn out of Alsace and brought back to the Nancy front.
They were put into action, while many French batteries were massed on
the Saffais plateau, a few miles south of Nancy.   The German advance
was halted, and the French, passing to the offensive, pushed the Germans
back materially.

Thus the German victory of Morhange was without real consequence.   It was a severe defeat for the French and wrecked their offensive.   But the defeated troops were able to rally and save Nancy.   In
the opening days of September and during the time of the Battle of the
Marne a new German attack on this front was beaten down, and the
French, although weakened by the transfer of several corps to the Marne,
were still able first to repulse a new and heavier attack and later to take
the offensive and push the Germans back to the frontier.   There a deadlock ensued which endured right through the next two years.   But
after September, 1914, the Nancy front became inactive.

Morhange was the first considerable Franco-German battle since the
War of 1870.   It was a real defeat for the French and, taken with the
defeats that followed, it unpleasantly suggested Wörth and the earlier

débâcle. But the French rally showed, as German official reports later conceded, that French armies were not like those of forty-four years before.

VI. NEUFCHÂTEAU AND CHARLEROI

At the moment when the Battle of Morhange was opening, two more French armies, north of Verdun, on a front from Luxemburg to the point where the Meuse quits France, were also taking the offensive. These were the armies of Ruffey, north of Verdun, and of De Langle de Cary, north of Sedan. A day after the defeat of Morhange these armies were heavily beaten in the same fashion. In the difficult region of the Ardennes they came suddenly in contact with armies of the German Crown Prince near Virton, south of Arlon and of the Duke of Würtemberg north of Neufchâteau. Once more the German heavy artillery triumphed, and the French, caught before barbwire entanglements, deprived of all artillery support, were repulsed in disorder, lost flags and guns, and surrendered the offensive.

Having won the encounter, the German troops now pressed forward. The French retired, first behind the Othain and the Semois and then behind the Meuse. Their retreat was more orderly than that of their fellows at Morhange. Behind the Semois and the Othain they were able to inflict heavy losses on the Germans and subsequently made good their position behind the Meuse, as Castelnau's troops had made good theirs before Nancy. Henceforth the retirements of these two armies— Ruffey's which passed to the command of Sarrail shortly, and De Langle de Cary's—were never seriously shaken. They shared in the general retreat because they were compelled to keep their alignment with the other armies. But as late as August 28th they inflicted heavy losses on the Germans, who were attempting to cross the Meuse all the way from Sedan to Dun.

These two opening engagements were French defeats and they contributed to raising German hopes and expectations, but the really decisive action was elsewhere. It was in the triangle between the Meuse and the Sambre and westward about Mons that the real blow was now

about to fall.   Against this triangle, in which four French regular corps
and some divisions of reserves and African troops were standing, their
left prolonged by the British army, thirteen German corps, the armies
of Kluck, Bülow, and Hausen, were now striking, having already disposed of the Belgian field army.

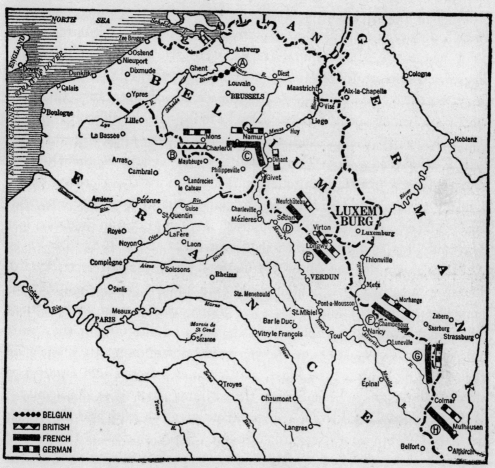

THE FIRST BATTLES, AUGUST 15TH-23D, 1914

A–Belgians   C–Lanzerac   E–Ruffey   G–Dubail
B–British   D–De Langle de Cary   F–Castelnau   H–Pau

On August 22d, two days after Morhange and one day after Neufchâteau, the French army commanded by Lanzerac, holding the crossings of the Sambre about Charleroi, was suddenly attacked by Bülow.
A terrific battle followed.   There was street fighting of the most desperate character, ground was taken and lost, the losses on both sides were

very heavy, and by night the French had been pushed back across the Sambre and the Germans held the river crossings. Lanzerac had lost the day but he was still capable of renewing the conflict. Unhappily at this time he learned that Namur was about to fall and that the army of Hausen, three corps strong and hitherto unsuspected, had forced the crossing of the Meuse at Dinant and was advancing across his rear, seeking to cut his line of retreat to France.

A retreat was inevitable and the French drew back rapidly until their flanks rested upon the forts at Givet and Maubeuge. By the next day all danger of envelopment was over, but the superior numbers of the enemy necessitated further retreat. The following day the misfortunes that had overtaken the British involved the Lanzerac army, soon to pass to the command of Franchet d'Esperey, and it was unable to stand again until it had reached the Oise. There, on August 30th, it inflicted a heavy check upon the Prussian Guard at Guise. But by this time its retreat, due to the British situation, had involved the armies of De Langle and Ruffey, which were compelled to leave the Meuse and retire south.

By August 23d, then, four French armies had been defeated on Belgian or German soil and driven back into French territory. Two had suffered something like routs at Morhange and at Neufchâteau; a third had lost a considerable battle at Charleroi but had left the field in order; all would soon be restored to fighting shape. The time had promptly passed when there was a chance that the first German victories would have decisive results. Already a new French army, under Foch, was ready to enter the line at the north between De Langle and Lanzerac.

To understand what followed, it is of prime importance to recognize that all the French armies were by August 30th in shape to attack again, and from the Oise to the Meuse north of Verdun the French line was intact. Only by grasping this fact is it possible to understand how the French, after another week of retreat, were able suddenly to pass to the offensive and win the decisive Battle of the Marne

VII. BRITISH DISASTER

In his original conception, it seems clear that Joffre had intended to hold the army of Lanzerac and the British at the French frontier facing Belgium until the magnitude of the German blow through Belgium could be measured. During this time he relied upon his armies to the east, and particularly the army operating from Nancy into Lorraine, to deal heavy blows that might compel the Germans to draw back troops from Belgium to reinforce their armies in Alsace and Lorraine. In this plan the British and Lanzerac's armies would have stood from the Scheldt to the Meuse resting upon Valenciennes, Maubeuge, and Givet.

Yielding to the appeals of the Belgians, and apparently to the urgings of French politicians, however, Joffre changed his plan and sent Lanzerac and the British northward to Charleroi and Mons just before the defeat of his Lorraine army ended all chance of lessening the force of the German blow coming from Belgium. This change in plan led to the subsequent disasters, for it threw two small armies, still imperfectly concentrated and amounting to barely seven corps, against the mass of Germans, thirteen corps strong. We are bound to conclude, too, that Joffre had no conception as to the numbers the Germans would send through Belgium or as to the rapidity of their movement, thanks to motor transport.

These miscalculations, together with an error not yet explained, were now to bring the British to the edge of ruin. On Sunday, August 23d, the British army, two corps strong, perhaps 80,000 men, took their positions behind a canal, extending their front from the Scheldt at Condé to a point of junction with Lanzerac north of the Sambre near Binche. Mons was the centre of their position. Here they were attacked, before they had time to entrench, by masses of German troops whose approach seems to have been almost totally unexpected.

The battle which followed was severe, but never reached a decisive point. At some places the British retired to straighten their line, and German heavy artillery caused material but not excessive losses. All the afternoon the British held on; there was nothing to suggest that they were facing a foe overwhelmingly superior in numbers, and not the smallest hint that they were threatened with envelopment on their left flank. At this moment the British army was at the extreme west or left of the whole Allied front, extending from Switzerland right up to Condé. West of Condé to Lille the British believed their flank was covered by French reserves.

But about five o'clock in the afternoon Field-Marshal French suddenly received a despatch from Joffre informing him that Namur had fallen, that the Lanzerac army had been in full retreat for many hours, and that there were in front of the British not two corps, as they had thought, but four, while a fifth was now swinging round their left flank, which they had believed was covered by French reserves, and was striking for their rear.

Why the message came so late, what had become of the French reserves toward Lille, why the British had not been informed earlier of the retreat of Lanzerac, why their own observation corps had failed to discover the size of the German army, these are questions that must wait until the end of the war for answer. But with this despatch the veil is lifted from German purpose. It was now plain that Kluck, who had been at Brussels on August 20th, had swung west and south; that with 300,000 troops he was now rushing forward in a desperate effort to get around the end of the whole Allied line, interpose between it and Paris, and produce a Sedan, tenfold magnified.

In his front, now, he had less than 80,000 British troops. His fifth corps—four were facing the British—had passed through Tournai and was moving toward Cambrai, while a vast horde of German cavalry were driving through northwestern France spreading panic and disorder and reaching for the British line of communications with the Channel. August 23d, the day after Charleroi, two days after Neufchâteau and three days after Morhange, is the day the campaign entered its decisive stage.

On this day we see very clearly that unless the British army can get away, unless its retreat can be effected and its left flank covered, Kluck will interpose between Paris and all the Allied armies. And Kluck is to play the decisive part in the German plan. Not until two weeks later, when he comes to grief in the opening phase of the Battle of the Marne, is he to lose the advantage gained through his appearance in an over-whelmingly superior force on the extreme flank of the Allied armies.

VIII. THE GREAT RETREAT

In the presence of an impending calamity, Field-Marshal French displayed that slowness of action which so long marred British operations in the war. Not for many hours did he actually begin his retreat; hours that were precious were lost; and lost, nearly brought ruin. By seven o'clock the next night, however, his army was back in France with its right resting on the forts of Maubeuge and the centre at Bavay. At this point French recognized the peril that confronted him. It was plain that the Germans were endeavouring to drive him in on Maubeuge, as Bazaine had been driven in on Metz in 1870. This would mean the ultimate capture of his army and would uncover the flank of all the French armies to the east. Accordingly, despite the weariness of his troops, French ordered the retreat to be continued through the night.

Now begins that period of terrible suffering for the British army, which tried the temper of the veterans, resulted in the loss of many prisoners and some guns but in the escape of the army. On the night of August 25th the two corps were widely separated: one was south of Cambrai to the west, and the other at Landrecies to the east. Here the First Corps, about Landrecies, was beaten upon by a terrific night attack, which it managed to repulse. But the troops were becoming totally exhausted. August 26th was "the most critical day of all." The burden was borne by the Second Corps, Smith-Dorrien's, rein-forced now by a fresh division just arrived. Ordered to resume the retreat at daybreak, Smith-Dorrien found it impossible and was compelled to fight until three o'clock in the afternoon before he could break off the engagement, which was fought about the town of Le Cateau but better known as the Battle of Cambrai. On this day an appeal for help made to Sordet, of the French cavalry, could not be answered, and the Second Corps stood alone, for the First Corps was still too far away to render any assistance.

But late in the afternoon the Germans, on their side, began to show weariness.   Smith-Dorrien was able to get his troops on the road.   All through the night and through the next day and night the retreat continued, but the crisis was passed.   August 28th, the British were back at the Oise from Noyon to La Fère and a new French army had come up on their left, the Army of Maunoury, sent by Joffre after he had measured the extent of the German thrust through Belgium.   Five days of fighting and marching, day and night, separated Mons from the British arrival at the Oise, but the army that reached the Oise was no longer in shape for the battle that Joffre was planning.   It was not, in fact, to regain its confidence or its cohesion until after the Battle of the Marne. Nor was it able, in that struggle, to perform the allotted task.   Yet it is difficult to believe that any, save a veteran army of professional soldiers, could have endured these five terrible days and lived.

In this whole period it was the pluck and the endurance of the individual soldiers that saved the day.   Just detrained, these men had suddenly been flung into a battle, their own corner of which was bigger than Waterloo, and their immediate enemy's numbers surpassed, three times over, those Napoleon brought on to his last battlefield.

While they were still holding their ground at Mons, the British were forced to retreat because the defeat of the French army at Charleroi had left the British to the west "in air."   Magnificently supported by the French army of Lanzerac on their right at Guise, they were not supported by French cavalry on their immediate left until the critical day of Cambrai-Le Cateau had passed.

At the time, British public opinion, misled by grotesque reports published in British newspapers and fired by the enthusiasm of having a fighting army on the Continent for the first time in sixty years—for the first time in a century one might say, for the Crimea hardly counted in popular imagination—fired by the undoubted rapidity and efficiency of British mobilization and transport, gave the British army in the retreat and at the Marne a rôle which it did not play.   Not only was the Marne a French battle, but the greatest blow struck at the Germans in the retreat was struck at Guise and not at Le Cateau, and by the French and not the British.   In point of fact the real glory of the British army in the opening months was earned at Ypres, where it died, as few armies ever have died.   But no praise can be too high for the manner in which the private soldiers met a great and utterly unforeseen crisis.

It is essential to point, here, the difference between the situation of the British army on August 28th and that of the French armies at its right and left.   All these latter were not only intact but in a condition to take the offensive.   Two fresh armies, those of Foch and Maunoury, had come up in the centre and at the left.   Joffre had now been able to correct the errors of his early concentration and to meet the unforeseen German concentration.   But the necessarily precipitate retreat of the British had opened a gap in his line.   This and the condition of the British army now combined to compel him to take the great decision, which led directly to the Battle of the Marne.

IX. JOFFRE'S LAST PLAN

In all his disappointments Joffre had never surrendered the idea of taking the offensive at the right moment.   He never conceived the opening reverses as anything but incidental, while German High Command wrongly interpreted them as evidences of complete collapse. Having been beaten at all points in his first attack, Joffre was prepared to fight again at the frontier.   This became impossible when the size of Kluck's army was disclosed.   By August 30th Joffre was again ready to attack along the lines of the Somme, the Oise, and the Aisne. He did attack at Guise and north of Rethel, winning a pretty little success at the former place.

But at this point he had to face the question of risking the decisive battle, with the British exhausted and in retreat far south of the Somme. He chose still to retreat, calling back his victorious troops from Guise; but the decision was not due to the early defeats the French had suffered, it was due to the collapse of the British, incident to the unforeseen strength of the armies that the Germans had sent through Belgium, the failure of French reserves to cover their flank, and the undreamed-of rapidity with which Kluck, thanks to motor transport, had pushed his advance south from Mons to the Somme.

On August 30th Joffre knew that Russian armies were in East Prussia and Galicia; he could calculate that Russian success inside of German territory would promptly compel the Germans to draw back troops from his front. This calculation was to be wrecked on the next day, when the Germans began the conflict at Tannenberg which was to destroy Russian pressure in Prussia. Believing that Russia would be able to fulfil her part, Joffre could afford to wait, even if waiting necessitated further retreat. But by August 30th all his armies were restored to fighting condition, had indeed been reorganized and strengthened, while Sarrail and D'Esperey had replaced Ruffey and Lanzerac.

Between August 20th, the date of Morhange, and August 30th, Joffre had, then, rearranged his armies, restored their cohesion, prepared the instrument he was to use. On the latter date he still found the opportunity lacking, hence he ordered a new retreat, but with fixed limits and with the clear purpose to attack again with only a brief delay. He had now escaped any great disaster, he knew his foe's plans, and he had the resources to prepare his own answer.

By September 1st the whole French line from Verdun to the Somme is in retreat, Maunoury's army is to come back on the entrenched line of Paris, Sarrail's is to swing in until one flank rests on Verdun, the other on the Ornain west of Bar-le-Duc, the remaining armies are to draw back south of the Marne, with the Seine as their southernmost limit of retreat. Meantime more troops are to be brought west from the Lorraine front. When this new concentration is complete, the French will have overcome all the handicaps imposed upon them by the size of German armies sent through Belgium and will have survived the initial defeats with only incidental losses. The morale of the French armies will not be impaired, their ammunition will be renewed, and the Germans will now begin to show the strain of their long, forced marches and begin to outrun both their ammunition and their heavy guns.

To understand the French strategy it is essential to remember that the French Commander-in-Chief necessarily kept in mind the events of 1870. Then the first battles had resulted in heavy defeats for the French armies. But following them these armies had been separated, Bazaine had been shut up in Metz, and MacMahon, driven by political pressure, had led his army to the disaster of Sedan. In 1914 the initial defeats had come, all the offensive plans had been wrecked, but the central idea of preserving the cohesion of all the armies and preventing isolation or envelopment had been rigidly adhered to from the outset.

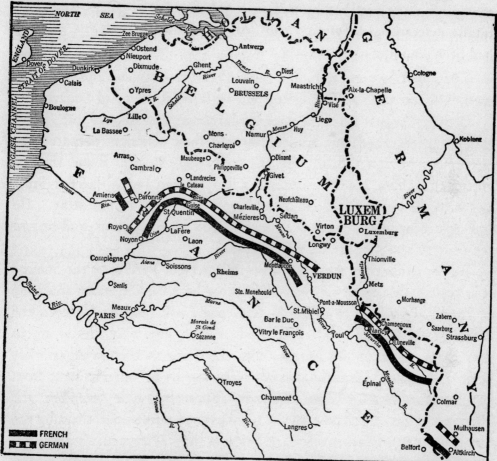

THE SITUATION OF THE FRENCH AND GERMAN ARMIES ON AUGUST 30, 1914
Between August 20th, the date of Morhange, and August 30th, Joffre had rearranged his armies, restored their cohesion, prepared the instrument he was to use

On the battlefield, French commanders showed themselves gravely inferior to German in the opening engagements, but French High Command was never shaken by the first reverses, never provoked into premature offensives, never permitted political pressure to drive it to risk a decisive engagement under unfavourable conditions. And by September

1st the advantage passed sharply to the French side; it was the German strategy that now began to break down. If the French Commander was totally deceived as to the magnitude of the German thrust through Belgium and as to the efficacy of German heavy artillery, the German General Staff was utterly misled as to the condition of French armies after the first battles and soon permitted itself to be led into a fatally defective position and thus lost the decisive battle for which it had been planning for over forty years.

CHAPTER SIX

THE BATTLE OF THE MARNE

I
SEPTEMBER 5

On September 5, 1914, at noon, a French battery of "75's" leaving the village of Iverny, something less than twenty miles due east of Paris and less than five from Meaux, suddenly came under the fire of a German battery on the Monthyon-Penchard hills, a little to the east. The captain was killed and the battery made a hasty retreat. These were the first shots fired in the Battle of the Marne. The next four days saw the greatest battle of modern history, fought by far more than two million men over a front of not less than one hundred and fifty miles—from the environs of Paris to the forts of Verdun.

In this battle, a German army, which had moved from victory to victory, whose marching flank had passed from Liége through Brussels almost to the gates of Paris, was turned back, compelled to retreat, on one flank not less than seventy miles, leaving behind it guns, flags, and prisoners. More than this, the decisive battle, for which German military men had been preparing for forty years, was lost; the promise of a swift, short, and irresistible blow, which the violation of Belgian neutrality held out, was vitiated; the offensive was lost, and a beaten army was compelled to dig itself into trenches from which it would be able to make no considerable advance during the next two years of the war.

This is what the French call the "Miracle of the Marne." While it was going forward, no detailed accounts were possible. After it was completed, the great events that followed robbed it of public interest. I shall endeavour to set forth briefly the story of the decisive phases of this battle as it was told to me on the battlefields by French officers, a year and a half later, or as it is disclosed in the writings of French military critics unhappily little translated as yet.

To understand the course of this gigantic struggle it is necessary first to dismiss the familiar legend that the French armies, which won the battle—the British contribution was insignificant—were ever routed. The battle was not the sudden rally of thousands and hundreds of thousands of soldiers, who had been for days fleeing before a victorious enemy. It was the result of a clear, cool, and deliberate plan, and it was in obedience to this plan that the several French armies, together with the small British force which fought at the Marne, had been drawn back from the frontier to the field of the conflict.

The sole purpose of French strategy in the opening days of the war had been to keep these armies intact until the direction and nature of the main German thrust were disclosed. Incident to this plan, and not for political or sentimental reasons, as was asserted at the time, Joffre had undertaken several minor offensives, in Alsace, in Lorraine, and in Belgian Luxemburg. These had resulted in the defeats of Morhange, Neufchâteau, and the useless victory, after initial defeat, about Mühlhausen.

All the armies engaged in these battles had retired to their earlier positions and made good their lines, repulsing all attacks. But the French army sent north toward Belgium, together with the British expeditionary force, had been beaten upon by an unexpectedly large German mass coming in three armies through Belgium. The French army had suffered defeat at Charleroi and had retreated in good order; the British army had almost found destruction, because upon it the full force of the German blow had fallen.

All this was clear to Joffre in the first days of the last week of August. The Germans, having the initiative, had elected to send a huge mass of troops through Belgium, and the troops were not discovered in full numbers until they had reached and passed the Franco-Belgian frontier.

But starting about August 25th, Joffre set himself to the task of matching his troops against the Germans, of reconcentrating his armies until he should have equal or superior numbers at the decisive point; he was never to have equal numbers at all points. While this reconcentration was going on he always foresaw a new French offensive. About September 1st it looked as if the moment had arrived. He had assembled two new armies, one in the centre and one on the left, on the flank of the British, thus abolishing the peril that Kluck's army had had for him after Mons.   On the line of the Somme, the Oise, and the Aisne, from Amiens to Verdun, the French armies were ready, but unhappily the British army, having suffered disproportionately, had

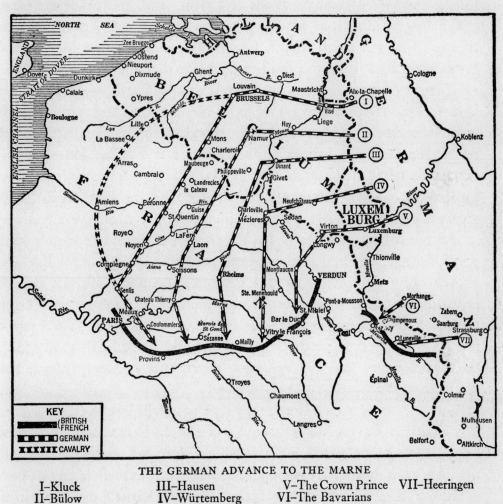

THE GERMAN ADVANCE TO THE MARNE

| I–Kluck | III–Hausen | V–The Crown Prince | VII–Heeringen |
| II–Bülow | IV–Würtemberg | VI–The Bavarians | |

retreated too far.   Therefore, despite local advantage in several conflicts, notably at Guise, Joffre determined on a new retreat.   When this was accomplished, his line would rest at either end on Paris and Verdun. His centre would curve south almost to the Seine.   From this point he planned to attack the Germans.

This retreat, which began about September 1st and ended by September 4th, placed the Germans in a difficult dilemma. In retreating south of Paris, Joffre offered Kluck, on the German right, the chance to attack the city. It was a tempting bait, but Kluck wisely refused it. Such an operation would consume too much time and would require weakening the line elsewhere to get necessary numbers. But, having refused it, Kluck had no choice—since he was compelled to keep in touch with Bülow—but to turn southeastward and march straight across the face of the forts of Paris. His objective was the left wing of the French field armies; the purpose of the whole German host was, of course, to smash the field forces of France.

II. KLUCK TURNS SOUTHEAST

Kluck's turn southeast was safe only if there was but a small garrison in Paris. If there was an army, then, when his front had got south of Paris, his flank and rear would be open to attack from this direction and he would be in exactly the position that the British had been in at Mons and at Cambrai. And as the British were on the end of the whole Anglo-French line from the Vosges, west, and it was thus exposed, so the whole German line would now be exposed.

We now touch on the first of the two determining circumstances of the Battle of the Marne, which in French history are known as the Battle of the Ourcq and of La Fère-Champenoise, respectively. Kluck, in common with all German generals, seems to have been satisfied that the opening conflicts of the war had been decisive; he seems to have been sure that he had before him only beaten troops, and he had no suspicion of the fact that Joffre had concentrated before Paris a new and strong army, that of Maunoury, which was now prepared to strike on his flank as he had struck on the Anglo-French flank from Mons to the Oise.

It was in the evening of September 3d that General Gallieni, commanding the Paris camp, learned from his observers that Kluck's army had begun to turn away from Paris and was marching southeast from Senlis toward Meaux and the crossings of the Marne. He communicated the fact to Joffre by telephone, and on the next day there was arranged the plan which precipitated the Battle of the Marne. The credit for this plan is still disputed by partisans of the two generals. It was on the day following (September 5th) that Joffre published his famous order announcing that the moment to attack had come, thanks to the blunders of the enemy; that failure would not be forgiven, and troops that could not advance must die on their positions.

Actually, it was planned that the Maunoury army, emerging from the intrenched camp of Paris and moving due east, should attack the small flank guards which Kluck had left facing Paris; drive them east across the Ourcq River, which runs from the north down into the Marne above Meaux; and, passing the Ourcq, cut across the rear both of Kluck's and Bülow's armies. The mass of Kluck's army was far south of the Marne, in front of the British and the Fifth French Army, under Franchet d'Esperey. A very good parallel for Maunoury's blow, as planned, is that delivered by "Stonewall" Jackson on Hooker's right at Chancellorsville.

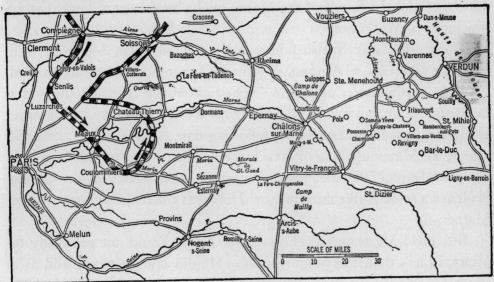

KLUCK'S CIRCLE

About Sept. 1st, at Senlis, Kluck began to move eastward away from Paris. On Sept. 5th the van of his army was south of the Marne beyond Coulommiers. At that time his rear and flank guard just north of Meaux was attacked by Maunoury coming from Paris. Kluck then drew back the mass of his troops in a complete circle north of the Marne and west of the Ourcq. On Sept. 9th, following the reverse of Hausen, he began his retreat upon Soissons

To the British was assigned precisely the rôle that Napoleon assigned to Grouchy in the Waterloo campaign. Field-Marshal French's army was expected to engage and hold Kluck's army while Maunoury struck its flank and rear. Kluck had two corps south of the Marne facing the British, in addition to cavalry; the British had three corps facing the Kluck army, and on its right the line was prolonged by General Conneau's cavalry to the left of D'Esperey.

III. BRITISH FAILURE

In this particular mission the British failed exactly as did Grouchy, and the consequence of their failure was the escape of Kluck and the restriction of the extent of the Allied victory. The failure long remained unknown to the British public, which was early informed and generally believed that the British had won the Battle of the Marne and saved France. The fact was quite different. Not only were the British not actively engaged at the Marne, but had they been able to do that which had been hoped, if not expected of them, Kluck might have been destroyed and the Battle of the Marne might have been as immediately conclusive as Waterloo.

The story of the British failure is simply told. On September 4th Generals Gallieni and Maunoury went by automobile to Field-Marshal French's headquarters at Melun. They asked the British commander to change front and attack the two corps of Kluck's army facing him; this attack was requested for the following day, September 5th. At the same time Maunoury was to attack the flank and rear guards of Kluck along the Ourcq. Such an operation would crush Kluck in the closing blades of a scissors-like movement. Here was the major strategy of the Marne.

But Field-Marshal French declared that he could not get ready to attack in less than forty-eight hours. He did not get ready and as a result Kluck drew his two corps out of the front of the British, put them in against Maunoury, totally wrecking the whole strategic conception of the French High Command and coming within the narrowest margin of destroying the Maunoury army under the walls of Paris.

MARSHAL FOCH

This is the man whose tremendous thrust routed the Prussian Guard at the Battle of the Marne. Launched at exactly the right moment it went through the Guard "as a knife goes through cheese," routed the whole army of Hausen, and earned for Foch, Joffre's verbal decoration as "the first strategist in Europe." A few weeks later, through his generalship and the help of the flower of the British Army, Foch's troops won the terrible struggle that we call Ypres. There is a legend that this time he won commendation from Lord Roberts who, after studying his plans, is said to have remarked to officers of his staff, "You have a great general." His appointment as Generalissimo of the Allied forces marked the beginning of their final forward drive to victory.

All that was left in front of the British was a cavalry screen, but this sufficed to hold up the British advance. Field-Marshal French's army did not get across the Marne until September 9th, and the British left, whose aid was most desired, did not get across the river in time to help Maunoury at all.

Thus to all intents and purposes the British were not engaged in the Marne at all. On this point the British and French commentators of any authority are completely in agreement. Here is the end of the legend that the British saved anything at the Marne; the sole question must be whether what was lost by reason of their failure was unavoidably lost. Could French have moved more swiftly? Did he let the supreme opportunity of the war slip through his fingers? Unmistakably this is the view of the French military commentators and to this view British military criticism now points clearly.

Field-Marshal French's apologists insist that Maunoury struck too soon and that the responsibility for the failure was his and not the British commander's. But will such a defence hold? We know now that the decisive blow in the battle was struck by Foch on September 9th and at La Fère-Champenoise. We know that it was struck when his army was in a critical condition and that it succeeded only because Maunoury's attack, opened on September 5th, had just produced that dislocation in the German lines which opened the gap through which Foch penetrated.

We may say without hesitation, then, that Maunoury did not attack prematurely. He attacked at the moment fixed by Joffre, who was surveying the whole battlefield of which Field-Marshal French saw but one corner, and he attacked because Joffre perceived that the hour had come beyond which it was dangerous to wait. What happened on September 9th, prior to the moment Foch seized the chance to save himself and France, completely demonstrated the correctness of Joffre's view.

This would show that Maunoury's attack was not premature, but it would not prove that Field-Marshal French was tardy, or "over cautious" to use the severe words of one British commentator. But, unfortunately for French, his whole record is against him. He delayed at Mons; he procrastinated in the retreat, notably at the moment of Guise, under conditions that had tragic consequences for one French commander; he was late in sending up supports at Neuve-Chapelle and Loos. All these delays were fatal to success at the moment, and the cumulative effect of them led to his retirement from the command of the British army in France.

On his own record, supported as it is by a wealth of testimony with

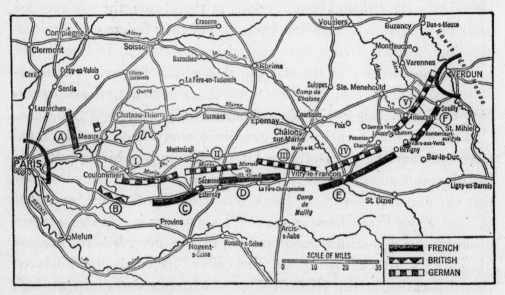

BATTLE OF THE MARNE, SEPT. 5TH

A—Maunoury   D—Foch   I—Kluck   IV—Würtemberg
B—British   E—De Langle de Cary   II—Bülow   V—Crown Prince
C—Franchet d'Esperey F—Sarrail   III—Hausen

Note—The small black and white square above Meaux represents the Fourth Reserve Corps left by Kluck to cover his flank

respect to his actions during the Battle of the Marne—when he continued to appeal to the hard-pressed Maunoury to send him reinforcements, after he had permitted all of Kluck's army but a cavalry screen to escape from his front and attack Maunoury—it is difficult to escape the conviction that Field-Marshal French failed to rise to the greatest opportunity of the war, either because he did not perceive it or lacked the necessary energy and initiative.

At all events, as to the main fact there can be no doubt. The British

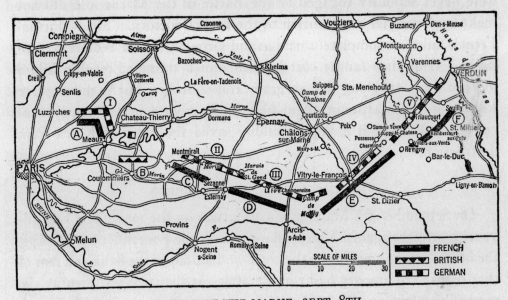

BATTLE OF THE MARNE, SEPT. 8TH

Armies distinguished by same symbols as on previous map. The small square north of the
British represents the cavalry corps

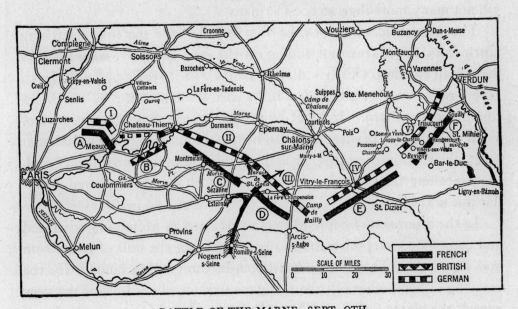

BATTLE OF THE MARNE, SEPT. 9TH

Armies distinguished as above. The arrow shows attack by Foch's Forty-second Division which
won the Battle of La Fère-Champenoise

were never seriously engaged at the Battle of the Marne and did not make any material contribution to the French victory. Field-Marshal French failed as completely here as did Grouchy in the Waterloo campaign. Grouchy's failure cost his Emperor a throne; French's failure did not have anything like so grave consequences, but it did deprive France of the maximum of possible profit from a magnificently conceived stroke, and it almost infallibly saved the army of Kluck from destruction.

IV. THE BATTLE OF THE OURCQ

On September 5th Maunoury's army was on the move, one half advancing straight against Kluck's flank guard, the Fourth Reserve Corps, the other circling round from the north and aiming at the flank and rear of that corps. Maunoury had considerably less than 100,000 men at the outset; his army was doubled as the engagement proceeded, but it was made up of very heterogeneous elements, Algerian and Moroccan troops, reservists, and only a few first-line units. It had before it on September 5th not many more than 40,000 Germans.

The battlefield of the Ourcq is a broad, level plateau, stretching north from the Marne and ending on the east abruptly, where it falls down into the deep Ourcq Valley. To the eye it seems perfectly level, save for two wooded hills, a few miles east of Meaux, the hills of Monthyon and Penchard. It is cut by several brooks, contains a number of small villages, but is without walls, hedges, or anything that would offer great obstruction to troops, or artillery fire. Several large farm buildings, recalling the Château of Hougoumont at Waterloo, played a similar rôle in the battle.

In the afternoon of September 5th this army of Maunoury advanced and came in contact with the German troops on the hills of Monthyon and Penchard. These hills were taken in the evening hours. By the morning of September 6th the Germans were recoiling toward the very edge of the plateau, with the Ourcq Valley at their backs. A number of villages were taken by storm, notably Barcy and Étrépilly, and the French from the north were able to threaten a flanking movement which promised to turn the Fourth Reserve Corps out of their position.

But now comes the change. Kluck seems to have appreciated the full extent of the peril incredibly swiftly. By September 6th he was drawing his troops from the front of the British. Actually he was able to withdraw first the Second (active) Corps and then the Fourth (active) Corps, leaving only cavalry under Marwitz to hold the British. With these troops he counter-attacked Maunoury, threw him back materially on September 8th, and on the next day bent the northern flank of the French army back until it stood at right angles to the rest of the line, and on this day seemed destined to drive Maunoury back into Paris. On the night of September 9-10, the Paris garrison stood to arms and Maunoury's troops waited anxiously for daybreak, still with orders to attack, but expecting to be attacked and destroyed. After three and a half days of fighting they were at the end of their strength.

When daylight came on September 10th the Germans were gone. For Kluck the retreat to the Aisne had begun, but it was not a retreat due to his own defeat. The first blow of the French had been parried; the failure of the British to retain even one corps of Kluck's army before them, their extreme slowness of movement, had permitted Kluck to reconcentrate his army, escape from the vicious position in which he stood when battle began, had enabled him to throw back Maunoury's army, insure his retreat, and to come within an ace of winning a decisive battle.

V. LA FÈRE-CHAMPENOISE

If it had failed in its chief purpose, still the effect of Maunoury's attack had been to dislocate not only Kluck's army, but that of Bülow to the east, the army which had won Charleroi and now faced the Fifth French Army along the Grand Morin, south of Montmirail and east to the marshes of St. Gond. This army drew back to keep its alignment with Kluck, heavily pursued and fighting many minor engagements right across the battlefields of the famous Napoleonic campaign of 1814. Montmirail, Vauchamps, and Champaubert woke from a century of peace to new carnage. But the fight between D'Esperey and Bülow was not to the finish, because Bülow was steadily compelled to retire to keep his contact with Kluck. Hence this part of the whole Battle of the Marne is of relatively minor importance. Had Kluck attacked Paris, D'Esperey's army might have played another and decisive rôle, for Joffre had also prepared for this consequence.

To the east of D'Esperey was the army of Foch, which now played the decisive part. This army stood, at first, with its advance guards on the north side of the famous marshes of St. Gond, a strange swamp full of stagnant ponds and crossed by only a few highways. This was a considerable military obstacle. Behind it ran a line of hills, north of the town of Sézanne and dropping away to the southeast, looking down on La Fère-Champenoise from the Plateau of Euvy and losing themselves in the monotonous plain of the Camp de Mailly.

When Maunoury's attack compelled the immediate retreat of Kluck's troops south of the Marne and the ultimate retrogression of Bülow, the German High Command resolved to seek victory by a redoubled pressure upon Foch, who held the French centre. In a word, the Germans undertook to break the French line, the whole line from Paris to Verdun, and to break it at the exact centre, which was where Foch stood. Foch was heavily outnumbered, and although he began, on September 7th, a brave offensive, he was steadily driven south and suffered great losses. The fighting here was the most sanguinary of the whole engagement, and there are ten thousand graves in the little town of La Fère-Champenoise alone.

Nor was this the worst. Not only was Foch driven south, but his right or eastern flank was driven very far south, until his army, instead of facing north, faced nearly east, and a wide gap began to open in the whole French line between Foch and the French army of De Langle de Cary to the east.

September 9th is here, as at the Ourcq, the decisive day. On this day Franchet d'Esperey, having cleared Bülow from the banks of the Petit Morin and finding his Tenth Corps freed by Bülow's withdrawal to the northwest, toward Kluck, lends this corps to Foch, and it now begins to act on the western flank of the German centre.

This aid assures the safety of Foch's western flank and he now withdraws his 42d Division from this flank, transports it eastward to Linthes, and very late in the afternoon suddenly launches it in a terrific drive at the Prussian Guard between the marshes of St. Gond and La Fère-Champenoise.

At this point the German line has been thinned as a result first of the withdrawal of Bülow toward Kluck and secondly in consequence of the eagerness of the Germans to press their advantage to the south, where they were at the point of piercing the whole French line about Gourgan-çon. These two movements, going on at the same moment, stretch the lines of the Prussian Guard—which is charged with preserving the contact between Bülow's army on the west and Hausen's in the centre facing Foch—as an elastic is stretched by pulling both ends. The 42d Division goes through the Guard as a knife cuts through cheese, as the French afterward explained; it throws the Saxons in and about La Fère-Champenoise into disorder which becomes a rout, for Foch at the same moment launches a general attack.

This tremendous thrust earned for Foch Joffre's verbal decoration as "the first strategist in Europe." It routed the Prussian Guard, which lost most of its artillery; it crumpled up the flank of the two Saxon corps; it routed the entire army of Hausen, who was forthwith retired in disgrace. It resulted in the wild retreat of the whole Hausen army as well as that of the Prussian Guard. Here, and only here, was there anything approaching a great battlefield triumph. Bülow had retired with little or no disorder; Kluck had retrieved his earlier reverses, and, at the moment when Foch struck his blow, was winning the Battle of the Ourcq.

But the retirement of Kluck and Bülow and the disaster which had overtaken the German centre, under Hausen, together decided the fate of the battle. It was on the receipt of news of this disaster that Kluck started his rapid retreat to the Aisne; that Bülow at last gave over his effort to regain control of the north bank of the Marne, which he had too hastily abandoned; and from Paris to Vitry-le-François the German armies all took the homeward roads.

VI. DE LANGLE DE CARY AND SARRAIL

It remains very briefly to mention the incidents to the east. Here, behind the Ornain, the army of De Langle de Cary stood for three days rigidly on the defensive, beating off German attacks made by the army of Würtemberg on a front from Vitry-le-François to Revigny. More physical destruction was done here than anywhere along the battle-field, and the ruins of Sermaize supply evidence of the wanton fury of the Bavarians. But like the battles around Montmirail, these contests were without issue, because the decision at La Fère-Champenoise ultimately compelled the Bavarians to retire.

As for the army of Sarrail, standing from Revigny north to Souilly, where it touched the positions held by the garrison of Verdun, it resisted all attacks of the army of the Crown Prince, operating east of the Argonne, to penetrate its front and isolate Verdun. It had a bad moment when its rear was threatened along the Meuse at Forts Tryon and Liouville by a drive coming from Metz, but the garrisons of these forts held out until aid came, and the destruction of the bridges of the Meuse proved sufficient to bar the Germans.

For the armies of Kluck, Bülow, and Hausen the day of September 9th was decisive, and as early as September 6th the first two were in partial retreat. But both the Würtemberg army and that of the Crown Prince held on for several days more and retired in good order in the end, when the recoil of the armies to the west made their retreat necessary to keep the alignment. Of the five German armies only those of Kluck and Hausen actually put forth their whole strength, and of these only that of Hausen was decisively beaten. Of the French armies, only those of Maunoury and Foch were engaged to the limit, and Maunoury failed to accomplish his purpose because he did not get the help from the British that was expected.

Had the plan conceived by Joffre or Gallieni, or by both together, been realized, the Germans would have suffered a decisive defeat and would have been unable to remain in France. Had Hausen been able to break the French centre, even after Maunoury's attack and the retreat of Kluck and Bülow, the Battle of the Marne would have ended in a decisive victory for the Germans and the French army would have been cut in two, one fragment driven in on Paris, the other on the barrier fortresses to the east.

There was a time when it was generally believed that the Battle of the Marne was won by the operations near Paris, and there is a legend of a victory won by the transport of troops through Paris in taxicabs. The troops were transported in taxis, but they arrived not in time to win the Battle of the Marne, but only in time to save the Battle of the Ourcq. Equally fallacious is the story of the British part in the battle. The British were never actively engaged in the battle at all; they never had anything but rearguards to deal with, and these rearguards held them up until the chance for a supreme success had totally disappeared.

It is open to question whether Foch would have been able to deal his decisive blow if Maunoury's thrust had not compelled the retirement of Bülow, by making Kluck draw his corps north of the Marne and west of the Ourcq, thus dislocating the whole German front. But it is not open to question that the blow of Foch was decisive. It was delivered by a beaten army almost at the last gasp, an army which had been recoiling under pressure for three days and had suffered losses that amounted to extermination in the case of some of its units. American army officers who visited the battlefield before the bodies had been removed will some day supply conclusive evidence of the bitterness of the conflict as measured by the carnage.

VII. THE CONSEQUENCES

No estimate of total losses, of prisoners, of booty, has ever been published. But it seems conservative to estimate that of the 2,250,000 men engaged between Verdun and Paris there were more than 300,000 killed or wounded. The French loss was not less than the German; it may have been more, for the French in many fields did the attacking. Certainly between the opening of the campaign and the end of the German retreat after the Marne the French losses exceeded the German

—the losses in killed and wounded—while the total of prisoners taken by the Germans in the various fortified positions, Maubeuge, Longwy, etc., were very much greater.

It is reasonably certain that the Germans outnumbered the French on the battlefield, but owing to faults of German concentration and deploying the French certainly got much more out of their inferior numbers, while the Germans seem to have handled their masses badly and to have suffered from an excess of numbers at certain unimportant points.

The consequences of the battle were wholly misunderstood at first by both the French and the Germans. The French believed that they had won a victory which would turn the Germans out of France. The Germans believed that they had merely suffered a minor reverse and that after a new concentration they would be able to take the offensive again and renew their bid for a decision. Both illusions perished at the Aisne. Here the Germans were able to repulse the French and dig in, but on their side they never were able to get on their feet and advance again.

Actually the Battle of the Marne broke the German offensive, wrecked their whole strategy, which was to bring the French to a decisive battle in the first six weeks of the war, win that battle, and put the French out of the war. They advanced to the Marne seeking a second Sedan, and the French there won an Antietam. All the original German conceptions were definitely defeated in this battle; they were compelled to retreat, to give over the offensive, to accept a long war. But, save for the Prussian Guard and the Saxons of Hausen, they were nowhere routed, and they were able within a week after the decisive day of the Marne, September 9th, to halt the Allies along the Aisne, establish their front unbroken from the Aisne to the Meuse, and even to undertake a new attack. But this failed almost instantly.

It is essential—as has been said before and cannot be said too often—to keep in mind, in examining the Battle of the Marne, the story of the opening weeks of the Franco-Prussian War. The two conflicts began in much the same way. In both cases German mobilization put more troops and better-equipped troops into the field. In both cases all the

NOVEL PHASES OF MODERN WARFARE SHOWN IN PICTURES

A HIDDEN AND DEFENDED MACHINE GUN

Except for the noise, which resembles a pneumatic rivetting machine, this gun gives the enemy no indication of its whereabouts. It fires through a painted net curtain.

THE "AGENT DE LIAISON"

This French soldier's official designation is as sinister as his appearance. He is an *agent de liaison*. It is a relief to know that this means simply telephone operator. He wears his mask as a protection against poison-gas bombs. A hand grenade is in the pouch suspended from his belt.

Photograph by Paul Thompson

"POISON GAS" IN THE WAR

The upper picture shows the cylindrical containers from which the poison gas emanates. The Austrians left them behind when the Russians drove them from this position. Trenches have to be dug sometimes when gas-bombs and shells are exploding close at hand. These British "Tommies" are wearing respirators as a protection against poisonous fumes.

MACHINE-GUN POSITION IN THE OPEN

Where guns and men are protected only by small dugouts and shell-craters—conditions
which obtain during an advance

PERISCOPE AND METAL HELMET

The French soldiers soon bowed to grim necessity and gave up the blue tunics and red trousers endeared to them
by a romantic and glorious tradition.   These entrenched *poilus* are sensibly making themselves as safe and comfortable
as they can.   Clad in serviceable and inconspicuous "horizon" blue uniforms with metal helmets, one man is trying
a pot-shot with his rifle, which is equipped with a periscope so that he need expose himself no more than is necessary,
while his comrade is solacing himself with a glance at his favorite Paris newspaper.

THIS IS THE RESULT WHEN A FOREST BECOMES A BATTLEFIELD

BUCKLER, HAND-GRENADE, AND HELM

History repeats itself in war as in other human relationships. In 1913 the world thought the day of warriors with steel helmets and shields had passed forever. But here is one very much alive. He is a grenadier, too, in the original sense of the term, for he stands ready to throw a hand-grenade in the face of his enemy.

Photograph by the International News Service

BARBED WIRE ENTANGLEMENTS

Barbed wire has been used in the World War on an unprecedented scale. These troops (*upper picture*) are advancing upon an abandoned fort by the side of a formidable entanglement which has been firmly anchored by stout posts. The French have invented a gun (*lower picture*) which fires into the midst of the wire entanglement a hook attached to a cable. The hook is then hauled back, supposedly bringing with it large masses of the wire.

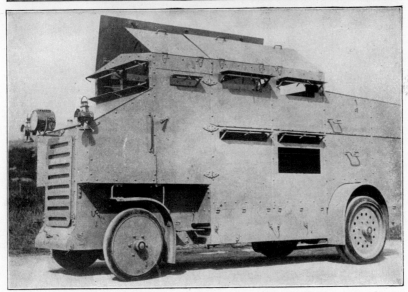

THE GASOLINE ENGINE

The gasoline engine has greatly increased the mobility of modern troops. The lower picture shows a little British fortress that can be moved at the rate of twenty-five or thirty miles an hour, wherever there is a decent road. The upper and middle pictures show one method the Germans have adopted for increasing the mobility of their artillery. The armoured car affords protection to the gun-crew while in transit to the point at which they are needed. Arrived on the ground the car's armour is removed (as shown in the centre picture and the gun cleared for action in two or three minutes.

WORK AND PLAY AT THE FRONT

These French gunners (*upper picture*) are working to excellent purpose in a dugout carefully concealed from the air-scouts of the enemy.

This seems a strange place for a candy-shop, yet it is doing a big business. The Young Men's Christian Association maintains many little booths like this, just back of the firing line. The soldier's small change is apt to burn a hole in his pocket, and he highly appreciates such opportunities to get rid of it in exchange for sweets and other little luxuries.

opening battles were won by the Germans. But at this point the parallel stops short. Instead of Mars-la-Tour and Sedan, with their fatal terminations, you have an orderly retreat of all French armies until a new concentration permits a fresh offensive, and when this happens you have a German retreat followed by a German rally, which ends in a deadlock and more than three years of trench war.

This, after all, is the "Miracle of the Marne." The German High Command said: "We have more men, better guns, better troops; we will violate the neutrality of Belgium, turn the French fortresses and, arriving in the plains of northern France, we will destroy the French armies, take Paris, and then turn east and dispose of Russia. We shall win the war in six weeks and take Paris in seven. We shall hold France to ransom and dispose of the French danger for all time."

Not one detail of this grandiose plan was realized. Not one detail has been realized after three years of war. We all see that if France had failed, Russia would have been conquered, and even the British Empire would have come to the edge of ruin. But France did not fail. She won her greatest victory in a wonderful history with but the least possible support from Britain; she saved herself, Britain and Russia, and after the Marne the war had new horizons and different possibilities. Thus in every sense the Battle of the Marne was one of the few truly decisive battles in all human history, a battle whose consequences, though we may not yet accurately measure them, seem, at the distance of nearly three years, incomparably greater than on the day when the world first learned that the German invasion would not reach Paris.

VIII. THE SECOND BATTLE OF NANCY

During the whole of the first week of September, ending before the Battle of the Marne reached its decisive stage, another contest was going forward on the front which had been successfully maintained by the French after their defeat at Morhange. Coördinating their movements with those of the armies to the west, eight German corps under the Crown Prince of Bavaria and General Heeringen, in the decisive hours, acting under the eyes of the Kaiser himself, undertook to cut their way through the gap in the French barrier forts between Toul and Épinal and thus arrive on the flank and rear of all the French armies fighting from Verdun to Paris.

Had this drive succeeded, the decision of the Marne would have been reversed, and German strategy would have triumphed despite the checks elsewhere. It did not succeed, because, although his armies were heavily depleted to reinforce armies to the west, General de Castelnau was able to repulse all attacks in fighting which was unquestionably the most costly to the Germans in the whole period of the war preceding the struggles in Flanders. Unfortunately the larger issues at the Marne, the proximity of the western battlefield to Paris, have served to obscure these operations. Thus, precisely as the victory of Foch at La Fère-Champenoise is little known save to military men; although it did, in fact, decide the Marne, the success of De Castelnau, which permitted the victory of the Marne and held the whole eastern line of the French field armies, has, as yet, no place in current history.

When the German attack began, De Castelnau stood thus: his left or northern flank rested on the Moselle south of Pont-à-Mousson and on the Plateau of Ste. Geneviève, a gentle hill, which is the northern extremity of the Grand-Couronne. Thence it followed the Grand-Couronne, facing the little Seille River, to the Plateau d'Amance, at the southern end of the Grand-Couronne. Here the ground falls sharply and the French line passing through the Forest of Champenoux and a dozen little towns, scenes of desperate fighting, still unknown, crossed the Meurthe at the foot of the Plateau of Saffais-Belchamps, due south of Nancy, and extended along the ridge between the Meurthe and the Moselle, south toward the Vosges.

This was a position long ago surveyed as the final line of French resistance if the German attack came from Alsace-Lorraine. Every higher officer in France knew it. Here, if anywhere, the French could be expected to make a successful resistance—and they did.

The first attack came upon Ste. Geneviève. The Germans advanced south on both sides of the Moselle, took Pont-à-Mousson, entered the Forest of the Advance Guard, and opened a cross fire upon the French at Ste. Geneviève. Despite orders to retire, the French, only a battalion strong, held on and repulsed massed attacks, after which the Germans left 4,000 bodies in the Bois de Facq. Finally, just as he was withdrawing in obedience to peremptory orders, the French Commander perceived that the Germans were also drawing out, whereupon he returned to his lines.

The second and main attack came at the other end of the Grand-Couronne on the edge of the Plateau d'Amance and through the large Forest of Champenoux. No more desperate fighting in the whole war has occurred than here. Heavily outnumbered, the French were driven back to the western edge of the forest; the Germans for a brief hour seized a small farm at the foot of the Plateau D'Amance but were driven out. Terrific fighting and enormous losses marked the engagements to the south, notably about the little village of Corbessaux. In front of the Plateau of Saffais-Belchamps the Germans were slaughtered in masses, attempting to cross the Meurthe.

A final attack, around Amance and the Forest of Champenoux—currently believed to have been made while the Kaiser, surrounded by his guard in white uniform, waited at Eply to enter Nancy—was rolled back. Before Foch had won his great struggle at La Fère-Champenoise, the drive through Lorraine was over and the Second Battle of Nancy had saved the eastern barrier to France. Afterward, as the Germans began to draw troops out of this line to meet the new situation in the west, the French pushed out, retook Pont-à-Mousson and Lunéville, and reëstablished their front along the frontier from the Vosges to Pont-à-Mousson.

The Second Battle of Nancy was a defensive battle to save the main French operation, westward at the Marne. It was really a vital phase of the Marne itself, the foundation on which Joffre built his whole strategy; it was probably bloodier than any fight at the Marne, and its relative value must be recognized to appreciate the whole picture of the Marne campaign. It was won by the army that had been defeated at Morhange, but by only a fraction of the force that fought in that disastrous engagement, for Joffre had long ago depleted it to supply troops for his new armies and to reinforce the others, while the Battle of the Marne was still in progress.

IX. TANNENBERG

To complete the story of the Marne, it is necessary to recount now the disaster that overtook the Russian army, which had invaded East Prussia from Warsaw. In the general Franco-Russian plan, it was

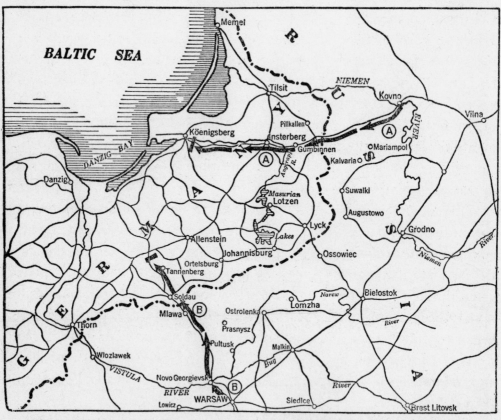

FIRST RUSSIAN INVASION OF EAST PRUSSIA, CHECKED BY HINDENBURG AT TANNENBERG, AUG. 31, 1914

Two Russian armies were sent into East Prussia, one from the Niemen front and the other north from Warsaw. Hindenburg defeated the Warsaw army decisively at Tannenberg and the other army then drew back

A–Rennenkampf   B–Samsonoff

agreed that Russia should promptly invade East Prussia if Germany sent her masses through Belgium and against France. It was believed that such an operation would mean that Germany would have to leave her eastern front insecurely guarded and that a Russian inva-

HINDENBURG, VICTOR OF TANNENBERG

When the Russians surprised the Germans by their quick mobilization and invasion of East Prussia, in August, 1914, the German Emperor summoned General Hindenburg from retirement and gave him command in the region which he had made a life study. He concentrated most of his forces about the Russian Warsaw army in the region he knew so well. Having drawn a net about his victims he massed his heavy artillery and practically annihilated the Russian army, which lost about 100,000 troops with guns and flags innumerable. This was the victory of Tannenberg, which made Hindenburg the idol of the German people.

sion would promptly force her to withdraw troops from France in advance of the decisive engagement.

Accordingly two Russian armies were at once sent into East Prussia, one from the Niemen front and the other north from Warsaw. Both won immediate and considerable successes, and the Germans on the day they reached Brussels learned that Russian armies were carrying the whole eastern frontier and advancing after victories at Gumbinnen and Insterburg, toward Königsberg and toward the east bank of the Vistula north of Thorn. Refugees fleeing before the storm were flowing into Berlin at the precise moment that French and Belgian exiles were reaching Paris.

So far the Allied plan had worked amazingly well and the promptness of Russian invasion had taken the Germans by surprise.

Now, however, the Emperor summoned Hindenburg from retirement and gave him command in the region which he had made a life study. Hindenburg acted promptly. Leaving only a screen of troops in front of the Russian army advancing from the east, he concentrated his forces about the Russian Warsaw army in the difficult swamp region he knew so well. Having drawn a net about his victims, he massed his heavy artillery and practically annihilated the Russian army, which lost more than 100,000 troops with guns and flags innumerable. This was the victory of Tannenberg, celebrated on Sedan Day by all Germany as a deliverance from deadly peril.

After Tannenberg, the other Russian army drew back safely and Hindenburg still lacked the numbers to press it hard, but he was able to clear German territory, and the mass of German armies in France were permitted to go forward to their decisive battle without fear for this eastern front. Half the Franco-Russian strategic conception had been wrecked. After the Marne the Germans would not be forced to face immediate peril in the east as well as the west. They could still concentrate their energies on retrieving the situation at the Aisne.

The French victory at the Marne and the great Russian triumph at Lemberg obscured the Allied mind and the mind of the neutral world as to the value of Tannenberg. It has not even now, outside of Germany, received its just appraisal. Yet, to judge it rightly it is only necessary to consider what would have been the German situation if, at the moment the Marne had been lost, Russian troops had occupied all of Prussia east of the Vistula. This would have happened but for Tannenberg; it would have happened infallibly if the action of the two Russian armies had been properly coördinated, for their combined strength was far greater than Hindenburg's.

For this disaster Lemberg was no counterweight, because Germany and not Austria was the true enemy and German disaster might have ended the war. Had the Germans been driven behind the Lower Vistula all their later and successful campaigns would have been impossible and, taken with the collapse of Austria at Lemberg and the defeat of the Marne, the Central Powers would have found themselves at the close of the second month of war in a situation difficult in the extreme, if not well-nigh desperate.

All this was avoided by Hindenburg's amazing victory, one of the most complete in history and rivalling any Napoleonic combination in skill and effectiveness. More than all else this German victory at the other end of Europe robbed the Marne of its greatest possible fruits and condemned northern France to a German occupation which still persists. The victory on the eastern front enabled Germany to go forward to the Marne without hesitation; it did not enable her to win this battle, but after the retreat to the Aisne it permitted her to concentrate her energies and her resources in new attacks upon the west which did not terminate until the Battle of Flanders in mid-November.

Therefore, just as the Marne deprived Germany of any chance to get a quick decision on her main front, the disaster of Tannenberg deprived the Allies of any similar chance for a prompt victory. Later historians will certainly do fuller justice to the importance and service of Tannenberg to Germany. It was not the greatest German victory of the war, but certainly it was the most useful, and as such it can rank only second to the Marne in the first two years of the contest. It is hardly too much to say that it saved Germany almost as unmistakably as the Marne saved France.

CHAPTER SEVEN

DEADLOCK IN THE WEST

I

THE BATTLE OF THE AISNE

On the morrow of the victory of the Marne, French purpose is clear. A great strategic victory has been won, the whole German conception has been broken. All the German armies are in retreat. It is essential to pursue these armies; to turn the retreat into a rout, if possible; in any event, to prevent the Germans from taking root in France and from presently stepping out in a new general offensive, reopening the decision of the Marne. In all save the last of these purposes French strategy failed.

This failure, although materially affected by the condition of the French army after its long struggle and the disorganization of French cavalry, was due primarily to the fact that only one German army, and that the smallest, Hausen's, had actually been beaten on the battlefield. German armies had allowed themselves to be drawn into a hopelessly bad position; they had suffered heavy losses and, in the case of the Saxon army, a real rout; but they had, in the main, seen the danger in time; drawn themselves out of the trap with great skill and speed; and begun a retreat, which if rapid was, in the main, orderly, and successful. In justice to the British, it should be added that if their share in the Battle of the Marne was insignificant, their part in the pursuit was considerable and they not only did exceedingly well but, having recovered from the disorganization incident to their long retreat, came into this operation relatively fresh and thus in condition to do what would have been beyond the strength of their exhausted allies had they been unaided.

In this same time the purpose of German strategy was to take a new position in France; reëstablish contact between the various armies separated by the movements of the battle; and then seek, in a new contest, to win that decisive battle which they had lost at the Marne. The German official statements did not admit the loss of the Battle of the Marne. From September 3d to September 13th they preserved a complete silence on western operations. It is clear, too, that German High Command, even as late as September 25th, did not regard the Marne as the decisive action, and remained confident that a new battle would win whatever had been temporarily lost.

And in this time German High Command lost forever the chance to seize the French and Belgian seacoasts, which lay open to their occupation from the moment that they passed the Somme until their new efforts from the Oise to the Meuse had been checked. We shall see, a few weeks later, a frantic effort to repair this great error, when it was too late. For this blunder, together with rumoured mistakes in the Battle of the Marne not yet established, the younger and lesser Moltke was presently to lose his great position as master of the German General Staff, turning over his office to the Kaiser's favorite, Falkenhayn, whose star was to set before Verdun as Moltke's set on the road to Calais.

German armies were able to realize many of the hopes and conceptions of their commanders in the weeks following the Marne. They did make good their position in France, behind the deep Aisne, resting on the hills from Noyon to the Craonne Plateau. They did restore contact between all their armies and they were able, within ten days after the decisive day of the Marne, to renew the offensive. But they were not able to reopen the decision of the Marne, because, while they were beginning a new offensive between Noyon and Verdun and striking a heavy blow south of Verdun, at St. Mihiel, French High Command opened a great turning movement, west of the Oise, which compelled the Germans to displace their armies, sending masses from Lorraine and Champagne to Picardy and Artois, and thus resigning their plans farther east.

All these operations, very complex when read in official bulletins and utterly confusing to the public at the time they took place, become perfectly simple if the main purposes are kept in mind. You have first the French and British pursuit, begun on September 10th. You have next the complete check of this pursuit, after September 13th, when Kluck stands behind the Aisne, digs himself in and, reinforced by the troops and guns which are freed by the capture of Maubeuge on September 7th, stops Field-Marshal French, Maunoury, and D'Esperey. By

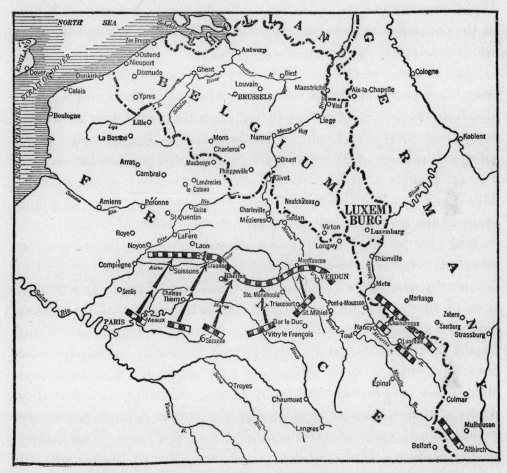

THE GERMAN RETREAT TO THE AISNE, SEPT. 10TH–15TH, 1914

The purpose of German strategy was to take a new position in France, reëstablish contact between the various armies, and then seek, in a new contest, to win that decisive battle which they had lost at the Marne

September 18th Kluck is able to take the offensive and drive the British and French out of some of the ground they have taken north of the Aisne.

Meantime to the east, Bülow, Einem (who succeeds Hausen), Würtemberg, and the Crown Prince, have retired slowly, save for the

Saxons, who disappear soon as an army. The German line curves around Rheims and through the Argonne. By the third week in September, Bülow, who has held up Foch just outside of Rheims, attacks, takes the forts of Brimont and Nogent-l'Abbesse, bombards the cathedral at Rheims, but is checked. Würtemberg and the Crown Prince make a considerable advance west and east of the Argonne, but are stopped in turn. Troops from Metz make a sudden and successful attack upon the barrier forts south of Verdun, and take St. Mihiel.

No one of these three attacks had immediately important military consequences, yet all three are of permanent interest—that of Bülow, because of the bombardment of the Cathedral of Rheims, which had a greater moral effect upon the French nation than anything but the victory of the Marne; that of the Crown Prince because, taken together with the operations about St. Mihiel, it had a very great value in a later phase of the war, when the Germans attacked Verdun.

The Crown Prince was checked after a few days. But he got forward sufficiently on the road along which he had recently retreated to occupy the town of Varennes, and from this and other points was able, with his heavy artillery, to cut the Paris-Verdun railroad by indirect fire. Even more complete was the success to the south, where the Germans, by taking Fort Camp des Romains and occupying the west bank of the Meuse, facing St. Mihiel, were able to cut the Commercy-Verdun line. There was a moment when it seemed possible that they might actually penetrate through the breach they had opened in the French barrier and join hands with the Crown Prince. This danger passed; Verdun was not enveloped, but it was left practically without rail communication with the rest of France, a circumstance which contributed gravely to its danger when the Germans returned to the attack in February, 1916.

About September 20th Joffre, now assured that he cannot break the German lines, which have become a wall of trenches from the Vosges to the Oise, begins to send troops to work around the German right, which does not extend west of the Oise. These troops come east from Amiens and aim at St. Quentin and the whole network of railroads on which the German armies depend for their supplies. So confident are the French of the success of this thrust that at this time Millerand, the French Minister of War, forecasts the immediate retirement of the Germans from France, and London has a rumour that Kluck has surrendered.

Nothing like this happens. Instead, the Germans begin to answer the French flanking operation by bringing troops of their own from their main front and putting them in west of the Oise. These troops very quickly put an end to the first French flanking operation; they retake Péronne, Roye, Lassigny, and win an action at Bapaume, establishing in this sector that front which will endure up to the time of the great Battle of the Somme in the summer of 1916.

II. THE RACE TO THE SEA

But Joffre sticks to his plan. He has brought De Castelnau from Lorraine with much of the army which had defended Nancy. Oddly enough the army of De Castelnau, which has long faced the army of Rupprecht of Bavaria east of the Moselle, arrives west of the Oise just in time to meet the same German army. A general dislocation of French and German armies is going forward, General Mand'huy, brought from the Aisne and put in command of a new army, encounters Bülow, brought over from before Rheims. Finally the Grand Duke of Würtemberg arrives from the Argonne and faces Foch but recently commanding the army which had reconquered Rheims.

And with this general dislocation the German hope of resuming the offensive between the Oise and the Moselle expires. The campaign enters the second phase. The front from Noyon to Nancy becomes relatively unimportant and the deadlock of trench war along this line becomes absolute. Now the field of operations is between the Oise and the sea and the centre of conflict mounts day by day to the north. The French and the Germans are exactly in the situation of two boys building rival towers out of blocks and each trying to build the higher structure. Joffre puts De Castelnau in about Roye and he encounters Rupprecht of Bavaria. He puts Mand'huy in and he meets Bülow

east of Arras.   He puts Foch in and Foch encounters, not merely Würtemberg come from the Argonne but Besseler, striking south, when the
Antwerp episode is completed.   Even Field-Marshal French, quitting
his trenches near Soissons, will presently arrive at Ypres.

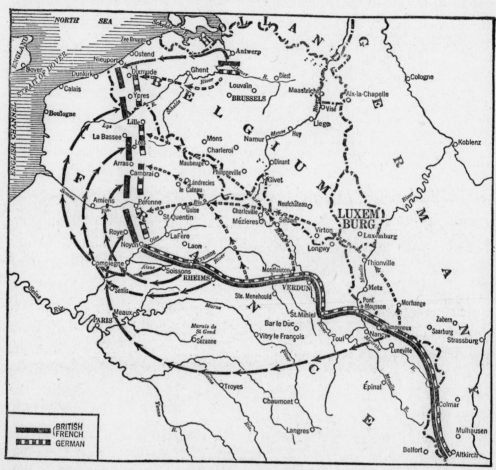

THE RACE TO THE SEA

Now the field of operations is between the Oise and the sea, and the centre of conflict mounts
day by day to the north.   The French and the Germans are exactly in the situation of two boys
building rival towers out of blocks and each trying to build the higher structure

The French strategy begins to reveal itself.   As the French line
mounts to the north it points first toward Lille, lost in the first hours of
the invasion and subsequently retaken, then toward Antwerp, where
the Belgian army still stands, with a line of retreat open to the south,
on the west bank of the Scheldt.

What this means the German High Command at last perceives. It can no longer continue its effort to advance between the Oise and the Meuse, it has been compelled to draw off troops in Lorraine and Champagne to meet the new thrust in Picardy and Artois. Already the active front has mounted into Flanders. Unless a change comes promptly the French line will extend until it reaches Belgium, joins with the Belgian front behind the Scheldt, and not only will there ensue a trench deadlock from Holland to Switzerland, but the Germans will be permanently excluded from the Belgian seacoast. If such a deadlock ensues, then there is an end to all hope—and already this hope is becoming remote—of a quick decision over France, and a short war.

There remains in late September only a gap forty miles wide between the French lines in position from Lille southward and the Channel. Unless German troops can penetrate this gap and come south, sweeping behind the Channel ports of Calais and Boulogne, the whole western campaign will have ended in a stalemate and the French, British, and Belgians will hold an unbroken line from Antwerp to Belfort.

Hence in the latter half of September begins the new and final German concentration. German strategy has now three purposes: to take Antwerp and capture the Belgian army, thus preventing a junction of the Belgians with their allies; to move south through the gap between Lille and the Channel, taking the Channel ports and finally, if possible, thus regaining the initiative; to reopen the decision of the Marne and win a real victory north of Amiens. Even if this last object is not realized the Germans can hope to shorten their front by establishing their western flank on the sea near the mouth of the Somme and at the same time complete the occupation of northern France and that seacoast which would be the logical base for operations against Britain. And for the German people this last phase is summed up by the word "Calais," as the earlier drive was comprehended in the magic term "Paris."

For clarity and convenience we may regard the Battle of the Aisne as covering all the operations between Soissons and St. Mihiel in the time in which the Germans endeavoured to regain the initiative and advance over the ground they had covered on the road to the Marne. We may regard the "Race to the Sea" as describing the complicated operations following the effort of the French to outflank the Germans between the Oise and the Channel, which resulted in extending the deadlock of trench warfare at right angles to the old front nearly as far north as the city of Lille.

Then comes the German effort to destroy the Belgian army in Antwerp and drive south through the open gap between Lille and the sea, which results in the capture of Antwerp and the advance south as far as the Yser and Ypres, the occupation of most of the Belgian seacoast, and finally the bloody defeats at the Yser and Ypres, where the French and British close the last gap in the line from the sea to Switzerland and thus checkmate German strategy.

In capturing Antwerp the Germans won a moral not a military victory, since the Belgian army escaped. But the occupation of the Belgian seacoast was a considerable material advantage and it was due primarily to the fatal interposition of Winston Churchill, who made his celebrated entrance into Antwerp after King Albert and the French General Staff had agreed upon an evacuation, inevitable by reason of German progress through the Belgian defences. Yielding to the importunities of Churchill, King Albert delayed his evacuation for two days. When he did leave he lost a whole division, crowded into Dutch territory by the Germans; his army was disorganized by its pressed retreat; it was no longer possible to hold the line of the Scheldt; and the Germans were not only able to take Ostend and the Belgian seacoast, but also to seize Lille, the greatest manufacturing city of northern France, which they still hold after two years and a half.

Only by a narrow margin did the intervention of Churchill miss causing the capture of King Albert's whole army and a great Allied disaster. Never was there a better example of the folly of political interference with military operations, no single blunder in the whole opening days of the war was more costly to the Allies than this grotesque venture of a British Cabinet Minister into the realms of higher strategy.

III. ANTWERP

It was the Siege of Antwerp which supplied the single unmistakable circumstance of the October fighting and on the human side the only dramatic incident in a war which had now become a bewildering tangle of operations obscure to the contemporary observer and without immediately apparent result.   From the attack on Liége to the Battle of the Aisne the world had looked eagerly for a Sedan or a Waterloo.   But in October it was plain that the time for Sedans and Waterloos was passing.

Thus it was that the first shots of the German cannon before Antwerp on September 29th instantly drew the attention of the world to an action which was easily comprehensible, and already promised to be promptly decisive.   More than this, there was in the final stand of Belgian patriotism an appeal to American admiration, lacking in all else in a war between rival cultures, ambitions, races.   For a nation whose own history began at Lexington, the resistance of the weak to the strong, the defence of liberty by the few against the many at the cost of life, of all that men could hold dear, was a moving spectacle.   For Americans there was bound to be in the final tragedy of the Belgians a claim on sympathy.   Already to the neutral eyes beyond the Atlantic the Belgian resistance had taken on the character of that of Holland to Spain, of the Greeks to the Persians.

On the military side the German attack upon Antwerp was easily explicable.   German attempts to force a short road into northern France by taking Verdun had failed.   West of the Oise and the Scheldt the Allied advance was pushing north toward Antwerp.   If the Allies and the Belgians should join hands, German hold on Belgium would be precarious, for Antwerp was now like the citadel of a captured fortress, which still held out.   But far more serious was the fact that such a junction would close the last open gap on the western front and rob Germany of her only remaining chance not merely to reverse the decision of the Marne, but also to reach the Channel and the North Sea, facing the British coast.

Already Belgian resistance had contributed seriously to impeding German plans. In the days when every German soldier was needed in France, an army corps had to be kept in Belgium to protect the German lines of communication and contain the Belgian field army in Antwerp. At the moment of the Battle of Charleroi the Belgian army had made a sortie, in the course of which it had almost reached Louvain. The destruction of this city followed this fighting, and was an act of reprisal by the Germans, who ruthlessly executed many men and women. This deed promptly filled the civilized world with horror and awakened protest in all lands. Again, at the Battle of the Marne, a second Belgian sortie had detained troops which were starting south and held them until the critical days of the retreat to the Aisne were passed.

To rid themselves of this annoyance, to clear their flanks, to prepare the way for a final attack to the south, the Germans now resolved to have done with King Albert and his gallant little army. The closing days of September, therefore, saw Belgium approaching her final agony.

In all military history of the future the capture of Antwerp must necessarily be a landmark. Here, briefly, terribly, the superiority of the gun over the fort, of the mechanic over the engineer, was demonstrated. Aside from Paris, there was no city believed to be as strongly fortified as Antwerp, and the fate of Antwerp gave a new value to the French for the recent deliverance of Paris. Unlike Paris, however, its position on the neutralized Scheldt and near the Dutch frontier prevented complete investment. Along its southern front, ten miles distant, the Nèthe flowed through deep marshes, forming a natural moat, strengthened by forts once held to be impregnable.

Before these forts, in trenches long ago prepared, stood the whole Belgian field army, reinforced in its last days by British marines. All that the art of the engineer, all that the courage of brave men fighting with their backs to the wall could contribute to making a fortress impregnable, were to be found in the ancient Flemish city.

Yet before the German artillery, Antwerp's defences crumbled with incredible rapidity. What the 42-centimetre gun and the Austrian "305" had accomplished at Liége, at Namur, at Maubeuge, but hith-

"ST. GEORGE FOR ENGLAND!"

FRANCE AND ENGLAND STAND TOGETHER

BRITISH HIGHLANDERS LANDING AT BOULOGNE

"VIVE LA RÉPUBLIQUE!"

GENERAL JOFFRE

GENERAL GALLIENI

General Joffre commanded the French during the first seventeen months of the war, was then retired as Marshal of France, and in April, 1917, came to America as a member of the French War Commission. He was the idol of the soldiers who spoke of him affectionately as "Grand-papa" and "Our Joffre." His ringing message to the army before the Battle of the Marne will long be remembered: "Cost what it may, the hour for the advance has come; let each man die in his place, rather than fall back."

General Gallieni was the defender of Paris. On the evening of September 3d, he learned from his observers that Kluck's army had begun to turn away from Paris and was marching southeast toward Meaux and the Marne. He telephoned this news to Joffre and the next day the plan for the Battle of the Marne was arranged.

THREE FRENCH GENERALS

These generals were all active during the first year of the war. "Grand-papa Joffre" stands in a characteristic attitude with field-glasses "mobilized." At Joffre's right and left are Castelnau and Pau. All three are good-naturedly quizzing the orderly who stands at attention while the man at the extreme left enjoys seeing his comrade "on the carpet."

LORD KITCHENER AND SIR JOHN FRENCH

There were persistent rumors of differences between Lord Kitchener, British Secretary of State for War, and Sir John French, Commander of the British Expeditionary Army. General French was relieved of his command six months before Lord Kitchener's tragic death at sea, June 5, 1916.

The British believed for some time that their help enabled the French to win the Battle of the Marne. But to all intents and purposes the British were not engaged in the Marne at all. When Joffre asked for instant action, Field Marshal French replied that he needed forty-eight hours in which to get ready. He failed to rise to the greatest opportunity of the War, either because he did not perceive it or because he lacked the necessary energy and initiative. That is the verdict of French criticism and British students of the war are being driven to the same conclusion.

GENERAL SIR DOUGLAS HAIG AND GENERAL SIR HORACE LOCKWOOD SMITH-DORRIEN

Sir Douglas Haig succeeded Sir John French in command of the British forces in France. He is a more active man than his predecessor and nearly ten years younger, having been born in 1861. Throughout his military career he has been concerned chiefly with cavalry, and he possesses all the cavalryman's traditional fire and dash.

General Smith-Dorrien commanded the Second Corps of the British Army during the terrible days of the retreat which preceded the Marne.

FRENCH ARMY JOINS BELGIANS

The advance guard of the French Army on their way to join the Belgians.
French marines welcomed by the residents of Ghent.

British Artillery in a Rearguard Action in Belgium.

When the British Marines disembarked at Ostend they received a rousing welcome from the Belgians.

BRITISH ARTILLERY IN ACTION

When the average British soldier actually gets to work he is happy. Even life in the trenches then becomes "a little bit of all right," as he expresses it.

THE PRINCE OF WALES WITH HIS REGIMENT

The Prince has seen service abroad and many anecdotes are current illustrative of his good-humor and democratic ways.

Photograph by Paul Thompson

ON THE MARNE FRONT

These men are constructing a series of caves—called "Robinson Crusoes" in military slang.

Photograph by the International News Service

FRENCH DRAGOONS WITH CAPTIVE UHLANS

This is what happened to some of the German Uhlans, who figured so prominently in newspaper headlines during the first days of the War. They were captured by French dragoons who have seized their caps to send off as souvenirs to French wives and sweethearts. General Joffre afterwards forbade this practise by an explicit command couched in very severe terms.

THE ADVANCE OF FRENCH MACHINE GUNNERS AND RIFLEMEN

Some types of machine guns may be carried by one man. Others are carried piecemeal by two or more. In this case the second man has the gun itself on his shoulder while the third man follows with the tripod.

A BIG FRENCH GUN ON THE RAILROAD AT VERDUN

The big German 42-centimetre guns seemed in the early days of the War to be irresistible and incomparable. But with the appearance of such creations as this the French artillery regained its traditional superiority.

TWO REMARKABLE AIRPLANE PHOTOGRAPHS ON THE FRENCH FRONT

(*Above*). The devastated city of Clermont, in the Argonne region. It was burned by the Germans at the Battle of the Marne. Roofless ruined walls are all that remain in the foreground. Up the road toward the top of the picture a cluster of buildings is seen which must have been just beyond the zone of fire.

(*Below*.) The French aviation camp near Verdun. One can plainly see the hangars with the insect-like war-planes in front of them. Behind the hangars motor trucks are parked, and behind these are tents, the living quarters of the aviators.

erto behind a veil, they now did in the full sight of the whole world. In less than a week these forts which had been pronounced impregnable were heaps of dust and ashes, and German troops had forced the river defences and the field trenches, driving the Belgians before them. By October 7th the Krupp shells were falling about the noble tower of the Antwerp Cathedral. The city and the suburbs were breaking out in flames. The end was in sight.

The next day the field army of Belgium, commanded by its still-undaunted King, crossed the Scheldt on pontoons, moved west along the Dutch frontier, accompanied by the British contingent, and made good its escape to join the Allied armies, still moving up from the south, although 20,000 Belgians forced across the Dutch frontier were disarmed and interned. Meanwhile, by every ship, train, road, thousands of refugees, fleeing from the shells that were falling in Antwerp, flowed out to Holland, to England, to France. A new migration of a people had begun.

The end came on October 9th, when the city surrendered, the remaining Belgian forces escaping to Holland and there laying down the arms they had wielded so valiantly. Not a city, but a nation, had fallen. For England only less than for Belgium, the fall of Antwerp had been a terrible blow. The "pistol pointed at the heart of England," as Napoleon had described the city, was now in the hands of William II.

With the fall of Antwerp and that of Ostend, which promptly followed on October 15th, British public opinion at last recognized that a new Napoleonic war, with the same issues and many of the same circumstances, was before them. British observers already foretold accurately the launching of German submarines and German Zeppelins from Zeebrugge. A new Napoleon had reached the Channel. Once more it was for the British people to watch the narrow strip of sea as they had a century before. But now it was necessary also to watch the skies for that new engine which had added so much to the terror of war.

IV. THE BATTLES OF FLANDERS

In late October there opened between La Bassée and the sea the most deadly campaign the war had yet seen. For the next six weeks, on a front of barely forty miles, some hundreds of thousands of men struggled by day and by night for the possession of a score of villages lying straight across the pathway of the new German advance, between the Lys and the mouth of the Yser.   When it had ended, in part through the exhaustion of both combatants, the Germans had gained a few parcels of territory, a few wrecked villages, but in the main the line stood as it had stood in the opening hours of the conflict, despite the fact that the German Emperor had come himself to spur on his brave but beaten soldiers and that the whole German nation had set its heart upon Calais.

The purpose of the German strategy was plain.   Antwerp taken, Ostend captured, there was an apparent opportunity to sweep down the coast past Calais and Boulogne; to seize Dunkirk, the last French fortress in the north; to take root on the eastern shore of the Straits of Dover; to bring by canal and river the submarines, already so fatal to British warships, to threaten England with invasion as Napoleon had threatened it; to menace London by Zeppelin fleets; by heavy artillery and mines, to close the Straits of Dover and leave the port of London as dead as that of Hamburg.   Underlying all these magnificent details, too, was the dominant determination to regain the offensive, to take up again the road to France.

Once Antwerp fell, the army corps released from this operation drove south upon the heels of the retreating Belgians.   From every corner of the German Empire garrisons and artillery were gathered up for a supreme thrust, a thrust through France but in part aimed at England, the nation now become the object of the concentrated hatred and wrath of all Germany.

Not less rapid was the concentration of the Allies.   Coming north across the French frontier, French regular troops, British forces withdrawn from the Aisne in early October, Sikhs, Ghurkas, all the Indian contingent now to have their baptism of fire, Senegalese and Moroccan riflemen, Turcos and Légionnaires—finally the retreating remnant of the Belgians reinforced by French and British divisions—gathered around the sleepy little Flemish town of Ypres, on the shores of the North Sea at Nieuport, and behind the Yser River and the canal that joined it to the Lys, to meet the storm. And once more the post of honour and danger fell to Foch under whose supreme command the Britons and the Belgians, as well as the French, fought.

A more admirable country for defence than the Yser front it is difficult to imagine. Eastward from the dunes stretched an intricate maze of river, canal, and ditch—much of the land subject to inundation, once the sluices were open; all of it certain to become a swamp when the first storms of winter began. On this front a dozen large and small villages and hundreds of little stone farmhouses offered cover. Trenches dug to-day might be flooded to-morrow; artillery dragged within range over level fields one day might be submerged and bemired the next.

Such was the country between the Yser and the sea. Here and about Ypres for more than a month there continued, with slight interruption, one of the most intricate, confused, and indescribable conflicts in all the history of war, fought by men of more races, religions, colours, and nationalities than any battlefield in western Europe had known since the onrush of the soldiers of Islam was halted on the field of Tours. Asia, Africa, and even America and Australia shared in the glory and the slaughter.

The first blow fell along the seacoast south of Ostend, fell upon the remnant of Belgian forces, led by their intrepid King standing behind the Yser River at Nieuport, where it enters the sea. Here for days the Belgians maintained an unequal combat. At the critical moment a British fleet took station beyond the dunes and with its heavy artillery beat down the German advance, after a slaughter which was terrible.

Halted here, the Germans moved inland and came on again about Dixmude, half way between Ypres and Nieuport. Here once more they made progress until the Belgians in their despair opened the sluices and the water flowed over fertile fields carrying ruin with it, turning the whole country into a lake, drowning the invaders in numbers, creating an obstacle impassable for the present, repeating the exploit of the Dutch in their glorious fight against Alva.

Eastward from Dixmude, which presently, after the most desperate of struggles and after changing hands many times, remained with the

Germans—who were halted in its ruin by the ever-memorable resistance of the famous Fusiliers Marins, the "Golden Lads" of Brittany—the attack was directed at Ypres. Here the British stood. Here the Kaiser's wish was gratified and the troops of England met the gallant Bavarians; but they did not succumb. At points the line bent back. Such real gains as were made, were made by the Germans, but the line held. Day and night the slaughter went on. Trenches, hills, farmhouses were taken and retaken. Villages and towns were transformed into heaps of ashes.

To add to the horror autumn began, and sleet and rain, finally snow, fell, transforming the whole country into a swamp. In the inextricable tangle of roads, buildings, and ruined towns, the bodies of men lay unburied for days. The streams and ditches were choked with the human wreckage. All semblance of strategy vanished.

Tactical considerations were subordinated to the simple, single purpose of an advance by the mere weight of numbers. It became not a struggle based on the application of modern theories, but a death grapple between thousands and hundreds of thousands of men, transformed by suffering, by deprivation, by the misery of the autumn storms, to mere animals, clad in clothes reduced to rags or undiscoverable beneath the outward layers of mud.

Again and again more losses, frightful attrition, seemed to bring the German effort to a standstill. Yet always in a few hours or days new thousands returned to the charge. Always, too, they came forward fearlessly, a song upon their lips. Regiments of youths took the place of the older men of the first line, but the boys were not less brave than the men, the recruits than the veterans.

V. CHECKMATE

Such were the battles of Flanders, the Battle of the Yser, won by the Belgians and the French, the Battle of Ypres won by the British and the French. Never was a race more closely run. Never was victory nearer to the Germans than in the early days of November. The jerry-built dyke that Joffre had stretched across the last open gap on his front barely held. On November 15th, when the last effort of the Prussian Guard failed, the British Expeditionary Army had become almost a memory and its losses had passed anything in British history. At Ypres fifty thousand British were killed, wounded, or captured—a third of the whole Expeditionary Army. On the same field the French lost seventy thousand and the Belgians twenty thousand. As for the German loss, it certainly passed a quarter of a million.

Memorable, hereafter, will be the fact that as the last German attacks before Ypres were failing, there died within the British lines the one British soldier who had foreseen what was now happening, whose words had been greeted with sneers, whose voice had almost been silenced by the cheap and empty optimism of Liberal and Radical politicians. Come to France at the moment of the crisis, come to cheer his well-loved Indian troops, now fighting bravely on the western line, Lord Roberts died on the eve of a great victory, which saved his own country from the worst he had feared for it. Worth repeating, too, is the legend, credited to De Souza, that having studied the maps, having examined the plans and preparations of the French general, who held supreme command over British and French troops alike, Lord Roberts said to staff officers of Foch: "You have a great general."

At Ypres the British troops did all that was expected of them, and more could not be expected of any troops. "Wipers" of the English "Tommy" deserves a place beside Waterloo and Blenheim in British military history. Yet here, as elsewhere, it was the British soldier who shone, for the generalship was French and the victory was won through the genius of that general who had delivered the decisive thrust at the Marne. And for Foch the supreme test came in the midnight hours of a day in which his son and son-in-law had died on the field of honour.

But however close the race, the decision was absolute. The whole German conception of a swift, terrible, decisive thrust at France had ended in the bloody shambles of the Yser and Ypres. Not a French army had been destroyed, not a French army had been captured. The great battle that was to come six weeks after the declaration of war had come; it had been a French victory, not a Waterloo or a Sedan, but a victory compelling a general German retreat dislocating their whole strategic conception. After that retreat it had never been possible to regain the offensive and renew the bid for a decision. Each separate

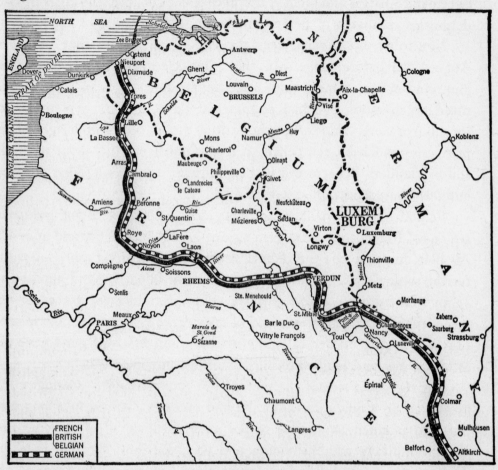

DEADLOCK IN THE WEST, NOV. 15, 1914

November 15th sees the end of the effort that began on August 5th before Liége. Behind her trench lines Germany held most of the industrial regions of France and the larger part of French machinery and minerals. All Belgium, save one tiny morsel, was in her hands. France was in no position to take the initiative, and almost two years were to pass before Britain could put sufficient forces in the trenches to permit the beginning of a considerable offensive

offensive effort from St. Mihiel to Nieuport had been beaten down almost where it had started.

Save for Russian defeat at Tannenberg, the defeat at the Marne might have necessitated a retreat to the Rhine. Hindenburg's victory had given Germany two more months in the west. She had used them up and now the eastern situation had become critical. Russian pressure in East Prussia had not recalled German corps from the Marne or before the Marne. But Russian victories in Galicia, the disasters that had overtaken Austria and seemed to forecast her collapse, the crisis in Hindenburg's campaign in Poland cried out for attention.

November 15th, then, sees the end of the effort that began on August 5th before Liége. In that time Germany had overrun Belgium and occupied more than 8,000 square miles of France and devastated much more; she had approached Paris, and on September 5th its suburbs were visible where her armies stood, but, within sight of the prize, she had been compelled to recoil, and from that hour until the end in Flanders, her strategy had conformed to Joffre's and her purposes had all wrecked in conflict with his will.

Behind her trench lines Germany now held most of the industrial regions of France and the larger share of French machinery and minerals. All Belgium, save one tiny morsel, was in her hands. France, after her terrific struggle, was in no shape to take the offensive, and almost two years were to pass before Britain could put sufficient forces in the trenches to permit the beginning of considerable offensive. Germany's prevision in the matter of heavy artillery and machine guns gave her armies a real and long-enduring advantage in trench war.

But the other side of the picture was unmistakable. Germany had staked all on a quick decision; she had become involved in a long war. She had planned to dispose of her enemies in detail, destroying first French military establishments and then Russian; she had failed to destroy France, and Russian armies were now pounding down to the Carpathians.

Despite her manifest gains and her brilliant preliminary victories, Germany had, then, lost the first round of the war. She had lost it at the Marne and all her desperate struggles from the Marne to the Yser had availed her nothing. Now at last she must go east and deal with Russia; new horizons and new victories beckoned; but while she turned her face east, Britain and France, behind the dyke they had erected in the west, began to gather up their strength for a renewal of their offensive in a future which was far more distant than they could dream.

With the close of the fighting about Ypres the western battle falls to the level of a deadlock, which endured until March, 1917, with no material change in the battle fronts.

CHAPTER EIGHT

THE EASTERN FIELD

I

RUSSIAN AND GERMAN PURPOSES

With the failure of the German effort at Ypres, the western field loses its importance for more than a year and a quarter. It is not until the colossal bid for Verdun in February, 1916, that the events on the French and Belgian front take on that importance which they had in the opening days of the war. It is, of course, true that long before the battles of Flanders in October and November the eastern field had been the scene of many terrific engagements, and of campaigns whose relation to those in the west is not patent, yet, for the purpose of narration, it is simpler to deal first with the western operations right through the Battle of the Marne until the decision there had been made absolute in Flanders, and then examine in detail the eastern operations from the morning of hostilities.

These operations were seen only confusedly and understood but little in the early days of conflict. There is lacking still and will remain wanting for many years, perhaps, that complete detail which we already possess in the case of the French operations in the west. But it is possible to perceive, upon the least scientific study, that from the opening days of the eastern struggle until the German victory at the Dunajec transformed the whole eastern situation, two very clear and well-defined plans were working out.

In the last days of August, acting in strict conformity with a prearranged plan made by the French and Russian General Staffs, two Russian armies were sent into East Prussia, where one found disaster at Tannenberg and the other was compelled to fall back to the frontier and assume a defensive posture. Despite subsequent ventures, leading directly to a second disaster, the Battle of the Masurian Lakes, the

East Prussian field was thenceforth of secondary interest and importance.

On the other hand, concomitant with the Russian defeat at Tannenberg was the first of the two great Russian victories about Lemberg, which exercised a permanent influence upon the eastern campaign down to the Battle of the Dunajec. In these battles about Lemberg the military establishment of Austria was temporarily wrecked and Russian strategy henceforth was concentrated upon the effort to make absolute the consequences of the early victories, to enforce the decision of Lemberg, and put Austria out of the war.

This purpose led to the steady pressure upon Austria on the Galician front, to the advance to the San, to the suburbs of Cracow, and finally, when further progress in this direction was proven impossible, to the gigantic campaign in the Carpathians, which aimed at passing the crests of this range and pouring down into the Hungarian Plain. In the course of the effort many battles, most of them Russian victories, were fought, and the great fortress of Przemysl, with a huge garrison, was captured. The disaster at the Dunajec occurred while the fighting in the Carpathians was still going in the Russian favour, but it is nevertheless true that Russia had failed to achieve her main purpose, when she was forced to give it over.

By contrast with the Russian campaign and purpose, the German efforts in the east were directed at preventing Russia from crushing Austria. These efforts were not originally or mainly confined to supporting Austria in Galicia; rather the Germans undertook, by a campaign of their own, to compel Russia to turn her attention away from Austria and give the Austrians time, under German direction, to get on their feet again. In addition, the German plan had the local object to take Warsaw, seize the west bank of the Vistula River, one of the most serious military obstacles in Europe, and thus insure their own eastern front.

When they began their operations in Poland in October, at the moment they were also attacking Antwerp and preparing for their final effort to break the decision of the Marne, the Germans had only small effectives, and their advance to the outskirts of Warsaw suggests Early's dash for Washington in 1864, designed primarily to shake Grant's grip on Petersburg and Richmond. Even if they did not get Warsaw, which was a gamble, the Germans expected, justly, to compel the Russians to send troops from Galicia and thus give Austria respite. In this they were entirely successful.

The second drive, begun in November and leading promptly to the terrible Battle of Lodz, was a more serious undertaking. This time the Germans not only expected to relieve the pressure on the Austrians but also to get Warsaw. Temporarily they helped the Austrians, but they failed wholly in the attempt to get Warsaw, and the Austrians were soon in danger again.

November saw, in the west, the final surrender of the German purpose to abolish the decision of the Marne. This was given over, not because it was proven hopeless—in fact, the Germans were almost at the point of victory when they stopped at Ypres—but because it was no longer safe to attempt to deal with their eastern front with the slender effectives which they had there. Up to this moment the Russian campaign had not materially affected the western. It had drawn two Austrian corps out of Alsace at the perilous moment of the Marne, but it had not compelled the Germans to withdraw troops from the western front. On the contrary, they had sent at least six new corps to Belgium for the Ypres and Yser battles.

Had the Russians won at Tannenberg their pressure would have begun to affect the Germans in the west before the Battle of the Marne. When the Russians failed, the Germans were able to go right ahead with their western campaign until November. But at this point the Battle of Lemberg began to have consequences, which the Battle of Tannenberg would have had, had it been a Russian victory. With her western campaign unwon, Germany had to go east in November. So far, the Franco-Russian strategy had prevailed over the German, but the result had been reached so tardily that German armies in the west had been able to dig in on French and Belgian soil from the Vosges to the sea.

After Lodz, Germany turns east and gives her main attention to the Russian front.   When she began in November, it is clear that her High Command expected to take Warsaw and beat down the Russian danger before spring, using several corps borrowed from the western front, which had now fallen to the level of trench war.   Her High Command obviously had expected to return to the west in the spring and try again to abolish that Marne decision, always weighing upon Germany, because if this decision were to stand, time would be allowed Britain to arm, equip, and munition her millions.

Once Germany did turn east she began a tremendous effort.   In December, in January, and in February there are terrific attacks on the whole Polish front facing Warsaw and one great attempt to get to Warsaw and behind Warsaw from East Prussia.   But all these fail.   The February failure establishes the fact that Warsaw cannot be taken from the north or from the west and new Russian victories in Galicia make it clear that the Germans' effort to relieve Austria by her campaign for Warsaw has failed.

Sometime in February at the latest, Germany discovers that it will not be possible to shake Russia off in time to go back west and renew her effort to get France, still her main foe, out of the war in the spring and summer of 1915.   Instead, it is clear that Austria must be kept in the war by a major effort directed against Russia.   It is then become essential, since Russia must be attacked, that the blow shall be sufficiently heavy to put Russia out of the war altogether and leave German hands free to deal with France, reinforced by Britain, before Britain has reached the point in her preparation where she will be strong enough to lend France the necessary aid.

Here is the genesis of the great German campaign of the summer of 1916, which begins in Galicia and ends far in Russian territory.   With this campaign we are not concerned now.   But what it is necessary to recognize is that Russia succeeded in defending Warsaw and holding back Germany, while beating in upon Austria, just long enough to prevent Germany from returning to the western field in 1915.   In doing this she gave France and Britain fifteen months to prepare.   The service was invaluable. In performing it, Russia invited that German attack which brought her to the edge of ruin. But she, also, escaped.

Here, then, is the whole story of the eastern campaign in the period which we are now to examine. In this time Russia is crowding more and more steadily in upon stricken Austria, pushing her back from Lemberg, from the San; coming close up to Cracow and then, checked here, turning toward the Carpathians and struggling up and in places over summits. And in the same time Germany is attempting, with ever-diminishing success, to compel Russia to let up on Austria by attacking Russia in Poland. German pressure is great enough to rob Russia's blow of just that weight which would have made it completely decisive, but it fails to divert Russian attention sufficiently. So at last we come to the decision to spend the summer in the east and direct the main blow in the spring and summer against the eastern enemy.

While all this is happening in the eastern field, Great Britain and France are making every effort to get their military forces into shape to take the pressure off their Russian ally in the spring. But the task is far too great and too long for the British. More than a year is to pass after the Battle of the Dunajec before Britain can be armed or munitioned; France, after the sacrifices of the Marne, is not strong enough, alone, to break the German lines in the west. The failure of all the French and British efforts from Alsace to Flanders supplies the German High Command with proof that their campaign against Russia can be pushed in the spring without danger to their western front. It is the failure of Allied efforts in the west straight through the winter, that makes the Russian burden so great, and it is the failure in the spring that precipitates the catastrophe of the Dunajec.

II. TURKEY'S ENTRANCE

The whole course of the eastern operations was affected and Russian disaster finally achieved through the intervention of Turkey on the side of the Central Powers. In the days when Antwerp had fallen and Warsaw seemed on the point of yielding to Hindenburg, the Turk suddenly put his sword at the service of the two Kaisers. Conceivably this

Turkish decision could not have been prevented either by Allied diplomacy or Allied naval action, but the event is the first in a long series of reverses for Allied statesmanship and High Command in the Near East, which changed the whole course of the war in its second year.

The military effect of Turkey's decision was not measured by the new front it opened on the Russian Caucasus or the British lines at Suez. Turkish military operations were neither fortunate nor influential, aside from the defence of Gallipoli. But when Turkey entered the war, Russia was automatically cut off from the outer world for many months by winter on the north and by Turkish forts at the Bosporus. The result was that her munitionment was gravely affected. Before spring she had exhausted all her stocks of ammunition, and when the German blow came in April she was almost without heavy shells. This was the prime cause of all the subsequent reverses. This was Turkey's real service to her allies and her terrible revenge upon her hereditary enemy.

The political causes of Turkey's entrance are not hard to fathom. With the rapprochement of Russia and Britain, the latter resigned, in fact if not by formal engagement, her long-standing rôle of the defender of the Turk. It was well understood in Stamboul, as elsewhere, that the Persian bargain between Russia and Sir Edward Grey had an implied consent to eventual Russian possession at the Straits. Under the stress of circumstances, because British title to the Suez Canal had been made absolute by the French withdrawal from Egyptian ambitions—a part of the 1904 bargain—Constantinople lost its old value for the British, England resigned her position as the first friend of the Sultan, and the Kaiser instantly and eagerly replaced his rival at the Golden Horn.

When the Balkan States attacked Turkey, Germany and Austria hoped for their defeat. Britain and her Russian and French friends hoped for their victory, and Russia and France contributed materially to training and munitioning the armies that won at Lule Burgas, Kumanovo, and Yenidze-Vardar. It was, too, by virtue of an understanding with France, Russia, and Great Britain, that Italy attacked Turkey and took Tripoli.

No Turkish statesman could mistake the fact that France and Britain had abandoned the policy which produced the Crimean War and the abrogation of the Treaty of San Stefano. No Turkish statesman could misunderstand the evidence that proved that Russia would never again have to resign Czarigrad at British behest. So far as London, Paris, and for that matter Rome, were concerned, Russia was free to take Constantinople. Therefore a victory of Russia and her allies in the war that had now broken out meant a Russian attack upon Turkey, with the consent of Russia's allies.

Turkey could have no illusion as to German ambitions. An Osmanli Empire administered by Prussian officials was as hateful to the Turk as a lost Constantinople, but this peril, if patent, was not immediate; he could hope that the outcome of the war would leave the enemies of Germany strong enough to prevent this, even though they were defeated. He could hope that the turn of events might save him as it had saved him for so many decades. But the Russian danger was immediate, unmistakable, carried with it a death sentence for him.

Actually the Turkish decision was procured by the intervention of two German warships, the *Goeben* and the *Breslau*, which were caught in the western Mediterranean at the moment of the declaration of war and fled via Palermo to the Dardanelles, escaping the whole French and British fleets. Had British and French warships followed them up the Straits, sunk them under the very eyes of the Turkish Government, the course of events might have been altered and the worst of Allied disasters avoided. But Allied purpose had not yet reached this point; Allied admirals lacked the courage of Nelson in the case of Copenhagen.

With the safe arrival of these ships, Turkey was lost to the enemies of Germany. Aided by their presence, Enver Pasha was able to throw his government into the hands of the Germans. More than this, these same ships, at last issuing forth from the Bosporus and attacking Russian ports and shipping, provoked that Russian declaration of war which placed Turkey definitely on the side of the Central Powers. Count d'Erlon's blundering march and countermarch in the Waterloo campaign was only one degree more disastrous to his Emperor than was this failure of British naval officers to the Allied cause—French ships were then engaged in covering the transport of French troops from Morocco and Algeria to France—to the whole Allied cause in the spring and summer of 1915.

GLIMPSES OF THE SQUADRONS OF THE AIR

AMERICANS WHO FLEW FOR FRANCE

This picture shows some of the members of the Escadrille Lafayette, an organization made up of American aviators. From left to right: Lieutenant de Laage de Mieux (the French instructor), Johnson, Rumsey, McConnell, Thaw, Lufbery, Rockwell, Masson, Prince, and Hall. Within a short time after this photograph was taken, McConnell, Rockwell, and Prince, had been killed in action.

THE DREADNOUGHT OF THE AIR

The huge Brequet air cruiser, used for bombardment purposes and carrying machine
guns as well as racks for launching bombs.

THE BATTLE CRUISER OF THE AIR

The new model Nieuport fighting machine mounts at great speed, rising to 7,000 feet in six minutes, and flies as
high as 20,000 feet.   The machine gun is mounted on the hood and shoots through the rapidly revolving propeller.

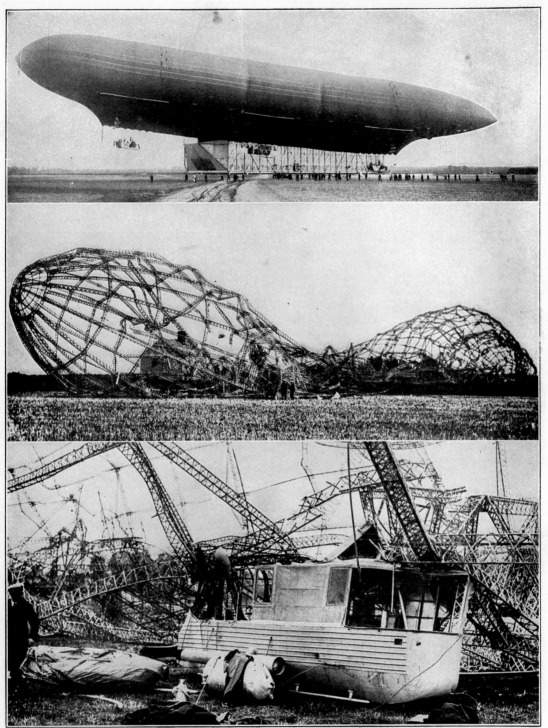

THE WAR IN THE AIR

This giant Zeppelin was brought down in the suburbs of London by anti-aircraft guns. The envelope burned up but the gondola was barely scorched. The whole incident afforded the British an excellent opportunity for studying the secrets of German Zeppelin construction. The upper picture shows a German dirigible intact.

WOMEN VOLUNTEERS FOR THE FRENCH AËRIAL SERVICE

This picture reminds one of the photographs of the crater-pitted face of the moon. But in reality it is an aviator's photograph of a modern battlefield. The numerous spots are the craters made by shell-explosions. The heavy lines drawn with mathematical precision are fortifications; and the lighter lines, more or less wavering, are the trenches.

A PAIR OF ABLE-BODIED ZOUAVES FROM THE GOLD COAST OF AFRICA

Decent Europeans at the front were often hard put to it, to explain the horrors of war to half-civilized men like these, who were familiar with such scenes among savage men and beasts in the African jungles. But as missionaries had assured them that such behaviour was abhorred by civilized men, they were much puzzled by the "frightfulness" rampant in France and Belgium.

TURCOS

In this war of many nations, men and costumes of all sorts were to be met with. This picture shows a group of French Turcos from Algeria, solicitous as to the manner of preparation of their midday coffee.

CANADIAN TROOPS

A large proportion of the sparse population of Canada crossed the sea to fight for the mother country. With them went many Americans. After a period of training in England the Canadians and the Americans stood shoulder to shoulder in the trenches in France.

A TRUE WORLD WAR

From all quarters of the globe men come together to resist aggression by the Hohenzollern and the Hapsburg. Never before in the history of the world—not even in the Crusades—were men of such diverse and wide-scattered races banded together in a common cause. Here are Cossacks from Russia, Sikhs from India, and English Colonials from New South Wales.

A SENEGALESE INFANTRYMAN

ANNAMESE SOLDIERS

MEN OF ASIA AND AFRICA

Few realize that there were troops of Mongolian race on the battlegrounds of Europe. The Japanese have taken a hand only upon the sea and at Kiao Chau. But here (*upper picture*) is a column of soldiery from French Cochin-China marching to their camp near Versailles. The lower picture shows a French Senegalese battalion going forward into action in the great Somme offensive.

CHAPTER NINE

THE BATTLE OF LEMBERG

I

RUSSIAN MOBILIZATION

Russian mobilization, for which the preliminary orders were given as early as July 25th, was conditioned upon circumstances of Russia's western frontier. Here Poland projects, like a fist against a pillow, to use a familiar figure, deep into the block of Teutonic territories. Thus Russian armies operating about Warsaw or to the west of Warsaw would be fatally exposed to German or Austrian attacks coming south out of East Prussia or north out of Galicia, which touches the longitude of Brest-Litovsk, more than a hundred miles east of Warsaw.

This situation Russia was in the process of remedying when the war broke out. North of Warsaw from the Vistula, at the point where the Bug enters it, to the Niemen, the Russians had stretched a line of forts, beginning at Novogeorgievsk and ending at Kovno on the Niemen. This was the famous Bobr-Narew-Niemen barrier, but it derived its main strength not from fortifications but from the swamps and from the rivers that give it the name it bears. Westward, Warsaw had once been guarded by forts, but these had been demolished and Russian armies had planned, when the scheme of fortifications was complete, to stand before Warsaw, on the Blonie line, a system of field fortifications suggesting the Chatalja lines. Thence southward the Vistula supplied an admirable defensive position being in itself a serious military obstacle, a broad deep river with high wooded banks.

But Russian preparation had only begun, and south of the Vistula, from Ivangorod to the Volhynian province, there was a gap, between Lublin and Cholm, through which Austrian armies could advance upon Brest-Litovsk, operating far in the rear of Warsaw and behind the line of the Vistula. Until this gap had been closed, all positions to the westward were gravely imperilled. And it is worth noting that the German advance to Warsaw, when it came, was successful because of this gap.

In this posture Russia was compelled to mobilize behind the Bug instead of the Vistula, using the Niemen and the three fortresses of the Volhynian triangle, Rovno, Dubno, and Lutsk, to guard her flanks. Only covering troops were left in Warsaw, and it was not until the strength of German numbers going west and the weakness of the army left in the east were disclosed, that Russia began her forward movement in Poland, the first positive evidence of which was the army pushed north out of Warsaw to the disastrous Battle of Tannenberg.

It seems now unquestioned that Russian mobilization, slow as it was because of the vastness of Russian area and the paucity of Russian railroads, took both the Germans and the Austrians by surprise and later led them to make angry charges about Russian preparations before the Serbian crisis. But this is a debate for the future. What is clear is that, by the middle of August, Russian armies were beginning to move. This movement was in two distinct areas. Two armies, one from the Niemen and one from the Vistula at Warsaw, pushed into East Prussia, met with considerable success in the third and fourth weeks of August, and were then brought to a dead halt by the disaster at Tannenberg, which destroyed one of the armies and eventually forced the retirement of the other.

The second group of armies was the more considerable and did not number less than a million, at least twice the strength of the other two armies combined. This group was divided into three armies commanded by Ivanoff, Russky, and Brusiloff, names that were to become famous in the history of the war. Ivanoff's army was based upon Brest-Litovsk and by the middle of August was moving south covering Lublin and the gap that opened toward Brest-Litovsk. His mission was to hold any Austrian invasion south of Lublin, but the main thrust was to be made by the other armies.

Russky's army came west along the Kiev-Lemberg railroad, having Kiev as its base, and advanced directly upon Lemberg, crossing the Galician frontier about Brody in the fourth week of August. Brusiloff brought his army up along the Odessa-Lemberg railroad, taking the field only when it became clear that Roumania intended to remain neutral. The original mission of this army was to protect Odessa and southwestern Russia from Roumanian attack, if Roumania remained faithful to her alliance with Austria and Germany. The release of this army actually made the victory of Lemberg possible and in this way Roumania

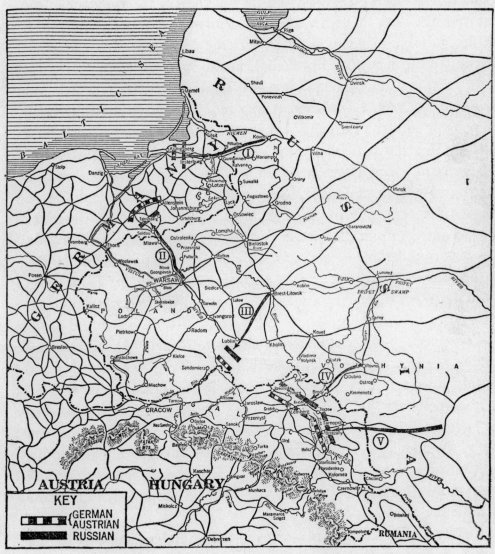

THE RUSSIAN OFFENSIVE ON ALL FRONTS, SEPT. 1ST, 1914

I–Rennenkampf	III–Ivanoff	V–Brusiloff
II–Samsonoff	IV–Russky	

served her old allies an evil turn quite comparable with that served them by Italy, when her proclamation of neutrality released French troops to fight at the Marne. Brusiloff crossed the frontier near Tarnopol, also east of Lemberg, and advanced toward this city, his flank along the Dniester. His junction with Russky was completed before the battle began and his part in the first engagement was decisive.

II. AUSTRIA'S PLANS

It was Austria's mission in Austro-German strategy to meet the main Russian thrust and parry it, while Germany was disposing of France. At the very outset it is plain that the High Command of the Dual Alliance fatally underestimated the speed and the force of the Russian blow. Thus Germany borrowed two of the best Austrian corps for her western drive and was putting them into operation in Alsace when Austrian disaster came. In addition, three or four more corps had been sent south to deal with Serbia. This latter army was far too small to fight an offensive campaign with the well-equipped and well-trained veterans of King Peter and suffered immediate and terrible disaster at the Jedar, while Russia was still just beginning to get across the frontier into Galicia, a full week before Tannenberg, and about the time of Charleroi.

It may be doubted whether Austria actually put in the field against Russia many more than 600,000 troops at the outset. In any event, she was outnumbered by at least two to one. She further invited disaster by dividing her armies. One (Auffenberg's) she stationed across Galicia from north to south, east of and covering Lemberg; its right or southern flank rested on Halicz on the Dniester, its northern flank was behind the Bug, and its centre behind the Zlota Lipa, on high ground. This position was excellent and it had been protected by well-constructed field works, but it was far too extended for the number of troops Austria had available.

The second Austrian army (Dankl's), leaving railhead at the San, moved straight north into the Lublin gap, aiming at Brest-Litovsk and having for its ultimate purpose to compel the Russians to evacuate Warsaw and all of Poland. This was an exceedingly ambitious thrust, it was entirely beyond the capacity of the army and the generals that first undertook it, but it did actually succeed less than a year later, and its success demonstrated the weakness of the Russian position and the wisdom of the original Russian strategic conception, which called for an evacuation of all the territory west of the Bug.

It will be noted that neither the Russians nor the Austro-Germans, in the opening days, undertook any operations in that part of Poland west of Warsaw. The Germans lacked the numbers for any such operation; the Russians were stopped by the concentration of Austrian armies opposite Lublin, which had a deadly menace for any army west of Warsaw. It is only after the German thrust at Warsaw, made possible by Tannenberg, had been undertaken and failed, that Russia ventures into this area, resigning the Galician field for the moment, and then she comes within a hairsbreadth of a crushing defeat at Lodz and makes no further effort in this field, standing stolidly on the defensive.

The opening of the last week in August, then, sees these two major efforts on foot. Russia is advancing with her two armies along the Kiev and on the Odessa railroads and standing firm with her Third Army about Lublin; Austria is holding one army before Lemberg and sending the other north into Volhynia and actually approaching Lublin, its presence already signalled by Austrian reports of victories about Krasnik. We may calculate that the Austrian armies are outnumbered about two to one and that as the armies before Lemberg begin the battle, the Austrians have learned that the Serbians have just won a sweeping victory at the Jedar and that Austrian invasion of Serbia has been abandoned.

Meantime, to complete the eastern picture, one Russian army is approaching Königsberg, having won a battle at Gumbinnen, and a second is approaching Allenstein in East Prussia, while Hindenburg is already preparing his amazing counterthrust. In the west Namur has fallen, the French have been beaten at Morhange and Charleroi, and all the Allied armies are beginning the great retreat which Berlin and Vienna interpret to be the collapse of French military power.

III. LEMBERG

The First Battle of Lemberg lasted not less than eight days. In its earlier stages it began along the Zlota Lipa, but the Austrians presently retired to their main front behind the Gnila Lipa, their southern flank still at Halicz and their centre about Krasne, on the Brody-Lemberg railroad, where it is joined by the Tarnopol-Odessa railroad there left behind the Bug. All this ground was again to be fought over by Brusiloff's great offensive in June, 1916.

The fact that the Austrian resistance finally collapsed has somewhat misled the world as to the nature of the struggle. It was exceedingly severe and for many days the Russians, despite heavy losses, were able to make no progress. Finally Brusiloff broke through to the south toward the Dniester and about Halicz, which he took. This success imperilled the whole Austrian line and it retreated through and beyond Lemberg—which fell on the first days of September, just at Tannenberg time—and took its stand behind the chain of Grodek lakes, a few miles west of Lemberg, its left flank reaching and passing Rawaruska.

This time the decisive thrust is made by Russky. His numbers are so much superior to Auffenberg's that he is able to turn his flank, and the Austrian line swings at right angles around Rawaruska and runs east and west; Russky takes Rawaruska, breaks the whole centre of the Austrians and throws the entire force, shaken by its defeats before Lemberg, into an utter rout.

Meantime Ivanoff, having at first retired before Dankl and permitted him to follow deep into Russian territory and become separated from Auffenberg, turns and delivers a heavy blow. Dankl's army is now left in air, its southern flank exposed by the collapse of Auffenberg, and he is compelled to make a disorderly retreat, approximating a flight, back to and across the San, giving up Jaroslav and coming back behind the Wisloka and approaching Cracow. Auffenberg's army retires over the Carpathian passes into Hungary. Before the Austrian flight had at last paused the Russians announced that they had taken 250,000 prisoners, vast numbers of guns, and an enormous store of munitions and material.

In point of fact, Lemberg was one of the complete disasters of military history; it brought the Austrian war establishment to the edge of ruin and disclosed a fundamental weakness, which, despite German effort and temporary success in the summer campaign of 1915, could not be quite cured and was revealed afresh on the same ground in the campaign that opened the summer of 1916. Differences of race, the manifest lack of

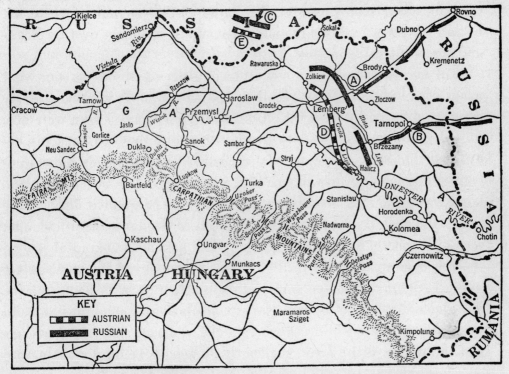

THE RUSSIAN INVASION OF GALICIA—BATTLE OF LEMBERG

A–Russky C–Ivanoff E–Dankl
B–Brusiloff D–Auffenberg

sympathy on the part of Slav contingents with their task of fighting Russians to please their German and Magyar masters, defective training and insufficient preparation, above all inadequate numbers for the task assigned, all these things combined to make Lemberg an Austrian disaster of first magnitude.

The immediate consequences were the loss of all of Galicia to the San, the advance of Russian troops beyond the San as far as the Wisloka, the investing of Przemysl, the passage of the Carpathians by Cossack raiding parties, and the first arrival of the invader in the Hungarian Plain. Austrian troops had to be recalled from Alsace and from Serbia to retrieve the lost situation and the first demand was made upon Germany to come to the aid of her Austrian ally. By the battle Austria lost 20,000 square miles of territory; Lemberg, a city of more than 200,000 people; the great oil district of eastern Galicia. She lost also not less than half of her first-line troops, counting the Jedar casualties, and, in addition, material of war which could only slowly be replaced.

Austrian defeat at Lemberg coincided with German repulse and retreat at the Marne. But for the unhappy disaster at Tannenberg, the second week in September would have seen all the armies of the Central Powers in retreat or rout. Had Tannenberg not released Hindenburg's army, it would have been from the western armies that Germany would have had to draw corps to repair the Galician situation. She was not now compelled to do this, but the consequences of Lemberg were ultimately to put a term to western operations for a year and a half.

The decision at Lemberg did not endure so long as did that of the Marne; the Germans abolished it at the Dunajec in April. But while the decision stood, it continued to hamper and embarrass German effort. Russia was temporarily compelled to withdraw from the region west of the San, by the first German drive at Warsaw; after Lodz, she was still before Cracow, and it required a new effort in Poland to compel her to abandon her thrust for Cracow. Then she turned to the Carpathians, and the immediate demand of Hungary compelled Germany to send troops to guard Hungarian passes.

In the end Germany had to give over the attack upon Warsaw through Poland and turn her main attention to Galicia. When she did this she reversed the decision of Lemberg and promptly turned the Russians out of Galicia, but this was only in the last days of April, and the Russian victory had begun in the last days of August. Lemberg is, then, the second great Allied victory of the war, ranking immediately after the Marne. It gave the world its first evidence of the new character of Russian armies, demonstrated that the evils of the Japanese War had been remedied, and that Russian generalship was as good as German or

French.   Disasters due to the failure of ammunition somewhat marred this new reputation, but in 1916, when munitions had been supplied, Russian armies began to win new victories of an impressive character.

It is fair to say that Lemberg and the Marne together demonstrated that Germany had terribly underestimated her Continental foes.   Two years were to pass before she was to reform her estimate as to British troops.   But by the middle of September she and her Austrian ally had fought three great battles, as she had planned, which should have decided the issue of the war, but two had been lost, and the third had only saved Germany from ruin and had not crushed France or Russia.

CHAPTER TEN

WARSAW

I
CONDITIONS OF THE FIRST BID

About October 1st the Russians had passed the San in Galicia and were moving toward Cracow, the first investment of Przemysl had begun, and Cossacks were pouring through the still-unfortified passes of the Carpathians and penetrating the Hungarian Plain. In the west the Siege of Antwerp was approaching its promptly decisive stage, and the German campaign to abolish the decision of the Marne by a final offensive through Flanders was taking final shape.

It was now necessary to aid the Austrians, but it was not possible to withdraw troops from the west, unless Germany was willing to accept a deadlock from Switzerland to the North Sea, and she was far from ready to do this. There remained the possibility of using the larger portion of the army of Hindenburg, which had won Tannenberg and pursued the second Russian army in East Prussia—that of Rennenkampf—from the very gates of Königsberg across the frontier. Gathering up the mass of this army and leaving the balance to retreat slowly before the Russians, the German General Staff might transport it rapidly, by those admirable strategic railroads which follow the frontier in a semicircle from East Prussia to Cracow; put it in at Lodz, which had fallen into German hands early in the war; call upon Austrian troops, returning from Serbia or from Alsace, and make a sudden drive at Warsaw.

If the drive achieved the maximum of success, Warsaw would be captured, together with Ivangorod to the south, the objective of the Austrian fraction of Hindenburg's army; Germany would, at a single thrust, win the west bank of the Vistula, an enormously strong military position. Behind this line she could hope to stand inexpugnably and

devote her efforts to preparing to renew the conflict in the west in the
spring.

But if this maximum was not realized, there was a minimum that
was assured, Russia had no troops of material consequence between
Lodz and Warsaw: most of her military strength was now in Galicia

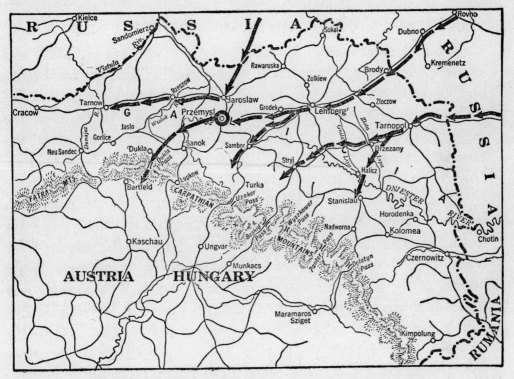

RUSSIAN INVASION OF GALICIA, ABOUT OCTOBER I, 1914

The Russians were moving toward Cracow, the first investment of Przemysl had begun,
and Cossacks were pouring through the still-unfortified passes of the Carpathians and penetrating
the Hungarian Plain

pressing against the Austrians and moving toward Cracow. Unquestionably the first sign of a German thrust for Warsaw would compel the
Russians to give over their Galician operations, draw out many corps
and send them to save Warsaw, and thus dislocate their whole Galician
concentration. When this began the Austrians could undertake a new
offensive in Galicia, designed to crush the weakened Russian armies,
and the danger to Cracow, as well as the menace to Hungary through
the Carpathians, would be abolished.

This was the main purpose of the offensive toward Warsaw. Austria must be helped. The help she required could still be furnished without any draft upon the western lines, but such help would not be sufficient to win a decisive battle, if Russia made a prompt concentration. It could only get Warsaw if speed enabled the Germans to seize that strong position before Russian numbers could be brought up. It was a serious bid for Warsaw, but it was a bid begun with the full recognition that it had at best no more than half a chance of success.

In the Civil War, Lee sent Early against Washington with precisely the same purpose in view. It was possible that Early might get Washington. If he did, the success would be of enormous political and moral value; but even if he failed he was likely to compel Grant, hanging doggedly to his footing before Petersburg, to weaken his front to relieve Washington, and this would give Lee a respite. It might lead Grant to abandon his whole effort to get Richmond, from his position south of the James. Early failed, as did Hindenburg, because troops from the other front arrived in time. But unlike Lee's thrust, that of Hindenburg succeeded in dislocating the other enemy concentration, that in Galicia.

There was further, a political purpose in the German thrust. The attitude of the Poles toward the conflicting nations was obscure. It was possible and reasonable for the Germans to hope that the Poles, if a German invasion carried Warsaw, might turn from their Russian allegiance and become the allies of the invader, as they had in the Napoleonic time when they furnished the great Emperor with at least one marshal and some of his best and bravest troops. This German hope was not realized, partly because the failure to get Warsaw necessitated a retreat, in which Poland was laid in ashes by contending armies, but it was an important consideration in the German mind and it was a possibility recognized fully by the Russians.

II. AT THE GATES OF WARSAW

Under these circumstances and about October 1st, Hindenburg began his advance in two columns—one following the railroad east from Kalisz

to Warsaw; the other, mainly composed of Austrians, moving north-
east along the railroad from Cracow to Ivangorod.   Combined, these
armies did not number six army corps, possibly there were but five;
certainly their total strength was less than that of Kluck's army in the
Marne campaign.   These armies had something like a hundred miles
to go; they had, when the advance began, practically no Russian

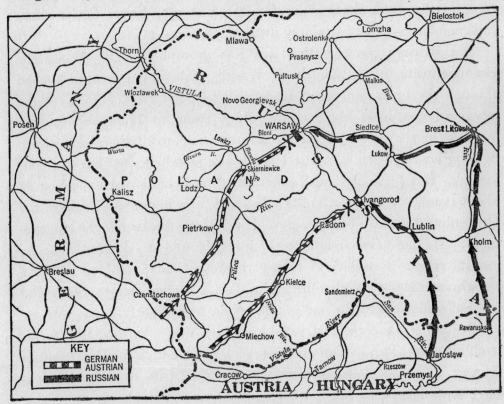

HINDENBURG'S FIRST CAMPAIGN FOR WARSAW, OCT. 20, 1914
The German thrust for Warsaw diverted the Russians from their operations in Galicia.
This was its main purpose.   In the Civil War, Lee sent Early against Washington with a pre-
cisely similar object in view

troops before them, and they had reasonably good roads to follow.
They began with the full expectation of taking Warsaw within the fort-
night, and the news of the fall of Antwerp overtook them on the road
and gave them new enthusiasm.

With little or no fighting, moving with almost incredible rapidity,
these two armies advanced until, on October 14th, one army stood on the

outskirts of Warsaw, in the suburb of Prushkow, seven miles from the centre of the city, while the other had cleared the west bank of the Vistula before Ivangorod. At this moment German shells fell within the Polish capital, German aeroplanes bombed the city, there was a general exodus of the population, and the world believed that Warsaw was to share the fate of Antwerp. So sure did German victory now seem to the Turk that, under German pressure, Enver Pasha chose this moment to put his country into the conflict.

But Russian concentration was just prompt enough. While the Germans were in the suburbs of Warsaw, Siberian regiments pushed through the town and began to defend the outskirts. They were the advanced guards of eight corps, which came to Ivangorod and to Warsaw in the next few days. For a whole week there was sharp fighting before Warsaw, where Hindenburg stood checked but not convinced. But presently the Russian reinforcements crossed the Vistula about Ivangorod and north of Warsaw and came in on both flanks of the Hindenburg forces. October 21st Hindenburg broke off the engagement. He had never fought to the limit; he had stood before Warsaw long after the possibility of taking the town had passed, to preserve the threat as long as possible. His Austrian allies before Ivangorod had suffered severely; he had gotten off far more lightly.

Beginning October 21st, the first thrust at Warsaw transforms itself into a swift and orderly retreat, such as Frederick the Great taught Europe to expect from his Prussians, and in trim columns Hindenburg moved back to the frontier. As he retreated, the fact was disclosed that he had constructed fieldworks along his route, foreseeing retreat, and these gave his rearguards admirable protection. In this retreat he destroyed roads, railroads, bridges, actually abolishing most of the means of communication in Poland.

Meanwhile, in Galicia, the effect of the Warsaw drive had been exactly what had been hoped. The Russians had come out of the Carpathians and retired behind the San. The Austrians had rallied and taken the offensive, reaching and in spots passing the river. Przemysl had been relieved; there was a moment when the reconquest of Galicia seemed to be within Austrian possibilities. But this moment passed. As the Germans retired from Warsaw the Russians in Galicia retook the offensive. This time, passing the San, they again—and as it turned out, finally—invested Przemysl and approached Cracow at the precise moment when the armies which had saved Warsaw and Ivangorod were coming southwest, and that of Ivangorod threatened Cracow from the north as the Galician army now threatened it from the east.

Thus the real benefit of Hindenburg's thrust was shortlived. By the time he had fallen back to the German and Austrian frontiers, his retreat was mainly toward the southwest, the Russian menace in Galicia had become even more serious than it had been when he started. He had but postponed the danger for a moment and he had now to deal with it in an aggravated form.

III. LODZ

We have now come to the moment when the western and eastern campaigns merge. Hindenburg is now compelled to make a second effort to relieve the Austrians in Galicia and save Cracow. He has still only very restricted numbers. The Germans are making their last desperate effort in Flanders; they have failed against the Belgians and French from Nieuport to Dixmude; they are attacking the British about Ypres, and the British are holding on doggedly while the French are striving to reinforce them. Unless the Germans can now break through in the west in a brief time, they will have to abandon the western effort and turn their attention eastward. The Russian pressure—which, in Allied plans, made before the war, should have become effective in the last days of August—is about to count in the last days of November.

For his second effort Hindenburg takes advantage again of the strategic railroads which run in a circle about the Russian frontier. In his drive at Warsaw he had used these railroads to move troops from East Prussia to Silesia. When he had failed at Warsaw he had retired southwest upon Cracow and Breslau, destroying Russian railroads as he retired. The Russian troops had followed him through Lodz and even to the Silesian boundary.   But, owing to the configuration of the territory, they were now farther from Warsaw than German troops at Thorn would be, and they had behind them only the ruined roads and railroads, which Hindenburg had wrecked.

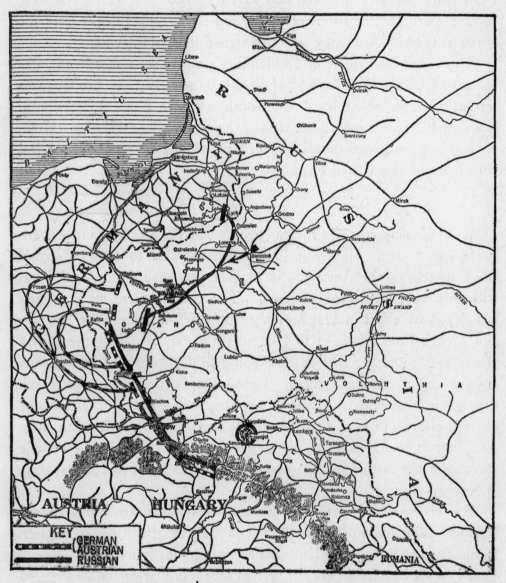

HINDENBURG'S SECOND DRIVE FOR WARSAW

Hindenburg left only Austrians to deal with the advancing Russians on the front from Cracow to Kalisz, moved north to the gap between the Vistula and Warthe rivers, and there sent in several corps under Mackensen

MEN AND GUNS OF
THE TWO KAISERS

THE IMPERIAL GUARD PASSES IN REVIEW BEFORE EMPEROR WILLIAM

At the left of the Kaiser is General Lowenfeldt, and at the extreme right General
Von Bülow.

GENERAL VON MOLTKE

GENERAL VON FALKENHAYN

GENERAL VON HEERINGEN

CROWN PRINCE RUPERT OF BAVARIA

General Von Moltke, nephew of the great Moltke of Bismarck's day was Chief of Staff at the outbreak of the World War. Because of his failure to seize and hold the French and Belgian seacoast when opportunity offered and because of rumored mistakes in the Battle of the Marne, Moltke lost his position and turned over his office to the Kaiser's favorite, Falkenhayn, whose star was to set before Verdun as Moltke's set on the road to Calais.

The armies of General Von Heeringen and Crown Prince Rupert of Bavaria met the French after they had penetrated German territory some fifteen or twenty miles, about a fortnight after the War began. The battle was an undoubted German victory. The French "75's" were outranged by the heavy German field artillery, and in three days the French were driven back across the border and the invasion of Lorraine was at an end.

A fortnight later, while the Battle of the Marne was on, these same generals fought another engagement on this same front—"the Second Battle of Nancy." They were opposed, as before, by the French general Castelnau. Their aim was to cut through the gap in the French barrier forts between Toul and Épinal and thus arrive on the flank and rear of all the French armies. Though fighting under the eyes of the Kaiser himself they were repulsed with great slaughter—else the Battle of the Marne might have ended very differently.

Photograph by Paul Thompson

GENERAL MACKENSEN

GENERAL LUDENDORFF

THE KAISER IN WARTIME

GENERAL VON KLUCK

General Mackensen, conqueror of the Russians under Dmitrieff at the Dunajec, in the spring of 1915. The trapped Roumanian army surrendered to him in December, 1916.

General Ludendorff, close associate of Hindenburg. He has been called "the brains of Hindenburg," and even the "real German dictator." His mastiff-like visage recalls the bull-dog countenance of Hindenburg and even more the resolute mask of the old "Iron Chancellor" Bismarck.

The Kaiser's wartime photographs betray the fact that he has aged greatly during the conflict. This shows him in his field uniform, with helmet covered so as to offer no glittering mark to sniping aviators. For all the dozens of gaudy uniforms in which he used to take so much delight, he has never been indiscreet enough to lead an army in person—except at manœuvres. He is said, however, to have waited "in shining armour" to take part in one or two triumphal entries which failed to come off.

General Von Kluck, about August 23d, made a desperate effort to "run around the end" of the Allied line, interposed between it and Paris and produce another Sedan. He did not quite succeed, and immediately found himself in a very dangerous position during the Battle of the Marne. Thanks to Sir John French's failure to rise to the occasion, Kluck was able by dint of desperate fighting against the gallant Maunoury to make good his retreat to the Aisne.

ONE OF HINDENBURG'S THRUSTS AT WARSAW

There is plenty of room on this broad road for ammunition and supply trains to advance along with the infantry.

AN INCIDENT DURING THE GERMAN EFFORT TO DRIVE THE RUSSIANS HOME FROM GALICIA

The German soldiers are coming out of the garrison church at Przemysl, after attending Sunday morning service.
Few civilians are in the street and the shop-windows are tightly shuttered.

EFFECT OF THE GERMAN BOMBARDMENT OF PRZEMYSL

Photograph by Paul Thompson

GENERAL VON AUFFENBERG (Right)

TYPICAL AUSTRIAN INFANTRYMEN

The unlucky Austrian general from whom the Russians captured a quarter of a million prisoners at the Battle of Lemberg, one of the great disasters of military history which brought the Austrian war establishment to the verge of ruin.

As is shown in another part of this book the Austrian makes a good and courageous soldier. Men of many diverse races fight under the colours of the Dual Monarchy yet no dissension has appeared.

PARCELS FROM FRIENDS AT HOME ARRIVE TO CHEER GERMAN ARTILLERY
OFFICERS BEFORE WARSAW

THE AUSTRIANS

It was Austria's mission in Austro-German strategy to meet the main Russian thrust and parry it, while Germany was disposing of France. But Austria was unable to carry out her part of the program, and when she had been defeated by the Serbians at the Jedar and by the Russians at Lemberg, Germany was compelled to draw troops from the western front to send to her rescue and thus lost her own chance for a quick victory over France.

The upper picture shows some of the celebrated Rangers Corps guarding a road; the lower one, a group of officers seated before one of the guns used in bombarding Antwerp.

ONE OF THE SKODA HOWITZERS THAT REDUCED LIEGÉ

On August 7th, the German infantry penetrated between the forts before Liegé and occupied the city and the citadel; but they were unable to take the forts. These maintained their fire till German and Austrian heavy guns were brought forward. Under this attack the forts crumbled almost instantly. They were the work of the famous Brialmont, and supposed to be very strong. But they had been allowed to fall into disrepair and their reduction proved to be child's play to the mighty new engines of destruction.

Accordingly Hindenburg left only the Austrians to deal with the advancing Russians on the front from Cracow to Kalisz and moved his mass right along the frontier north to Thorn and the gap between the Vistula and Warthe rivers and there sent in several corps under Mackensen, soon to earn world fame. These troops moved rapidly

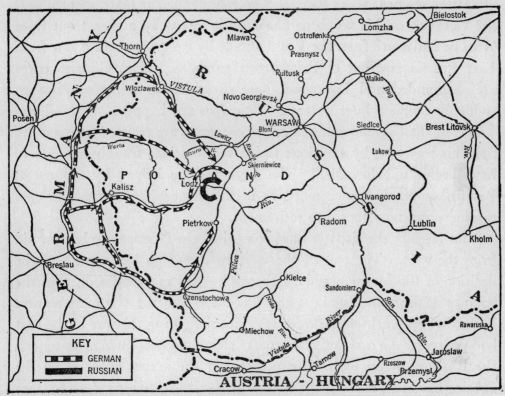

THE BATTLE OF LODZ, DURING HINDENBURG'S SECOND CAMPAIGN
FOR WARSAW

Troops hurried eastward soon turn the balance against the Russians, and December 6th the Germans reënter Lodz after six weeks of the most sanguinary fighting. German official reports claim 100,000 Russian prisoners

across the flank and rear of the Russians to the southeast, turned their flank and presently interposed between them and Warsaw, much as Kluck sought to interpose between the Anglo-French forces and Paris in the September campaign in the west.

Here, then, in the last days of November, while the Battle of Ypres is just ending, is the promise of a second Tannenberg, the capture of a large Russian army, and the ultimate fall of Warsaw. The position of the Russian army is desperate, it would seem, because its northern flank is turned by the Germans, while it is assailed in front by more Germans, and the Austrians have advanced north from Cracow, threatening its southern flank.   But the Russians escaped, showing again the same qualities which shone, even in disaster, in the Manchurian campaign.

At the moment when Russky, who commanded at Lodz, seemed lost, the Germans on his northern flank are involved by a thrust out from Warsaw and south from the Vistula made by troops brought down from East Prussia and out of the fortress garrisons.   Two German corps are surrounded and Petrograd, long silent in the midst of disaster, suddenly claims a huge success.   This does not happen.   General von François, the German commander whose corps are trapped, manages to fight his way out, by exertions which the Russians frankly concede to have been "unbelievable."   The Germans are helped by failures of Rennenkampf, who once more, as in the Tannenberg times, discloses tardiness and now goes into retirement.

But already the situation has compelled the Germans to borrow aid from the west.   The end of the western campaign has come and the decision of the Marne stands.   Troops hurried eastward soon turn the balance against the Russians and December 6th the Germans reënter Lodz after six weeks of the most sanguinary fighting the war in the east had yet seen.   German official reports claim 100,000 Russian prisoners; the Russians claim material captures, but the actual effect of all the fighting has been, in the immediate area of conflict, to reproduce western conditions of deadlock, and the Polish front rapidly tends to descend into the same state of trench warfare that has obtained on the Aisne since the middle of September.

IV. THE THIRD BID FOR WARSAW

When in October the Russians began their advance from Warsaw, following Hindenburg toward Cracow, it seems clear that they temporarily renounced the Galician field as the main theatre of operations and put forth their full strength in Poland.   After Lodz they again reverted to their old idea.   Lodz demonstrated clearly that it would be impossible to move west out of Poland. It was, in fact, as the Germans said in their official announcements at the time, a permanent check to Russian offensive toward Silesia and Posen.

On the other hand, while the first Hindenburg advance toward Warsaw had checked the Russian operations in Galicia and turned them into a retirement behind the San, the Lodz operation did not affect the Galician field and the Russians still continued to press on toward Cracow, after their Polish army had evacuated Lodz, and retired toward Lowicz and Skierniewice, covering Warsaw. A new effort was required to relieve the Galician situation. This new effort was made in Poland; in it we see, unmistakably, the contribution of troops brought from the west. The necessity for this operation was revealed in the severe defeat suffered by Austrian armies coming up out of the Carpathians and seeking to relieve Przemysl and redeem western Galicia.

Accordingly Hindenburg resumed his pressure in Poland; from the Lower Vistula south before Lodz he began a terrific frontal attack upon the Russians, employing the numbers he had now borrowed from the west. Under this pressure the Russians retired slowly, giving over Lowicz and Skierniewice and retiring upon Warsaw. They finally took their stand on the eastern banks of the Bzura and Rawka, little rivers which together stretch straight across the front of Warsaw from the Lower Vistula for many miles south. Below this system the Russians fortified the banks of the Pilitza and then of the Nida, which enters the Upper Vistula north of Tarnow.

The position was largely accidental. The Russians had intended to defend Warsaw from the Blonie lines, much nearer the city; the Bzura is more than twenty miles west of the Polish capital. But little by little they discovered that their lines held; they found that they had been driven into a defensible position, and they hung on. At the same time they drew back from before Cracow, north of the Vistula, standing behind the Nida, south of it behind the Dunajec. They had now entered the lines they were to hold from December until May between the Lower Vistula and the Carpathians, and until August before Warsaw.

The German attacks upon the Bzura-Rawka lines recalled the similar efforts in Flanders, at the Yser and before Ypres. German losses were exceedingly heavy; German gains were inconsiderable, a trench here, a farmhouse there. Meantime the weather had come to the rescue of Russia. An early and severe winter had destroyed Napoleon. The winter of 1914-1915 was one of the mildest in Polish history and the roads were turned into swamps. The superior mobility of the Germans was abolished as a factor and they were unable to use their heavy artillery because of the difficulties of transport. These conditions had materially affected the Lodz operation; they had an almost decisive influence now.

By January 1st the attempt to get Warsaw by frontal attack has failed. It will be resumed in January and February, combined with a thrust south from East Prussia, via Mlawa and along the railroad up which the Russians had marched to disaster in the Tannenberg time. But it will fail again, and this failure will be absolute. Meantime, the Russians will abandon their momentary plan to move west from Poland toward Breslau and through Galicia to Cracow. They will more and more direct their energies toward forcing the passes of the Carpathians and reaching the Hungarian Plain.

Well into February the Germans will continue their efforts to get Warsaw from the front and from the north. In all of this time they will content themselves with bolstering up Austrian defence in Galicia by more and more considerable reinforcement, and by a gradual taking over, first of High Command and then of the direction of the smaller units. It is not until the February attacks fail, and the Russian line before Warsaw is proven too strong to be broken, that Germany, in her turn, will go to Galicia and make her main effort in the field where, for many months, Russia has been steadily progressing.

January 1st, then, is a date when it is possible to dismiss the Warsaw operation as actually terminated, despite subsequent efforts. From the Baltic to the Carpathians the line begins to take the same stationary form that the western line has already assumed. There is a slight fluctuation in East Prussia; it will be February before the Germans,

having won the Battle of the Mazurian Lakes, can announce that East
Prussia is freed from the invaders. But actually the decision has been
reached, Warsaw cannot be taken from the north or from the west.
Germany must make up her mind to this, and when she makes up her
mind it will be too late to hope to resume the great western offensive in
the spring.

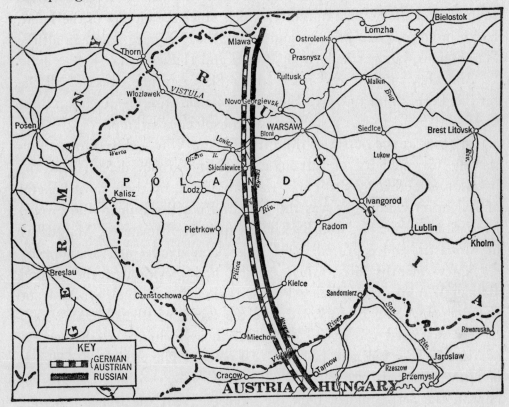

DEADLOCK IN POLAND, DEC., 1914–MAY, 1915

January 1st is the date when it is possible to dismiss the Warsaw operation as actually
terminated, despite subsequent efforts. The line begins to take the same stationary form that
the western line has already assumed

Instead, there must be prepared a new eastern campaign and that
campaign will have for its real purpose, not alone taking Warsaw and
the line of the Vistula, not merely abolishing the threat of Austria, but
destroying the military power of Russia and compelling a separate peace;
in a word, adopting against Russia the strategy and purpose which
failed against France at the Marne.

V. SERBIA TRIUMPHANT AGAIN

While the German advance from Lodz upon Warsaw was going forward, a fresh Austrian disaster attracted the attention of the world. As far back as the first days of November, Austria, hoping permanent relief from the German operations toward Lodz, had detached troops to dispose of the Serbian nuisance, which, since the victory of the Jedar, had injured Austrian prestige and imperilled Hapsburg power in all the Slav regions, but particularly in Bosnia and Herzegovina.

And once more it was reserved for Serbia, prime cause of all the terrible world conflict, to give Europe a great surprise, the fourth in three brief years, and to win a shining and conspicuous triumph.

In 1913, at the outset of the First Balkan War—when Europe preserving the memory of Slivnitza, forecast Serbian defeat, and the invasion of Serbia by the Turks was prophesied by those most hopeful of Bulgarian victory—it was the Serb and not the Bulgar who proved irresistible, invincible, won back Old Serbia at Kumanovo, Macedonia at Monastir, and captured the Turkish Commander at Adrianople.

A few months later, when Austria had precipitated the Second Balkan War to destroy King Peter's nation, it was the Serb and not the Bulgar who again prevailed, and the Battle of Bregalnitza as completely shattered the legend of Bulgarian invincibility as the reverse of Mars-la-Tour had wrecked that of France. The victims of a breach of faith, attacked by night and without warning, without declaration of war, the Serbs rallied, took the offensive, sent the Bulgars in rout back over the Rhodopians and restored to Serbia the southern half of the empire of the great Dushan.

Finally, in the opening month of the World War, when the fortune of the Allies in the west was most desperate, it was the victory of the Serb at the Jedar which opened the more prosperous period that culminated at the Marne. At the Jedar four Austrian army corps had been routed, Austrian prestige in the Balkans shattered, the first Slav triumph won in that long series which by December was to bring Austria to the lowest ebb in her history since the Hungarian Revolution.

On December 1st Serbia was once more in the presence of grave peril. The October drive of Germany had released several army corps of Austrians in Galicia and Poland, and these came south to complete the work of destroying the troops of King Peter, who had for months defended their frontiers. Before this overwhelming force the Serbs had retreated. All the corner of Serbia between the Save and the Drina was lost. Coming east from Bosnia the Austrian right approached Belgrad, which for four months had defied daily bombardment; the centre

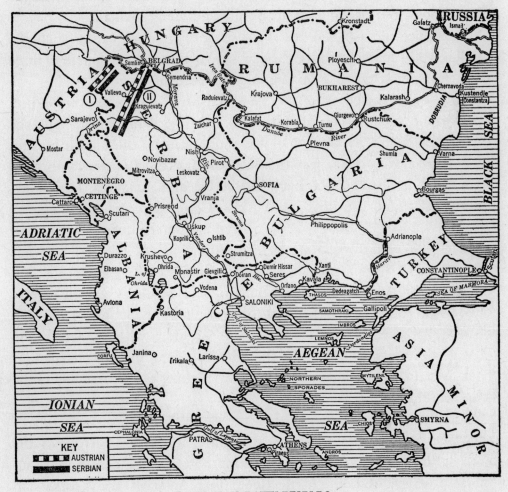

SERBIAN BATTLEFIELDS

I—The Jedar, August, 1914. In the opening month of the World War, when the fortune of the Allies in the west was most desperate, it was the victory of the Serb at the Jedar which opened the more prosperous period which culminated at the Marne

II—Valievo, December, 1914. One of the most complete of Austrian disasters reached Valievo, the left penetrated to Uchitza, on the Serbian Morava. Presently Belgrad fell, a birthday present to the aged Francis Joseph, the only conquest of his army in the whole struggle.

In the first week in December the fate of Serbia seemed sealed. A second Belgium, another little state destroyed in the contest between the great, seemed assured. Austrian armies appeared certain to reach Nish, the temporary Serbian capital, to open the Orient Railway to the Bulgarian frontier and persuade Bulgaria, still smarting from her defeat by Serbia, to cast her lot with the two Kaisers and open her territory for the passage of the Turks to the battlelines of western Europe.

In the moment of greatest peril, however, Serbia was saved—partly by her own courage, by her own determination, without which destruction was inescapable; partly by the new advance of the Russians. While the Austrian troops were still before Belgrad, Cossacks once more crossed the Carpathians, swept down into the Hungarian Plain; panic reached the very gates of Budapest, and three army corps were hurriedly recalled from Serbia to defend Hungary. Once more at the critical moment the Austro-German Alliance had to surrender triumph in one field because of deadly peril in another.

No sooner had the three corps been withdrawn than the Serbs again took the offensive. Old King Peter, now stricken in years and infirmities, but retaining something of the fire that earned him his cross of the Legion of Honour as a soldier of France in 1870, rode in front of his troops, mounted on a white charger, and harangued them as their chiefs of remote centuries were accustomed to do. Then followed one of the most complete of Austrian disasters. In a few days the whole force had fled across the frontiers, leaving thousands of prisoners, many cannon, and much material, behind them. Belgrad was retaken; by December 15th Serbia was free of Austrians, saved for the time being; saved until the third—and fatal—attack, the Balkan drive of Mackensen almost a year later.

CHAPTER ELEVEN

NEW HORIZONS AND NEW GERMAN PROBLEMS

I
NEW YEAR, 1915

The New Year—which was to witness the most brilliant military triumphs of Modern Germany, triumphs rivalling the Napoleonic cycle—opened dismally enough for Berlin. Five months of war and a million casualties had sufficed to complete the destruction of all the initial plans and hopes of Germany. The supreme hope, that of a short war, had gone glimmering and Lord Kitchener's forecast of a three-year war had begun to find converts even in Germany. And the prospect of a long war raised new problems, of which the military, if it was not the most pressing, was by no means the least.

In point of fact, new political considerations were now becoming apparent. There was the question of Austria, a question at once political and military; there was the problem of Italy, destined to become more and more grave as the months passed until the spring should see the House of Savoy again in the field against the House of Hapsburg. There was, too, the similar and only less serious problem of Roumania, which was not to find so speedy a solution as that of Italy, but was destined to prove even more dangerous to German safety. There was the additional necessity to care for Turkish defence, a necessity which would grow with the months and become pressing in the spring, when the Allied fleets knocked at the door of the Dardanelles and Allied armies took root on the Gallipoli Peninsula.

Finally, the problem of sea power was beginning to become acute. A world which too eagerly and too completely accepted the British view as to the effect of the British blockade was not completely mistaken in recognizing thus early that the British fleet would steadily and increasingly hamper the domestic economy of Germany and compel her to employ one expedient after another to meet the shortage incident to the blockade. Only in food did the reckoning prove radically mistaken and even in this department there was discomfort, without immediate or intolerable privation.

The sense of this closing net, the anger at the nation which thus struck the whole German people while it remained removed from the weight of German arms, was to drive the German Government, the naval school of Tirpitz, into a submarine campaign that would involve neutrals, and in the case of the greatest of all neutrals, the United States, produce a situation which after many clashes would at last add the United States to the nations at war with Germany.

The paralysis of the German merchant marine; the closing of the seas to the German flag while British, French, and even Belgian ships still sailed the ocean and brought to French and British ports the munitions and supplies essential to preserve them, while their own factories were still unready and their own industrial system not yet readjusted; the resources of ships and sailors, which permitted the transport of armies; the arrival of colonial troops from Australia, Canada, India, which permitted the nations to redress the balance which was with Germany at the outset, thanks to her superior preparation; these were things that exercised an ever-growing influence upon German thought and German action.

Nor could there be any mistaking the resentment in the whole Fatherland, as it was recognized that, so far as the world was concerned, Germany had become a besieged city, and German explanations and German statements, save for the few fugitive messages sent through the air, were condemned to satisfy German readers alone; while the world, the neutral world to which Germany desired to appeal, found its evidence and drew its conclusions from anti-German sources alone.

II. THE MILITARY PROBLEM

Looking first at the military problem, it was plain on January 1, 1915, that German prospects, without being desperate, were dark. It was true that men, the world over, too promptly began to compare the

posture of Germany in 1915 with that of Napoleon in 1813. The outside world neither understood the enormous accession of faith and confidence the restricted victories of the opening phase had brought to
Germans, and the unparalleled magnitude of German effort which was
to come, nor could they realize, as the Germans did, how futile were
many of the hopes in Allied quarters of the prompt arrival of Kitchener's millions and the limitless flow of Russian masses.

Yet, despite the exaggerations, the fundamental conception of the
non-Teutonic world was correct. Germany had failed at the Marne and
in her subsequent efforts to reverse the decision of the Marne. Her
armies now stood on the defensive in the west and there was no promise
that the initiative could be reclaimed. Two months of terrible slaughter before Warsaw had proven as sterile as the murder done in the battles
of Flanders. Warsaw stood as Calais and Boulogne stood.

Looking southward to Austria the picture was dismal in the extreme.
The defeat of Lemberg had shaken the whole fabric of Hapsburg military life. After Lemberg the efforts of German commanders to rally
and reorganize Austrian armies had saved the armies, but it had failed
to make them victorious. Temporary Russian retirements in Galicia
had again and again been followed by Russian victories, and in the last
days of the year a second Serb triumph had revealed the permanent
disorder of Austrian forces. The Russian armies were again pressing up
and over the Carpathians, and from Budapest came insistent demands
that Germany should guard the Magyar marshes against the Slav danger.

Reckoning on the basis of country occupied, it was true that Germany was now fighting in foreign lands, for the most part. The East
Prussian invasions had been repulsed, but not until grave injuries had
been done to Junker estates. Not less than 8,000 square miles of industrial France, holding in peace times 2,000,000 people, was occupied,
as was the bulk of Belgium and some 15,000 square miles of Russian
soil. But, to balance this, France clung to a corner of Alsace, Russia
to a paring of East Prussia, and Austria had lost in Galicia and Bukowina
nearly 35,000 square miles of territory including the oil-fields of Galicia.

If anything else were needed to incline the balance toward the Allied side, it could be found in the isolation and inevitable extinction of German colonial power. Togo and the Kamerun were both lost, Kiaou-Chau and the islands of the Pacific were gone. The doom of German Southwest Africa had been sealed by the failure of the Boer rebellion, and a Boer General, Louis Botha, was gathering up the troops which would presently conquer it. German East Africa still endured, but not even a German could believe that it would permanently escape the fate of the other colonies.

On the military side Germany had now once more to bend her energies to restore Austria. She had to reckon on the eventual demand of the Turk for guns, and men to man them. The chance of a resumption of the offensive in the west in the spring was already fading, but the failure meant more time for France and Britain, aided by the workshops of America, to restore the balance in numbers and preparation. The story of how Germany met the military problems is one of the most magnificent in military and industrial history. Unfortunately for her, the political problems were beyond her capacity—beyond all human capacity, probably—and, as it turned out, her military successes could only in part postpone the political perils that were now revealed.

III. ITALY

Of all the political problems, that of Italy was the most dangerous. Count Nigra had once said that Italy and Austria, in the nature of things, could only be allies or open enemies. The Triple Alliance had been denounced by Italy in the opening days of the war. With the denunciation of the fact of the Treaty, although the letter endured for some months thereafter, Italian hopes turned again to the Irredenta, and the Italian people, far more promptly than the Crown or the politicians, began to clamour for the acquisition of the Trentino and Triest, of the islands of the Adriatic and the lost Venetian province of Dalmatia, still adorned by some of the most splendid monuments of Ancient Rome.

Such an agitation could have but one consequence unless Austria were prepared to resign Triest and the Trentino, and Austria was not prepared for any such sacrifice. Under the influence of Germany she tardily, very tardily, consented to certain cessions, but they were too slight to satisfy Italian demand. Bismarck, in refusing to allow his ally of 1866 to acquire Trent, had sown the seeds of later disaster, and almost from the morning of the war it was clear that Italy would eventually enter the alliance against Germany.

Turkish participation merely increased Italian agitation for war,

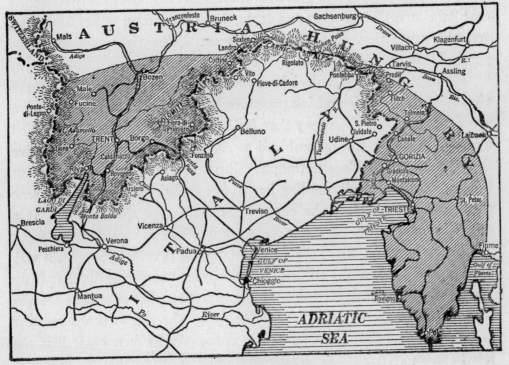

ITALIA IRREDENTA

As soon as the Triple Alliance was denounced, Italian hopes turned to the Irredenta, and the Italian people began to clamour for the acquisition of the Trentino and Triest

because the alliance of the Turk with the Central Powers, besides reopening the Tripolitan question, assured the latter of supremacy in the eastern Mediterranean, where Italy had great ambitions, all of which ran counter to those of Berlin and Vienna but found ready hearing and small opposition in Allied capitals. It was a desirable thing for Italy that Germany and Austria should be beaten. It would be a fatal thing for many Italian hopes if they won.

Nor was it less essential that Italy should contribute to the defeat of the Central Powers, if she was to share in the results. There were in Greece and Serbia eager aspirants for the eastern shores of the Adriatic and the islands and shores of Asia Minor. The noise of Allied fleets before the Dardanelles forts presently awoke echoes in Rome that German diplomacy could not silence. The hereditary antipathy to the Austrian and the longing for Triest mounted with the weeks until they reached a point in popular emotion where Prince Bülow grimly conceded that "the street" had won; and Italy, despite the fears of her Sovereign and the opposition of Giolitti, her most influential politician, was plunged into the world strife.

We shall see that the decision came too late to prevent the German victory of the Dunajec, which transformed the whole face of the eastern war for a year. We shall see that Italian hesitations, taken with Allied blunders in the Balkans, combined to clear the way for the great drive through Serbia to Constantinople. But also, at a still more distant time, we shall see Italy sending her troops to Saloniki, as she had sent them to Valona, before she entered the war. We shall see her, at a critical moment, extending her declaration of war to include Germany.

But in January, 1915, the Italian danger was only apparent, it was not yet imminent, and Berlin could believe for many months that Italy would remain neutral. To this end she exerted all her efforts, and it was with an eye to the moral effect in Rome that she prepared the greatest of her victories, the Dunajec, which, unhappily for her, came just too late to check Italy's course, although it did avail to restrict the influence of Italy in the war for nearly a year. Fatally, however, the prospect of a long war was beginning to weigh upon Berlin, for if a swift victory such as those of 1866 and 1870 might have left the neutrals still reconciled to their rôles, a long war held out attractions to their racial and national hopes which could not be mistaken.

IV. ROUMANIA

Not less real than the Italian was the Roumanian danger. Within Austrian and Hungarian frontiers there lived more than 3,250,000 people of Roumanian tongue and race. They were a majority in the great

Hungarian province of Transylvania; the largest group amongst the many races in numbers in Temesvar; a considerable element in Bukowina. All these provinces touched the Roumanian frontier. In every Roumanian heart there had been for many years a desire to achieve the re-union of Roumania, as that of Italy had been achieved in the previous century. Could the Austrian provinces be won, Roumania would become a compact state of nearly 100,000 square miles, as large as the mainland of Italy; if not a Great Power, second only to Spain among the lesser nations of Europe.

Such hopes had seemed impossible of realization until the Second Balkan War first revealed the weakness of Austrian policy and the crumbling of the Hapsburg edifice. Until that time Roumania had, perforce, consented to remain a minor member of the firm of the Triple Alliance, and, as Italy had been drawn to Berlin by the quarrel with France over Tunis, Roumania had been influenced in the same sense by the gross injustice and ingratitude of Russia after the Turkish War. In that conflict Roumanian troops had saved the Russian army at Plevna, but Russia had robbed Roumania of her portion of Bessarabia and flung her a morsel of the Bulgarian Dobrudja as an insufficient recompense.

Ruled by a Hohenzollern, who in the opening days of the World War sought to cast the lot of his country with the head of his House, Roumania had marched with Berlin, Vienna, and Rome—held not a little by the presence of Italy in the partnership, which enlisted the Roumanian tradition of Latin origin—from the era of the Congress of Berlin to the outbreak of the Balkan wars. But when Austria, eager to crush Serbia, had given her support to the creation of a Bulgaria even greater than that which had been erected by the Treaty of San Stefano and abolished by the Congress of Berlin, Roumanian allegiance faltered.

Bulgaria was the rival of Roumania in the Balkans and had openly declared her purpose to reclaim the Dobrudja. Bulgarian plans looked forward to achieving a hegemony in the Balkans comparable to that which Prussia had achieved in Modern Germany. To all such plans Roumania was necessarily hostile, because they both threatened her integrity and menaced her influence. When Austria sacrificed Bukharest for Sofia, Bukharest openly altered her policy; accepted Russian warrant for attacking Bulgaria; and, by her attack in 1913, completely demolished the whole structure of Austrian statecraft. Moreover, the Roumanian soldiers who invaded Bulgaria openly announced that they were taking this route to Transylvania and Bukowina.

Once the breach had been made, the consequences were inevitable. Roumania followed Italy in declaring her neutrality when the war came, despite the desire of the King, whose subsequent death soon removed a Teutonic ally not less potent than Constantine of Greece. When Italian policy began to drift toward the Allies, Roumania tacitly followed. More and more Roumanians looked over the Hungarian boundaries to where, beyond the Transylvanian Alps, millions of their race brothers suffered something approaching intellectual and moral slavery under the Magyar yoke.

When the first Russian victories brought the Slav to the Roumanian boundaries of Bukowina and even across the Carpathians into the Hungarian Plain, Roumanian patriots and politicians listened eagerly to Russian promises, based upon Roumanian participation. Only Russian disaster could abolish or postpone such participation. Had Russian diplomacy been a little less stiff or Roumanian demands a little less grandiose, Roumania might have followed Italy at once. As it was, the Dunajec postponed what it could not prevent. At Bukharest, as at Rome, German diplomacy was to perform miracles, but the ultimate failure was already assured, short of German victory in the war, when 1915 began.

V. AUSTRIA

The military side of the Austrian problem was plain. But the political aspects were not less patent to Berlin. Half of the Austrian population was Slav. In the opening battles Czech, Croat, Serb, and even Polish regiments fought with something less than half-hearted zeal. The Italians from Triest and the Trentino, the Roumanians from Transylvania and Temesvar, easily succumbed to the assault of enemies a degree less hateful to them than the races whose yoke they bore. The vast Russian captures after Lemberg, the Serbian disasters, the later

PICTURES OF TRENCH WARFARE

GERMAN SHELTERS OF SANDBAGS, IN THE DUNES ALONG
THE BELGIAN COAST

RELAI
DE
COUREURS

THE ELABORATION OF TRENCH WARFARE

A typical trench on the western front, braced to prevent caving in, with the usual boardwalk and the numerous telephone and telegraph lines needed in a modern communication system. The shell case, hanging from the cross beam, is struck when a gas attack is discovered, as a warning to all within hearing to put on masks. The inset shows an underground telephone exchange which is part of the system of communication between the front lines and headquarters in the rear.

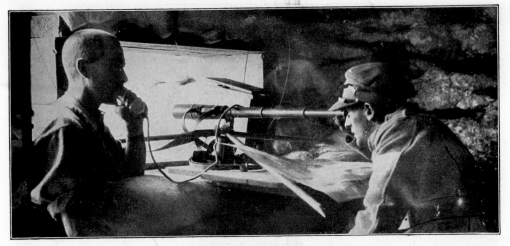

AN OBSERVATION STATION

These are placed in buildings, trees, shell craters, etc.—wherever the observer can see the effect of his batteries' fire. Telephone communication back to the gun is arranged and the observer then reports as to the range, the movements of his own and the enemy's infantry, etc.

AN UNDERGROUND PASSAGE DUG BY THE AUSTRIANS AT DUBUS, RUSSIA, WITH AN OUTLET
IN A CHURCH

WINTER QUARTERS

These German soldiers have made themselves very snug just behind the front in the Argonne region. The hut in the foreground is a field post office. The "corduroy" paths are reminiscent of pioneer days in America.

ANOTHER ASPECT OF LIFE IN THE TRENCHES

These Frenchmen are in the front line of trenches during a brisk bombardment. The shell-hole shows the Germans have got the range. The less venturesome of the pair finds his pipe useful in helping to preserve his sang-froid.

A LIGHT GUN ELABORATELY ENTRENCHED

Note the curtains which are closely drawn when there is danger of aërial observation. These guns are used to cut wire entanglements, destroy parapets, silence enemy artillery, and for barrage fire either with or without gas shells.

BELGIANS ENTRENCHED OUTSIDE ANTWERP

In this final stand of Belgian patriotism against the German invaders there is a strong appeal to American admiration. For a nation whose own history begins at Lexington, the resistance of the weak to the strong, the defense of liberty by the few against the many, at the cost of all that men hold dear, is a moving spectacle.

UNDERGROUND WITH THE BRITISH

(*Above*) King George inspects a trench won from the Germans.

(*Below*) These British Red Cross Officers have "dug themselves in" very comfortably and are just sitting down to dinner. Cave life is not always incompatible with good cheer.

Photograph by Underwood & Underwood

AUSTRO-HUNGARIAN SHELTERS IN THE ALPS

Galician defeats, were all due in some part to the failure of the subject races of Austria and Hungary.

Yet it was of prime importance to prevent this disintegration from spreading, because every evidence of crumbling was but a new incentive to Roumanian and Italian appetite, and every Austrian disaster had an echo in Bukharest and in Rome which no one could mistake. It was not alone that the crumbling of Austria weakened the Central Alliance directly, but it was also that each new crack, each fissure, in the Austrian unity was a new invitation to other nations to enlist and add their numbers and resources to the enemies of Germany.

Napoleon faced the same problem in 1813, when he lingered in eastern Germany, because he realized that a retreat behind the Rhine would mean that his German allies would, either from desire or necessity, enter the ranks of his foes; as they did, when, at last, after the disaster at Leipzig, he was compelled to retire behind the old frontiers. More than all else this political situation forced itself to German attention in the shaping of the campaigns of 1915. It compelled the abandonment of the west, quite as much as any military consideration. It compelled Germany to allow to Britain the time to begin to get her masses in the field, and it held Germany in the east until February, 1916.

More and more it became clear that, while Germany continued to win victories, she could count on the neutrality of Roumania and the annoying rather than dangerous hostilities of Italy. But only in victory was there safety. On the military side, the Austrian armies would take on new efficiency when a German general and German artillery had won the Dunajec, and the great Russian retreat from the Carpathians to the Beresina began. But once the Russian counter-offensive came, Austrian armies would crumble in a new disaster comparable to that of Lemberg and having more immediately unfavourable consequences.

More and more Austria became a burden, a deadweight upon German military and civil policy. Less and less useful became Austrian military assistance, and greater and greater became the share of Germany in the work of the Alliance. But in addition to this was the posi-

tive peril that grew out of the long-standing enmities Austrian policy
had engendered or out of the weaknesses inherent in the heterogeneous
nature of Hapsburg populations, weaknesses that at one time contributed to the breakdown of the Austrian army and to the growth of the
number of nations at war with Germany.

All this is clearer now than at the moment—yet little was hidden
from German eyes—when the Kaiser's Ministers, with the opening of
the new year, took up the problems of a long war and were compelled
to estimate the assets and liabilities of their new undertaking. These
influenced the military situation; they compelled strategy to bow before
considerations of state; they forced the Germans to make their main
effort in the east; and, even at this early date, they made clear the
consequences of immediate or eventual failure either in the east or the
west. From the task of destroying France, Germany was now definitely recalled to devote her best skill to the salvage of Austria.

CHAPTER TWELVE

ON THE EAST FRONT TO THE BATTLE OF THE DUNAJEC

I
IN THE CAUCASUS

The first days of January saw a considerable Turkish disaster on the Russian frontier in the Caucasus. Into this difficult region, where campaigning was made the more difficult by the severity of the winter, the Turks had, in obedience to German dictation, sent several of their best corps. The ostensible purpose was to recover the famous fortress of Kars, lost after a gallant defence in the last Russian war. But, in fact, Kars had small value for the Turks. The real purpose of their effort was to compel the Russians to divert troops to this front from the Austrian frontier and thus take off some of the pressure upon their hard-pressed German ally.

For the Turk there were much more pressing services to be performed near at hand. His entrance into the war had cost him the last, shadowy title to his ancient Egyptian estate, and the friendly Khedive had lost his throne. Britain had proclaimed a protectorate and placed an Anglophile ruler on the Khedivial throne, thus completing the work of making good her position in Egypt, recognized by France in the famous and fatal agreement of 1904. To Suez and to Cairo and to the lost African provinces, Tunis and Tripoli, opportunity seemed to beckon the Osmanli along the road that his Arab predecessors of the Caliphate had marched.

That such a venture might have succeeded seemed and seems possible. Britain still lacked the men to defend Egypt; the native troops were at least cold to their Christian masters, if they were not disloyal. Time had not been allowed for the fortification of the shores of the Suez Canal, which, less than a year after, were to face and master a Turkish attack. Could Suez have been reached, and the canal blocked, the injury to Britain would have been great, although by no means as considerable as German military writers announced a year later, when the road from Berlin to Byzantium had been opened and Germany found a Teutonic purpose to be served by Osmanli effort at Suez.

German control of Turkish military policy was, however, complete, and while the proclamation of the Holy War was still stirring the imagination of the world, even if it fell flat in Islam, beyond the immediate territories of the Turk; while the world was looking for revolts in India and Egypt, in Tripoli and Tunis; while it was expecting Turkish attack at Suez, several Turkish corps were making the difficult advance from Erzerum toward Kars, and the Russian troops, heavily outnumbered, were falling back into the Caucasian marshes, south and east of Batum and Trebizond.

In this difficult country, suffering from insufficient equipment and from the rigours of a terrible winter, the Turks, after brief preliminary successes, met complete disaster. Of three corps, one, with its Turkish and German officers, was captured. Two more, striving to cover the retreat, were heavily beaten, losing flags, guns, and prisoners. Not less than 100,000 Turkish troops were thus eliminated from the battleline, and German prestige suffered its first heavy blow in Constantinople, a blow from which it did not recover until the successful defence of the city a few months later.

From this moment and for more than a year the Caucasus front loses its importance. The subsequent changes in position were not considerable. The Russians did not bring many troops east from the Galician front; the German purpose was not served by the Turkish effort. But when, in the next winter, the Russians were ready to move in this Armenian district, the fall, first of Erzerum and then of Trebizond, to the sword of the Grand Duke Nicholas, gave the world the first hint of the renaissance of Russian military strength, so shaken at the Dunajec and after.

II. LAYING THE ROUMANIAN PERIL

In December and early January Austrian disaster had for the second time led the world to believe that a collapse of the Dual Empire might presently change the whole face of the conflict. While Russian armies again passed the central and eastern Carpathian passes, other forces swept Bukowina and approached Transylvania. The occupation of the Crownland was a fair invitation to Roumania to join the conflict on the Russian side and receive Bukowina as a bribe and Transylvania as a reward for participation.

For Germany the problem was promptly set to protect Hungary, grown impatient through disaster and anxious because of impending attack from Serbia, from Galicia and Bukowina, and because of the possibility of Roumanian hostility. The resignation of Count Berchtold and the selection of Baron Burian were evidences that, within the empire, Hungarian apprehensions were recognized. The visit of Count Tisza to the Kaiser was a sign that Germany had been warned.

This warning Germany received with all possible attention and acted upon with amazing promptness. Thus in January, while the Russian occupation of Transylvania was being discussed, German troops were brought south and concentrated in lower Hungary. Their purpose, it was duly announced from Vienna and Berlin, was a new invasion of victorious but stricken Serbia. Yet a few weeks later these troops appeared in Transylvania, and moved east, parallel to the Roumanian frontier, as a warning to the Hohenzollern king of this state that, to take Transylvania, he must fight the head of the House of Hohenzollern.

Under the pressure of these troops, Russian armies in Bukowina speedily began to give ground. Like the Shenandoah Valley in our Civil War, Bukowina was becoming a thoroughfare of invasion and a pathway of destruction. Step by step they were driven from before the Borgo and Kirilibaba passes; they were cleared out of the foothills of the Carpathians, and by the middle of February their retreat had halted at the Sereth River, a few miles south and west of Czernowitz and the Russian frontier; more than two thirds of Bukowina had been reconquered, and the Germans had interposed a wall of troops between the Czar and his prospective Roumanian ally.

At the same time there came from Budapest new rumours of Russian disaster, of the suicide of a Russian commander, and the capture of the

General Staff of the defeated army. These rumours were duly denied, but there remained the solid fact that Bukowina had been reconquered; the invitation to Roumania to participate in the war had been abruptly cancelled by German arms, and from Bukharest there came no more reports of the intervention of the Latin state without delay. On the contrary, there were credible reports of the release of vast stores of grain previously purchased by Germany and Austria, temporarily held up by the Roumanian Government, but now permitted to go north. A military campaign waged for obvious political ends had succeeded.

Nor did the quieting of Roumania end the success of German policy. A German loan to Bulgaria again stimulated rumour that Ferdinand and his Bulgarian subjects were contemplating an entrance into the war on the German side, were planning to retake Macedonia, to strike at Serbia and Greece, and, by cutting the Orient Railway, shut off the Slav state from Saloniki and foreign supplies, and, by invading the Valley of the Morava, open a road between Berlin and Constantinople and thus unite the Central European nations. This rumour, however idle at the moment, supplied an interesting forecast of what was to come, and gave Allied diplomacy a warning which it stupidly failed to take.

Finally, from Albania came a fresh incursion into Serbia along the marches of the Drina, directed at Prisrend and the territory still populated by Albanians but ceded to Servia and Montenegro by the Treaty of London. Here was new work for the Serbian army, calculated to keep it occupied, south of the Danube and away from Bosnia, until Germany had dealt with Russian activity in the southeast.

Such, briefly summarized, were the purpose and achievement of German arms in Bukowina. Thus promptly and completely had the Kaiser answered the appeal for help made a few weeks before; thus had he justified the affection and esteem in which he had long been held by the Hungarians, and temporarily silenced the whispers of discontent in Budapest.

III. THE BATTLE OF THE MASURIAN LAKES

To answer the Austro-German thrust through Bukowina and over the Carpathians, the Russians chose to strike at East Prussia. Strategically such a move was advantageous because it meant moving troops a far shorter distance away from Warsaw, which remained the centre of military operations in the whole eastern front. Practically, could East Prussia be overrun, the whole Russian front would be straightened; a great province, a source of food supply to Germany, would be conquered; and, ultimately, the German position between the Bzura and the Nida in Russian Poland would be exposed to attack in the flank and rear.

Thus, while the main Russian and German armies faced each other west of Warsaw on the lines they had taken when Hindenburg's great offensive against the Polish capital had been halted in December, new armies were directed against the German positions north of the Vistula and south of the Niemen, on a front from Tilsit to Johannisberg, while another force moved down the north bank of the Vistula toward Thorn.

Again, as in the case of Tannenberg, the geographical circumstances explain the military operations. Inside the eastern frontier of East Prussia some fifty miles there extends from north to south, between Insterburg and Johannisberg, that intricate tangle of water known as the Masurian Lakes, out of which flows the Angerapp River, which joins the Inster at Insterburg to make the Pregel, a stream that enters the sea at Königsberg. West of this region Samsonoff had suffered his great disaster in September at Tannenberg. To this obstacle the Russians had returned in October after defeating a German invasion of Suwalki Province at the Battle of Augustovo.

For three months Russian and German forces had faced each other in this region with little or no change of position. Now the Russians undertook to turn the Germans out of their strong position behind the Masurian Lakes by attacking from the north and south; that is, by coming in on the flanks. At the outset this move met with apparent success. Coming west on the solid ground between the Niemen and the Angerapp rivers, the Russians approached Tilsit, took Pilkallen, began to talk again of a siege of Königsberg. At the same time, to the south of the Masurian region, between the East Prussian frontier and the Vistula, they made headway toward Thorn.

In the first week in February, however, Hindenburg countered with terrific force. The first sign was a renewal of the German offensive south of the Vistula and along the Bzura-Rawka front. On this line the Germans began a series of desperate assaults, which were announced as a new drive at Warsaw. Petrograd proclaimed the slaughter in these

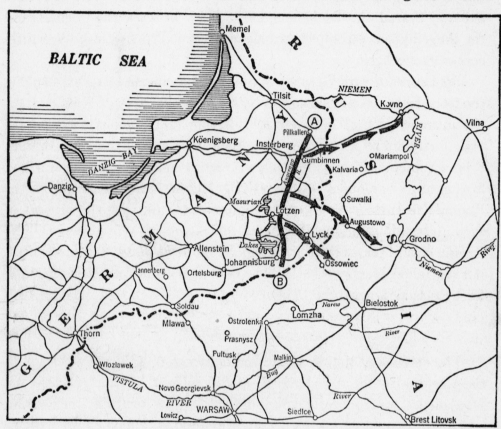

THE BATTLE OF THE MASURIAN LAKES

Seven months after the war had broken out German soil was practically free of Russians. Line *A-B* shows the Russian front before the battle. The *arrows* show the lines of the Russian retreat

fights the greatest in the whole war, and there were circumstantial reports that the Kaiser himself had been shocked by the sacrifice of life in a forlorn undertaking.

By the second week in this month, however, the truth became apparent. The German attacks had been mere screening movements to cover the withdrawal of troops from this front to East Prussia, and very soon Petrograd began to concede defeat and retreat in East Prussia, while Berlin announced a second Tannenberg and the capture of 40,000 Russians. In any event, it was clear that by the use of automobiles, by again employing the strategic railways along the East Prussian frontier, the Germans had rushed overwhelming forces into East Prussia, beaten the Russian flanking force between the Niemen and the Angerapp and completely redeemed East Prussia, save for a little corner about Lyck.

By February 15th German troops were advancing eastward all along the front from the Vistula to the Niemen, were across the Russian frontier in many places, and were still driving the Russians back toward their fortresses of Kovno, Grodno, Bielostok, and Ostrolenka; that is, behind the Niemen and the Narew. Seven months after the war had broken out German soil was practically free of Russians, and from the Roumanian frontier to the Baltic German troops, with the support of their Austro-Hungarian allies, were advancing. Their success in East Prussia was to tempt them to one more bid for Warsaw, from the north, but this failed, like the others. The road to Warsaw ran neither through East Prussia nor northern Poland.

IV. PRZEMYSL

The disaster of the Masurian Lakes, which divided the attention of the world with the Allied naval operations just beginning before the Dardanelles, was counterbalanced in the following month by the Russian capture of Przemysl on March 22d. Invested for a moment in September, relieved when Hindenburg made his first drive for Warsaw, and promptly surrounded again when the Russians resumed the road to Cracow before the Battle of Lodz, Przemysl had been shut in ever since. Its surrender was one of the most spectacular incidents in the war and it did much, temporarily, to destroy the effect of recent Russian reverses and checks. Since Bazaine had laid down his arms in Metz four decades before, Europe had seen no such capitulation, and Russian estimates placed the number of captives at 130,000.

Before his surrender, the Austrian commander, General Kusmanek, had destroyed all the forts, blown up the bridges, turned the rifles and cannon into useless junk. But this diminished the material rather than the moral effect of the victory. Actually the last considerable fortress of Galicia, east of the Dunajec and north of the Carpathians, had now fallen. As for the numbers of prisoners, they astonished the whole world and explained a surrender which took the Russians by surprise. Like Metz, Przemysl had fallen to hunger, and, like the Lorraine fortress, it had fallen because it was provisioned to hold a garrison, not a host.

The siege itself had been marked by no considerable military effort. The Russians had merely invested the place and sat down before it. A few brief attacks had demonstrated that it was beyond the resources of their artillery train. Now and again there had been sorties; a desperate effort by Hungarian troops just preceded the surrender. Several attempts on the part of the Germans and Austrians to relieve it had come close to success, but ultimately failed. Time and hunger did the rest.

In the closing days of the siege, cats and dogs had sold for prices recalling the Paris market in 1871. There seems to have been much mismanagement of resources, and the defence shed little lustre on Austrian arms. The last sortie of the Hungarians seemed to the Russians useless sacrifice, for it was promptly and completely checked.

With the fall of Przemysl the Galician campaign entered its final stage. The troops released by the surrender joined the armies that had long been battling in the Carpathians, advancing when opposed only by Austrians, retreating when German reinforcements came up. Each attack after retreat found the passes more strongly fortified, found the task more terrible. Still Russia stuck to it, and with the fall of Przemysl the world looked for the arrival of spring and the Russians together in the Hungarian Plain.

In this it was mistaken. Carpathian hopes, like the expectations aroused by the Allied fleet before the Dardanelles, were soon to be destroyed, and one failure after another was to meet Allied armies and fleets in the whole eastern field. Yet it is worth recalling that the moment when Przemysl fell was the most fortunate moment, from the Allied point of view, since the struggle had opened. Austrian collapse, German surrender, these were the things that the press of the world outside German and Austrian territories talked of at the very moment when Germany had gotten well forward in the preparation of that tremendous thrust at the Dunajec, which was to usher in a full year of Teutonic victories.

Przemysl is a high-water mark; dead low water in Allied prospects comes something more than a year later, with the disaster and surrender of the British at Kut-el-Amara. It remains, now, briefly to examine the final phases of the great Carpathian battle in which the Russian flood was finally checked, the Russian armies were exhausted and shaken by their terrible efforts and losses, and the failure of Russian munitions brought disaster comparable in modern military history only with that of Napoleon in the Moscow campaign.

V. THE BATTLE OF THE CARPATHIANS

There had been fighting in the Carpathians as early as September, after Lemberg, when the Cossacks crossed the range. There had been new and more serious fighting in October and November, when the Russians came west again and approached Cracow. But it was not until the new year that the Russians definitely abandoned the attack to the west and set their faces toward the south and strove to cross the Carpathians into Hungary. Their attempts to the south on the edge of Roumania, designed to influence Roumanian policy, had met a swift check at German hands, and Bukowina had been cleared of Slavs in January and February. Similar German operations, made in response to Hungarian appeals, had closed the passes immediately to the north of Bukowina, through which the shortest rail line to Lemberg goes.

By March, when the Battle of the Carpathians takes its final form, the Russian effort is concentrated upon the Dukla and Lupkow passes while the Austrians and Germans are now on the north side of the Carpathians from this point south to the frontiers of Roumania.

The passes by which the Russians were now seeking to reach Hungary are the lowest in the range. The Dukla is but 1,500 feet at the crest and opens easily into the headwaters of the affluents of the Hungarian Theiss.   In this pass, as in several of the others, there had been terrific fighting all through the winter and the casualties had been exceedingly heavy.   White uniforms had been adopted to deceive the outposts, every device had been employed to aid the assailant and the defender, alike.   And slowly but steadily the Russians had progressed in the Dukla until they were actually at the edge of the Hungarian Plain. But in the other passes the stiffening of German reinforcements had permanently checked the Slav.

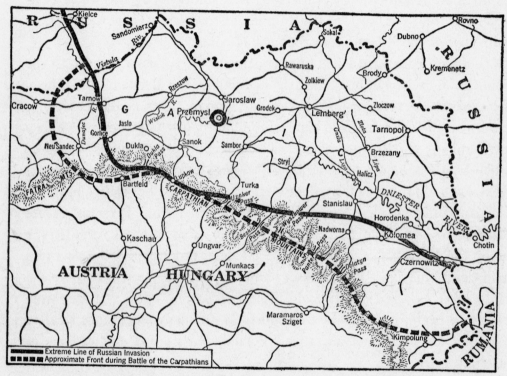

THE GALICIAN CAMPAIGN, SEPT, 1914–MAY, 1915
Russia's Carpathian Army literally beat itself to pieces against the barrier that faced it

The opening weeks of April saw the crisis.   A stupendous Russian effort gained still more ground at a frightful cost.   The world believed that Russia was forcing her way through the passes, when, by the third week in April, Ivanoff's army came to a practical but not an absolute standstill.   The cost had been beyond the resources of Russia in men, in guns, above all in ammunition.   To the south, Austrian troops, with

German contingents, were actually breaking out in the foothills of the Carpathians on the Galician side, threatening the flank of the Russians in the Dukla and the Lupkow.

Actually the Battle of the Carpathians was over, although it had two more weeks to run. Germany had succeeded at last in erecting a bulwark against Russian floods in Galicia, as she had promptly broken the force of Russian invasion twice in East Prussia. By the third week in April there is something approaching a deadlock along the whole eastern front from the Baltic to the Roumanian frontier. There is, as yet, no sure sign of the Russian halt, but it had come.

Looking backward we may now perceive that Russia had for all the months since November, since the opening of the Battle of Lodz, been bearing an ever-increasing burden of German effort. Her mission to deal with the Austrians had been triumphantly discharged by the victory of Lemberg and its immediate consequences. All German efforts to abolish this Lemberg decision by Polish and East Prussian drives upon Warsaw had failed. Only when Germany had sent her troops into Galicia and Bukowina had Russian advance slowed down. Przemysl, in late March, had been an authentic sign of Russian strength; the attack upon the Carpathian passes had been a final proof of Russian devotion and determination. But Russia had now reached the point where she must have aid, and effective aid, from her western allies. If they were ready to begin, if Anglo-French efforts in Flanders and France recalled German troops from Galicia and Poland, Russia was still capable of useful service.

But if this help did not come, Russia could no longer bear the burden she had been bearing through the months of furious fighting that separated Lemberg and Tannenberg from Przemysl and the Carpathians.

The best of Russia's officers and of her first-line soldiers had found their graves on the fields of victory and defeat in East Prussia, Poland, and Galicia. The Carpathian Army had literally beaten itself to pieces against the barriers that faced it. Russian military achievement had surpassed her own and her enemies' expectation, but no Russian warning, although there had been many, had sufficed to moderate the hopes and expectations of the western allies of the Slav.   They were soon to be undeceived.

It remains, now, to look westward and examine rapidly the progress of events from the German defeat at Ypres to the moment when Russian effort was checked at the summit of the Carpathians and Russia began to lack the strength to continue the work begun at Lemberg and carried forward, to the very great advantage of her western allies, up to the arrival of spring.   It is well to remember, too, that at this moment Russia had at last realized, through the failure of the Allied fleets in the Dardanelles, that she was to receive no immediate aid in munitionment or supplies, of which she stood in desperate need, from her western allies.

CHAPTER THIRTEEN

IN THE WEST, NOVEMBER, 1914, TO MAY, 1915

I
THE PROBLEM

When the German attack in Flanders ceased and the Germans began to transport some fraction of their main force eastward to relieve Hindenburg in his Lodz venture, to aid him in his later attacks upon Warsaw and finally to prop up the crumbling Austrian armies, they left a field upon which they had missed victory by the narrowest margin. Napoleon was never nearer to winning Waterloo than were the Germans to achieving a complete success about Ypres. Had Russian pressure been one whit less severe, had Austrian collapse been one degree less imminent, it is difficult to believe that the Germans would have missed arriving at Calais and crushing in the whole western flanks of the Allies.

When the German flood at last subsided it left behind it a victorious but well-nigh-annihilated foe in Flanders. To meet the storm the Allies had flung into the gap the most heterogeneous mass of men that Europe had known since the Mohammedan invasion. Asia and Africa, Australia and Canada, were represented by white, by black, and by yellow troops who fought beside the French, the Belgians, and the British. Sailor lads from Brittany marched shoulder to shoulder with the Senegalese; troops from British India held ground within sight of Arabs and Berbers from Algeria and Morocco. Languages, customs, religions of four continents and a score of races were represented in this strange horde.

Actually the Allies had striven, as men strive when there is a break in the dyke, to stop the rapidly growing gap by every conceivable and available resource. Never in military history was there such a jerry-built wall as stretched across the pathway of German floods, wavered and faltered under German attack, and just held at the final moment, when, with the eastern crisis becoming ever more insistent, the

Germans, under the eyes of their emperor, called upon the famous Prussian Guard to deliver the final blow.

And when the wave at last was spent, there stretched from Switzerland to the sea that long line of trenches which henceforth for more than two years was to be the western front.   Such an ending to a Franco-German campaign had been foreseen neither in Berlin nor in Paris. That such a condition would endure, not for months but for years, was a thing wholly hidden from German and French High Command in November, 1914.

For the Germans there was the firm belief that a few months of winter campaigning would dispose of the Russians, permit the capture of Warsaw, and that spring would see the return to the west of the troops borrowed from the west for the winter months.

As for the Allies, their forces already began to talk of that happy hour when Kitchener's "Million" would arrive, by Easter at the latest, and the long German lines would be broken, the whole of France delivered, and the decision of the Marne enforced along the Rhine.   No one yet foresaw the magnitude of German resources or effort; no one yet foresaw that the heavy artillery, prepared to win field battles and reduce fortresses; the machine guns, which only in the German army had been provided by thousands to obtain victory in the decisive battle in the open field, would give Germany an advantage in trench warfare enabling her to hold her lines, not for weeks or months, but beyond the date of the second anniversary of the war, with wholly insignificant changes.

Actually, the German problem had been posed in the east; it was the problem of disposing of Russia by spring and returning to the west to reopen the Marne verdict in the summer and win the war in the first year.   The problem of the Allies was to reorganize their shaken armies, to raise the British forces that could supply the necessary superiority of numbers in the west, and to provide that heavy artillery and ammunition which were utterly lacking and without which the attack, in the new conditions of war, was a mere murder.   All this it was imperatively necessary that the Allies should accomplish before Russia was beaten down by the whole weight of German attack—before the victory

THE SLAVS IN
THE WORLD WAR

PART OF THE CRACK CAVALRY CORPS FORMERLY KNOWN AS THE
CZAR'S OWN HUSSARS

PICTURES OF RUSSIAN AND
SERBIAN SOLDIERS

GRAND DUKE NICHOLAS

GENERAL RENNENKAMPF

GENERAL RUSSKY

GENERAL BRUSILOFF

FOUR RUSSIAN GENERALS

The Grand Duke Nicholas, uncle of the Czar, is a real soldier and an able soldier. Though a Romanoff his political tendency is toward liberalism. The Czar was probably jealous of him, and after his abdication a plot was launched to offer Grand Duke Nicholas the crown.

General Rennenkampf. After winning Tannenberg from one Russian army under Samsonoff, Hindenburg pursued a second, that of Rennenkampf, from the very gates of Königsberg across his frontier. Later, two German corps under Von Francois were surrounded and Petrograd claimed a victory. But it failed to materialize. The trapped Germans by exertions which the Russians frankly conceded to have been "incredible" found their way out, thanks to the tardiness of Rennenkampf, who went at once into retirement after this fiasco.

Russky and Brusiloff commanded two of the five armies which took part in the great Russian offensive in August and September, 1914. They operated in Galicia, while Rennenkampf and Samsonoff invaded East Prussia.

BATTERY OF RUSSIAN HOWITZERS ON THE POLISH FRONT

RUSSIAN SOLDIERS

The Russian muzhik makes a good soldier. To begin with there is an inexhaustible supply of him. He has great endurance, is patient, good-natured, and obedient, but lacks initiative. On the whole he has given a good account of himself in the war. He would have done better had he been equipped and supplied as efficiently as the soldiers of the other races. Moreover, there is good reason for the suspicion that he has sometimes been led to his undoing by traitorous pro-German generals.

THE FORMER CZAR'S BODYGUARD OF PICKED COSSACKS RIDING TO
THE DEFENCE OF WARSAW

RUSSIANS AND AUSTRIANS

When Russians and Austrians are pitted against each other as man to man in a fair encounter, this is apt to be the result. The Austrians march to the rear as prisoners. The Austrians have more spirit and dash, but they lack the stolid strength and steadfastness of the Russian peasants. Moreover, the Russians are racially a unit; while the Austro-Hungarians are of many races, and the Slavic blood in many makes them laggards in war against their kinsmen of the steppes.

SERBIA IN THE WAR

The raw material of which Serbian soldiers are made.

The finished product.

Gallant little Serbia was finally overcome by the overwhelming strength of her adversaries. But the world will not soon forget the splendid succession of victories which preceded her days of disaster. In the First Balkan War she defeated the Turks at Kumanovo, at Monastir, and at Adrianople; in the Second Balkan War she shattered the legend of Bulgarian invincibility at Bregalnitza; in the opening month of the World War when the fortune of the Allies was most desperate it was the victory of the Serb at Jedar which opened the more prosperous period which culminated at the Marne. In the early days of December Belgrad fell, but once again the Serbians rallied. Belgrad was retaken; by December 15, 1914, Serbia was free of Austrians, saved for the time being, saved until the third—and fatal—attack, the Balkan drive of Mackensen almost a year later. In October, 1918, the Serbian army again showed its mettle in its marvellous dash to final victory.

SERBIAN TROOPS ON THE MARCH NEAR THE AUSTRIAN BORDER

of Lemberg, which had given the Russians the initiative and the advantage in the east, should have lost its influence.

We have seen that the Germans failed in the east. All their mighty efforts were insufficient to abolish the consequences of the initial Austrian collapse and the early Russian triumphs in time to resume the western campaign in the spring. Not less absolute was the Allied failure in the west. For another year, after the critical spring, Kitchener's million, as an offensive force, was to be a myth. The task set for Britain was beyond the capacity of any nation, untrained to wars of the national sort and lacking the resources in trained men which conscription alone supplies.

Without Britain, France could not free her soil. Almost a million French had been killed, wounded, or captured in the first four months of the war. The industrial districts of France had been seized and were held. France could and did address herself to the task of organizing her national life within a brief time. But such organization was for long beyond the capacity of British Government or people. Months after the need for heavy explosives had been disclosed, the faults of the British military system—its inability to learn—combined to keep the munition works at the task of turning out useless shrapnel.

From political, military, and industrial aspects, the story of the British department of Allied effort, deduction of course being made for the Navy, remains the story of failure, of inability to perceive the character and magnitude of the war, of failure to understand the new horizons, the new conditions, to grasp the fundamental fact that the war could only be won when Britain conscripted her youth and set her maturity to the organized task of munitionment. Under the strain of the first really considerable war in British history, the whole fabric of British Imperial life broke down.

On the military side the British failure was complete in all but defensive operations. The world knew little of the original campaign of Field-Marshal Sir John French. The legend that he had saved the French before the Battle of the Marne and contributed the decisive thrust in this engagement served to deceive and delude the British themselves. Not even Neuve Chapelle opened their eyes and it required the dismal slaughter at Loos in September, 1915, to demonstrate the need of a new commander-in-chief and of a new system.

Field-Marshal Sir John French's services to his country and to the Allied cause at the Aisne and at Ypres were incontestably great. On the latter field the British army—the old army—died, holding a line whose collapse would have brought ruin to the Allied defence in the west. Not a little of the failure of the British commander must, in fact, be charged to Lord Kitchener.   We shall not know until history has cleared the ground how far the commander in the field was blocked, handicapped, finally exhausted by an administration of the War Department, which in such instances as that of heavy explosives starved the army in France because it misunderstood the conditions of the new warfare. Yet in the light of such evidence as exists, the recall of the Field-Marshal seems to have been inevitable and the responsibility for failure in the field in some part his own.

As for the British army, more was asked it than could fairly be asked of any army in the first year of the war.   And what it did was a larger portion of the impossible than was then conceivable. It fought with rifles against machine guns—with shrapnel against high explosives; it manufactured its bombs out of jam tins and matched them against the products of prepared machinery. It was often defeated but never conquered; and never—save between Mons and the Marne—greatly disorganized.

In the nature of things this British army was for nearly two years a "forlorn hope"; it could not be compared on the military side with the highly organized German armies or with the French conscript armies; yet, without its contribution, the war would have been irrevocably lost in the first year; and after the first year, its mounting strength and growing efficiency were recognized even by the foe.

During the first two years of the war, this British army never had an equal chance, most of its offensives were sheer sacrifices, made gallantly and willingly, but foredoomed to defeat because equipment was lacking and training was still to be acquired.   Political blunders, such as Antwerp and Gallipoli, added further burdens and led to further disastrous consequences. Many of the blunders were censurable and indefensible; many were the inevitable concomitants of national unpreparedness. Yet the critic who recognizes necessarily the failure, from the military point of view, feels his words unfair, in the presence of the spirit and the devotion of the men who held the line from the first Ypres battle to the coming of the new armies or died unhesitatingly in the opening days of the Somme, a sacrifice to the tuition of a nation which had to learn modern warfare in the most expensive of all schools.

With the weapons they had; with the officers that were available— officers as destitute of training as their men; under the burden of the most powerful attack military history records, both in numbers and in mechanical appliances, the British army hung on; and if the original "contemptible little army" died on the line, its presence there prevented an immediate disaster to the Allied cause and its tenacity insured the coming of the other British armies which were to know victory and regain the offensive.

The close of the period we are now to review was to reveal the fact that the Allies in the west were still unready. A moment was to come when, coincident with the fatal thrust that Mackensen was to deliver against Radko Dimitrieff at the Dunajec, German attacks in Flanders were to disclose the fact that Russia could not be relieved by pressure exerted on Germany's western front and must go from retreat to retreat until the coming of winter found her terribly beaten armies at the Beresina and Dwina.

The military operations in this period are of practically no value, compared to that attaching to the struggles in the east, because they resulted in no tactical or strategic advantage to either side— did, in fact, no more than contribute to revealing the fact that Russia could expect no help in the west, at the precise moment when the temporary success of Russia had compelled Germany to turn all her attention for the summer campaign toward Warsaw and not toward Calais.

II. JOFFRE'S "NIBBLING"

To the operations in the west in the period we are now to examine, and, indeed, for many months thereafter, there was applied the picturesque term of "nibbling." Actually, these operations were local offensives, undertaken in all but one of the more considerable instances by the French, and they were designed to keep as many German troops as possible occupied, to prevent the transfer to the east of any large number of army corps, to strain German resources in men and munition by a double pressure on the eastern and western fronts. Beside these purposes local objectives were insignificant.

The world misunderstood these operations completely. It saw in each activity from Switzerland to the North Sea the evidences of a grandiose attempt to reach the Rhine or the lower Meuse. It did not understand the weakness of the Allies, the difficulties of the British, the inadequate resources of the French—in men as a result of their terrible losses, and in munitions because of German occupation of so much of the industrial portion of France. From November to May the whole outside world waited for the new Allied "drive" in the west, were waiting for it when the German thrust at Ypres crushed in half of the whole salient and won a local success more considerable than any the Allies had achieved in all the months preceding.

The first of these "nibbles" was in some respects the most considerable and successful. In December French forces appeared along the western slopes of the Vosges and beyond the summits in that corner of Alsace to which the French had clung after they had abandoned Mühlhausen in August. They flowed down the valley of the Thur and reoccupied Thann; they approached the village of Cernay, which is the key to Mühlhausen, and, after long and desperate fighting, took the mountain of Hartmannsweilerkopf, from which they could look down into Mühlhausen a scant ten miles away.

But despite local successes in the villages of Steinbach and Anspach, despite a slight advance along the plain toward Altkirch, the larger purpose could not be realized. The French were unable to break the

German line at the point where it left the plain and approached the Vosges. Mühlhausen could not be taken, nor were any of the later efforts more successful. Some little territory was won north of the Thur, some more Alsatian villages were "redeemed," upward of 350 square miles of Alsace was reunited to France, but although each new general who came to the Vosges eagerly undertook, with the limited resources allowed him, to break through to Mühlhausen, the failure was absolute.

Checked in Alsace, the French turned to Champagne and endeavoured to push up the slopes of the hills north of Soissons and beyond the Aisne, where Kluck had held the British in September. Again there was a preliminary success in early January, the gain of several miles. But as promptly came a German counter-thrust and this time the French lost, not alone what they had gained, but the ground turned over to them by the British when Field-Marshal French had gone north in October. Only on the southern bank of the river were the French able to hold. Germany claimed a crushing victory and talked rather obscurely of Gravelotte; the French explained that the floods in the river behind them had made their position indefensible. Neither statement is worth considering. The Germans never tried to advance farther; the French were unable to progress on this front until April, 1917. The local operation promptly lost all importance.

In February the French undertook a still more ambitious operation in Champagne, on the ground which was to see the great and desperate attack in the following September. Over a narrow front and for the possession of insignificant ridges commanding a railroad line vital to German communications, the French and Germans fought for weeks. The battleline rested on the east upon the Argonne and from the western flank the cathedral of Rheims was visible. After casualties not much under 200,000 for the French and German combined—and the French loss was much the heavier—there ensued a new deadlock. The French had gained rather less than a quarter of a mile on a front less than a dozen. But there was never much promise that they would actually penetrate the German lines, and any original hope was promptly extinguished when German reserves arrived.

While this last attack was going forward the British undertook their first, and for the present period their last, offensive, attacking in the district south of Lille. This effort is worth examining in more detail because it disclosed the extent of the weakness of British organization and was the first of that series of failures, extending through Gallipoli and Loos, to Kut-el-Amara, which revealed how little British military training had kept pace with that of continental nations in later years, and how long was to be the task of organizing new British armies.

But in dismissing these early French operations it is well to recall that each of them was designed primarily to aid the Russians and to divert German attention from Galicia and from Poland; the Alsatian attack coincided with the great drive of Hindenburg to the Bzura-Rawka line; the Champagne attack with the opening of the Battle of the Carpathians; and the Soissons fight which just preceded it with the demand of the Hungarians for German aid to repulse the Russian menace in Bukowina and the growing Roumanian threat, due to Russian victories in the Crownland.

In this synchrony of operations east and west it is possible to see what the French were striving to do, not on their own frontier primarily but in the wide field of the continental strife. Nor can one doubt that, while their efforts were not fully successful in this larger field nor of any real consequence locally, they did materially reduce the pressure upon their Slav ally and postpone the day when Germany was able to regain the offensive in the east.

III. NEUVE CHAPELLE

On March 10th at Neuve Chapelle, a few miles southwest of the great city of Lille and just north of the strong German post of La Bassée, which had seen desperate fighting in October and November, the British launched a great attack upon a four-mile front. The immediate objective of the attack was the Aubers ridge, which in military comment is described as the key to the city of Lille itself.

This attack was preceded by the first of those avalanches of artillery bombardment to become familiar thereafter and to be described at once by the Germans, who gave it the enduring name of drum-fire. Under this storm of fire, delivered from 300 guns concentrated in a narrow area, the German first-line trenches disintegrated, even the second line was shaken, and the British infantry made its first advance with little or no serious opposition, finding the ground strewn with German dead, and capturing scores of men overcome by the noise and shock of the fire.

But beyond the first-line trenches the British came under machine-gun fire from scattered points in which the German second line had not been destroyed. They also suffered severely as a result of the miscalculation of their own guns, but the fatal circumstance was the failure of reserves to arrive.

There was a moment when it seemed as if the road to Lille was open. But the British could not seize the moment, and it passed forever. After two days the Germans were able to repulse all attacks with terrific slaughter. The British had gained a mile on a front of four; the ruins of the village of Neuve Chapelle were in their hands, but the larger success had been lost. British Command had failed to synchronize men with guns, to prepare reserves to follow the first waves of attack. What was to happen at Loos and Gallipoli on a far larger scale had now occurred at Neuve Chapelle.

In this battle, which filled the bulletins at the time but is now hardly more than a forgotten skirmish, the British first tasted the cup of bitterness which the Germans had drunk to the dregs in the Battle of Ypres. Under German artillery and machine-gun fire, the British losses surpassed that of the British contingents who fought with Wellington at Waterloo. The "butcher's bill" had been 13,000 casualties; the gains, a mile of territory, 2,000 German prisoners, and the privilege of burying 3,000 Germans fallen to British guns.

In Allied strategy this blow in Artois had been delivered in strict conjunction with the French offensive far off in Champagne and at the moment when the arrival of German reserves on the latter field disclosed the fact that Germany was weakening her line before the British. In September a similar double thrust was to be undertaken in Champagne and Artois, which would cost the French 120,000 casualties and the

British 60,000. Looking back to it, after the mighty struggles of the later months, Neuve Chapelle seems insignificant. Yet it was the first time that a considerable use was made of massed fire. It forecast exactly the tactics Mackensen was to employ in his great victory in Galicia not many weeks later, and it did come within sight of a considerable triumph that might have restored Lille to France.

In the first blush London celebrated Neuve Chapelle as the "battle bigger than Waterloo"; but the later disclosures changed the whole tone of British comment, and England presently realized that a meaningless local gain had been achieved at a frightful cost, because British troops had fallen under their own guns and British reserves had wholly failed to arrive at the moment when real victory was within easy grasp. Taken with the scandal over the shell supply,—which soon developed and revealed that the British High Command was still sending shrapnel in limited quantities to an army that required heavy explosives in enormous quantities and could not get them at all—Neuve Chapelle was a saddening incident to the British people.

IV. THE SECOND BATTLE OF YPRES

In early April the French undertook an interesting campaign to abolish the St. Mihiel salient, the single breach in the yoke of permanent French fortifications from Verdun to Switzerland, which the Germans had been able to make in September. Coming out from Metz and ascending the valley of the little Rupt de Mad, the Germans had actually crossed the Meuse, taken foot on the west bank, and also captured Fort Camp des Romains, above the town of St. Mihiel on the east bank.

The ground held by the Germans was a narrow spearhead thrust straight through the armour of France. Never had the Germans been able to widen the wound or deepen it after the first thrust, but they remained in possession of a portion of the hills of the Meuse and they cut the railroad from Commercy to Verdun. Now the French, coming north out of Toul and south out of Verdun, endeavoured to break this salient along its sides. Some initial success they had at Les Éparges;

they took several hills and a village or two. But then they were stopped. German heavy artillery in Fort Camp des Romains held them up. The local success did not hide the larger failure. A still more ambitious effort in July, and from the Bois-le-Prêtre, above the west of Pont-à-Mousson, similarly failed. Verdun was left in danger and the extent of the danger was to be disclosed in February, 1916.

Finally we come to the last of the battles in the west in the period under examination, the Second Battle of Ypres, which coincided almost exactly with the date at which the world believed that Kitchener's million were to begin their triumphal advance in the west; and it terminated in a local German success at the moment when Mackensen was to regain for Germany the initiative in the east.

The new blow fell on April 22d. It was delivered by relatively small contingents, and it is plain that the Germans had no expectation of anything but a local triumph, the moral effect of which would far surpass the military. Not only did it come in an hour when the news from the east was to fill the world, but the Allied failure at the Dardanelles had dashed the hopes of all the enemies of Germany and a shining Teutonic triumph held out a promise to hold Italy to neutrality. Again, the Allies were already collecting an army to send to the Dardanelles on the most foolish of all ventures and German pressure was conceivably calculated to withhold troops from the Near East.

The German attack was preceded by the first discharge of "poison gas" of the war. Not since the slaughter in Louvain and the bombardment of Rheims had any event made such a noise in the world as this first use of gas as a weapon of destruction. It added instantly to the horrors of conflict and it was in violation of all the restrictions that humanity and international agreement had placed about the conduct of war. It instantly changed the whole temper of the British, who suffered most severely, mainly in the Canadian contingent; it abolished quarter on the western front for many months, and it brought in its train a savagery and brutality that the wars of the Nineteenth Century did not know.

Even in its immediate purpose, this weapon was unsuccessful. It did not give Germany a shining triumph. It did not open a gap in the

Allied defence, it merely brought to horrible death a few thousands of Allied soldiers, and, before many weeks had passed, the Allies had prepared an apparatus protecting their soldiers and had in their turn adopted this hideous method of killing, which subsequently brought as many thousand Germans to terrible agony and frightful death.

In selecting the Ypres front as the point of attack, the Germans had pitched upon the point best known to the outside world in the whole Allied line from Belfort to Nieuport. Here the Germans had attacked in the autumn and by but a shadowy margin failed to get through. Belligerent and neutral nations, watching for the advance of the Kitchener army, still hardly taking shape, saw, instead, what seemed to be a new German drive for Calais and for several days a real German advance. Nor were the military reasons less weighty in determining the point of attack; Ypres was a salient on which the Germans from higher and encircling ground could pour down a converging fire, cutting all the lines of communication.

The original attack fell to the west of Ypres, at the moment when this beautiful city, with some of the most interesting monuments of Flemish art, was melting into dust and ashes under a terrific cannonade. At the point where the French and British lines touched—the French position held largely by native troops—the Germans launched immense clouds of gas. First amazement and then terror followed. The men who had endured artillery fire and faced death with unfaltering courage for many months broke and fled, a gap opened in the Allied front.

This break exposed the flank of the Canadians. They, too, had suffered from the gas, but less severely than their French neighbours. They did not break or immediately retreat. They extended to cover the exposed flank and hung on. No reserves were available for hours, and in these first hours nearly a third of the Canadian contingent died or were wounded and captured on their lines. Presently the crisis passed. Reinforcements arrived, the Belgians extended their aid to the French, the British brought up troops from the south. Ypres was not lost, the dyke between the Germans and Calais still held.

It is worth recalling, too, that for England, the Canadian contingent bore the brunt as the Australian Anzacs were to win equal glory at

Gallipoli.   In the history of the British Empire the Second Battle of Ypres may well prove memorable, for Canadian loyalty there gave shining answer to German forecasts of colonial secessions; while in German Southwest Africa, British South Africa was presently to emulate the example of Canada in Flanders and Australia and New Zealand at the Dardanelles.

The Second Battle of Ypres lasted five days; by the third the Germans no longer claimed to be making progress and at points they were presently pressed back, but the whole Ypres salient had to be flattened out.   Actually the British gave up more ground than they had surrendered in the First Battle, but solely because of the collapse of the French line to the west, under the poison gas attack.   Guns, prisoners, ground, the Germans had taken, but the triumph was local and of no permanent value on the military side.

Yet the lesson of the Second Battle of Ypres was unmistakable, although the world was long in learning it.   A swift, heavy blow had disclosed the fact that the Allies were unready.   Their previous offensives had disclosed the same weakness.   Now it was clear that only by heroic efforts could they check a German attack.   They could not break the German lines, they could only with difficulty hold their own.   The whole British front had been affected by the attack and new dispositions had to be made.

Before she went east, Germany had undertaken one attack to demonstrate that she need fear no real danger from the Anglo-French quarter.   She had established the fact.   Not until September would her western lines be threatened and not until July, 1916, would the British be ready to take an effective share in the western offensive operations. The legend of "Kitchener's Million" disappeared in thin air, the hope of the speedy deliverance of France vanished, the first authentic sign of German recovery was now perceived by the world which was to have a second and greater proof in a few hours.

In the major problem, to reorganize, to get forward in time to take the pressure off Russia, France and Britain had failed at the moment when the Russian strength was becoming inadequate for the task on the Russian front.

CHAPTER FOURTEEN

CONCLUSION

While the echoes of the guns about Ypres were filling the world, the Austro-German army of Mackensen attacked and almost destroyed the Russian army, commanded by Radko Dimitrieff—the victor of Lule Burgas—which stood behind the Dunajec River, in western Galicia. The immediate consequence of this disaster was the dislocation of the whole Russian front; the eventual result, the retreat from the Carpathians and the Vistula to the Dwina and the Beresina.

These great events do not concern the present narrative, they belong, as I see it, to the second phase of the war, the attack upon Russia. With the Battle of the Dunajec ends that first phase, comprehended in the attack upon France and the consequences of this attack. These consequences, since the attack failed, were the deadlock in the west and the loss to Germany of the initiative in the east and west. To obtain the necessary numbers to deal the colossal blow that should destroy France, Germany had weakened her eastern front and relied upon Austria to hold up Russia. Still relying upon Austria mainly, after the Marne, Germany had elected to endeavour to reopen the decision of the Marne in all the weeks from September to the middle of November.

Compelled at last to go east, while the Battle of Flanders was still unwon and the decision of the Marne stood, Germany had then to labour under the disadvantages which had resulted from the successes won by Russia over Austria and the position gained in Galicia. Not until the Dunajec did Germany finally restore the balance, not until the Dunajec did she escape from the consequences of the Marne campaign, consequences which affected the eastern quite as much as the western field.

Had the Allies been prepared to take the offensive in the west, when Germany at last turned eastward in November, they would have won the war. Had they been able in the spring, when the German attack at the Dunajec began, to make a similar attack in the west, German disaster would have been immediate. The failure in the autumn enabled Germany to erect those colossal dykes against the Allies in the west which extended from the North Sea to Switzerland. Failure in the spring condemned Russia to bear that terrible burden which almost brought irreparable disaster and real German victory.

In the spring of 1915 it was plain that the advantage belonged to the alliance which could strike the first heavy blow, but the superficial circumstances alike favoured the Allies and seemed to indicate that they would be able to retain the initiative which they had won at the Marne and bring Germany to swift and complete defeat. All this was impossible because Great Britain had been unable to transform herself into a military nation and to do in months what her Allies and enemies had achieved only by long years of patient and universal training. As for France, she lacked the numbers, now, to risk alone the supreme effort, for if it failed, German victory in the west, while Britain was still unprepared, was inevitable.

In this situation there was allowed to Germany a new opportunity, and as it turned out, another year, in which to win the war. If she could dispose of Russia and return to the west before Britain had at last organized her millions and her industries, she might hope for the complete victory that had escaped her in the Marne conflict. But if she failed in the east, if she were compelled to come west with the Russian task incomplete, as she had been compelled to go east while France still stood, then German failure in the second phase would be as patent as it was now in the first.

Only victory in the east, followed by triumph in the west, could permanently abolish the decision of the Marne. Unless it was abolished the time was bound to come when Germany would have to face fresh millions coming from Britain and find herself outnumbered and deprived of all the advantages that superior preparation and organization had given her at the start. This is what did happen, but not until the sum-

mer of 1916.   And as it did happen the decision of the Marne stood, and
stands, the one great event in the whole World War from August, 1914,
to September, 1916.

All that the science, knowledge, skill, genius of two races could mobilize met at the Marne in a struggle in which the fate of one race, at least,
was in the balance, and if France fought for life, Germany fought for a
world power that could hardly have escaped her had she prevailed.   But
she did not prevail; everything she hoped to attain escaped her on this
field.   Afterward she still had numbers, the fruits of her years of preparation remained in her hands, but the moment had escaped her and did not
return.   Had Napoleon won at Waterloo, his old domination of Europe
would not have been regained, but had Germany won at the Marne,
William II would have attained an eminence that Napoleon never
reached in his most fortunate hour.

At the Marne, France willed to live; in the gravest hour in the history of their race, French commanders and French soldiers alike displayed not merely the courage that was traditional and was equalled by
German devotion, but those qualities which have often given France the
supremacy in Europe and have never failed to save her when her condition seemed desperate.   And by her will to live, France saved Britain,
Russia, Europe, from a German domination, which in the German mind
was to renew the glories of the Roman Empire.

A second sacrifice and a second agony were to be demanded of the
French people at Verdun, but the stakes of that terrible contest were incomparably smaller, and the greatest possible fruit of German victory on
the Meuse would have been provinces and indemnities.   Nor was there
ever a grave danger of this harvest.   At the Marne, Germany fought for
a World; at Verdun, for a War; and while she fought at Verdun, her
statesmen talked of a victorious peace, which if it still indicated great
ambitions, no longer disclosed Napoleonic aspirations.

With all its mighty events, with all its noble and splendid pages, the
history of the first two years of the great conflict is the history of the
Battle of the Marne.   We have seen in these chapters how Germany
strove to abolish that decision; we shall see in those which describe the

attack upon Russia how she continued to strive to abolish it in tremendous struggles from the Straits of Dover to the Golden Horn, from the Meuse to the Beresina; but after splendid successes, we shall see the continuing failure. Like Marathon, the Marne was a mortal wound; but, unlike Marathon, it did not kill at once.

Mr. Simonds's History of the Progress
of the War Will Be Carried Forward in the Succeeding Volumes.

Editor

APPENDIX

THE EARLY FRENCH OFFENSIVE
By FRANK H. SIMONDS

APPENDIX

THE EARLY FRENCH OFFENSIVE
By FRANK H. SIMONDS

In the third week of August, 1914, a French army crossed the frontier of Alsace-Lorraine and entered the Promised Land, toward which all Frenchmen had looked in hope and sadness for forty-four years. The long-forgotten communiqués of that early period of the war reported success after success, until at last it was announced that the victorious French army had reached Saarburg and Morhange, and were astride the Strassburg-Metz railroad. And then Berlin took up the cry, and France and the world learned of a great German victory and of the defeat and rout of the invading army. Even Paris conceded that the retreat had begun and the "army of liberation" was crowding back beyond the frontier and far within French territory.

Then the curtain of the censorship fell and the world turned to the westward to watch the terrible battle for Paris. In the agony and glory of the Marne the struggle along the Moselle was forgotten; the Battle of Nancy, of Lorraine, was fought and won in the darkness, and when the safety of Paris was assured the world looked toward the Aisne, and then toward Flanders. So it came about that one of the greatest battles of the whole war, one of the most important of the French victories, the success that made the Marne possible, the rally and stand of the French armies about Nancy, escaped the fame it earned. Only in legend, in the romance of the Kaiser with his cavalry waiting on the hills to enter the Lorraine capital, did the battle live.

When I went to France one of the hopes I had cherished was that I might be permitted to visit this battlefield, to see the ground on which a great battle had been fought, that was still unknown country, in the main, for those who have written on the war. The Lorraine field was the field on which France and Germany had planned for a generation to fight. Had the Germans respected the neutrality of Belgium, it is by Nancy, by the gap between the Vosges and the hills of the Meuse, that they must have broken into France. The Marne was a battlefield which was reached by chance and fought over by hazard, but every foot of the Lorraine country had been studied for the fight long years in advance. Here war followed the natural course, followed the plans of the general staff prepared years in advance. Indeed I had treasured over years a plan of the Battle of Nancy, contained in a French book written long ago, which might serve as the basis for a history of what happened, as it was written as a prophecy of what was to come.

281

When the Great General Staff was pleased to grant my request to see the battlefield of Nancy I was advised to travel by train to that town accompanied by an officer from the General Staff, and informed that I should there meet an officer of the garrison, who would conduct me to all points of interest and explain in detail the various phases of the conflict. Thus it fell out, and I have to thank Commandant Leroux for the courtesy and consideration which made this excursion successful.

In peace time one goes from Paris to Nancy in five hours, and the distance is about that from New York to Boston, by Springfield. In war all is different, and the time almost doubled. Yet there are compensations. Think of the New York-Boston trip as bringing you beyond New Haven to the exact rear of battle, of battle but fifteen miles away, with the guns booming in the distance and the airplanes and balloons in full view. Think also of this same trip, which from Hartford to Worcester follows the line of a battle not yet two years old, a battle that has left its traces in ruined villages, in shattered houses. On either side of the railroad track the graves descend to meet the embankments; you can mark the advance and the retreat by the crosses which fill the fields. The gardens that touch the railroad and extend to the rear of houses in the little towns are filled with graves. Each enclosure has been fought for at the point of the bayonet, and every garden wall recalls the Château of Hougoumont, at Waterloo.

All this was two years ago, but there is to-day, also. East of Bar-le-Duc the main line is cut by German shell fire now. From Fort Camp des Romains above St. Mihiel German guns sweep the railroad near Commercy, and one has to turn south by a long detour, as if one went to Boston by Fitchburg, travel south through the country of Jeanne d'Arc and return by Toul, whose forts look out upon the invaded land. Thus one comes to Nancy by night, and only by night, for twenty miles beyond there are Germans and a German cannon, which not so long ago sent a shell into the town and removed a whole city block beside the railroad station. It is the sight of this ruin as you enter the town which reminds you that you are at the front, but there are other reminders.

As we ate our dinner in the café, facing the beautiful Place Stanislas, we were disturbed by a strange and curious drumming sound. Going out into the square, we saw an airplane, or rather its lights, red and green, like those of a ship. It was the first of several, the night patrol, rising slowly and steadily and then sweeping off in a wide curve toward the enemy's line. They were the sentries of the air which were to guard us while we slept, for men do sentry-go in the air as well as on the earth about the capital of Lorraine. Then the searchlights on the hills began to play, sweeping the horizon toward that same mysterious region where beyond the darkness there is war.

The next morning I woke with the sense of Fourth of July. Bang! Bang!

Bang! Such a barking of cannon crackers I had never heard. Still drowsy, I pushed open the French windows and looked down on the square. There I beheld a hundred or more men, women, and children, their eyes fixed on something in the air above and behind the hotel. Still the incessant barking of guns with the occasional boom of something more impressive. With difficulty I grasped the fact. I was in the midst of a Taube raid. Somewhere over my head, invisible to me because of the wall of my hotel, a German airplane was flying, and all the anti-aircraft guns were shooting at it. Was it carrying bombs? Should I presently see or feel the destruction following the descent of these?

But the Taube turned away, the guns fired less and less frequently, the people in the streets drifted away, the children to school, the men to work, the women to wait. It was just a detail in their lives, as familiar as the incoming steamer to the commuters on the North River ferryboat. Some portion of war has been the day's history of Nancy for nearly two years now. The children do not carry gas masks to school with them as they do at Pont-à-Mousson, a dozen miles to the north, but women and children have been killed by German shells, by bombs brought by Zeppelins and by airplanes. There is always excitement of sorts in the district of Nancy.

After a breakfast broken by the return of the airplanes we had seen departing the night before for the patrol, we entered our cars and set out for the front, for the near front, for the lines a few miles behind the present trenches, where Nancy was saved but two years ago. Our route lay north along the valley of the Meurthe, a smiling broad valley, marching north and south and meeting in a few miles that of the Moselle coming east. It was easy to believe that one was riding through the valley of the Susquehanna, with spring and peace in the air. Toward the east a wall of hills shut out the view. This was the shoulder of the Grand-Couronne, the wall against which German violence burst and broke in September, 1914.

Presently we came to a long stretch of road walled in on the river side by brown canvas, exactly the sort of thing that is used at foot-ball games to shut out the non-paying public. But it had another purpose here. We were within the vision of the Germans, across the river, on the heights behind the forest, which outlined itself at the skyline; there were the Kaiser's troops and that forest was the Bois-le-Prêtre, the familiar incident in so many communiqués since the war began. Thanks to the canvas, it was possible for the French to move troops along this road without inviting German shells. Yet it was impossible to derive any large feeling of security from a canvas wall, which alone interposed between you and German heavy artillery.

We passed through several villages and each was crowded with troops; cavalry, infantry, all the branches represented; it was still early and the soldiers were just beginning their day's work; war is so completely a business here-

Transport wagons marched along the roads, companies of soldiers filed by. Interspersed with the soldiers were civilians, the women and children, for none of the villages are evacuated. Not even the occasional boom of a gun far off could give to this thing the character of real war. It recalled the days of my soldiering in the militia camp at Framingham in Massachusetts. It was simply impossible to believe that it was real. Even the faces of the soldiers were smiling. There was no such sense of terribleness, of strain and weariness as I later found about Verdun. The Lorraine front is now inactive, tranquil; it has been quiet so long that men have forgotten all the carnage and horror of the earlier time.

We turned out of the valley and climbed abruptly up the hillside. In a moment we came into the centre of a tiny village and looked into a row of houses, whose roofs had been swept off by shell fire. Here and there a whole house was gone; next door the house was undisturbed and the women and children looked out of the doors. The village was St. Geneviève, and we were at what had been the extreme front of the French in August, and against this hill burst the flood of German invasion. Leaving the car we walked out of the village, and at the end of the street a sign warned the wayfarer not to enter the fields, for which we were bound: "War—do not trespass." This was the burden of the warning.

Once beyond this sign we came out suddenly upon an open plateau, upon trenches. Northward the slope descended to a valley at our feet. It was cut and seamed by trenches, and beyond the trenches stood the posts that carried the barbed-wire entanglements. Here and there, amidst the trenches, there were graves. I went down to the barbed-wire entanglements and examined them curiously. They at least were real. Once thousands of men had come up out of the little woods a quarter of a mile below; they had come on in that famous massed attack, they had come on in the face of machine gun and "seventy-fives." They had just reached the wires, which marked high water. In the woods below, the Bois-de-Facq, in the fields by the river, 4,000 Germans had been buried.

Looking out from the trenches the whole country unfolded. Northward the little village of Atton slept under the steep slope of Côte-de-Mousson, a round pinnacle crowned with an ancient château. From the hill the German artillery had swept the ground where I stood. Below the hill to the west was Pont-à-Mousson, the city of 150 bombardments, which the Germans took when they came south, and lost later. Above it was the Bois-le-Prêtre, in which guns were now booming occasionally. Far to the north was another hill, just visible, and its slope toward us was cut and seamed with yellow slashes. Those were the French trenches, then of the second or third line; beyond there was still another hill, it was slightly blurred in the haze, but it was not over five miles away, and it was occupied by the Germans. From the slope above me on a clear day it is possible to see Metz, so near are French and German lines to the old frontier.

Straight across the river to the west of us was another wood, with a glorious name, the Forest of the Advance Guard. It swept to the south of us. In that wood the Germans had also planted their guns on the day of battle. They had swept the trenches where I stood from three sides. Plainly it had been a warm corner. But the French had held on. Their commander had received a verbal order to retreat. He insisted that it should be put in writing, and this took time. The order came. It had to be obeyed, but he obeyed slowly. Reluctantly the men left the trenches they had held so long. They slipped southward along the road by which we had come. But suddenly their rear guards discovered that the Germans were also retreating. So the French came back and the line of St. Geneviève was held, the northern door to Nancy was not forced.

Looking down again it was not difficult to reconstitute that German assault, made at night. The thing was so simple the civilian could grasp it. A road ran through the valley and along it the Germans had formed; the slope they had to advance up was gentle, far more gradual than that of San Juan. They had been picked troops selected for a forlorn hope, and they had come back four times. The next morning the whole forest had been filled with dead and dying. Not less than a division—20,000 men—had made the terrible venture. Now there was a strange sense of emptiness in the country; war had come and gone, left its graves, its trenches, its barbed-wire entanglements; but these were all disappearing already. On this beautiful spring morning it was impossible to feel the reality of what happened here, what was happening now, in some measure, five miles or more to the north. Nature is certainly the greatest of all pacifists; she will not permit the signs of war to endure nor the mind to believe that war itself has existed and exists.

From St. Geneviève we went to the Grand Mont d'Amance, the most famous point in all the Lorraine front, the southeast corner of the Grand-Couronne, as St. Geneviève is the northern. Here, from a hill some 1,300 feet high, one looks eastward into the Promised Land of France—into German Lorraine. In the early days of August the great French invasion, resting one flank upon this hill, the other upon the distant Vosges, had stepped over the frontier. One could trace its route to the distant hills among which it had found disaster. In these hills the Germans had hidden their heavy guns, and the French, coming under their fire without warning, unsupported by heavy artillery, which was lacking to them, had broken. Then the German invasion had rolled back. You could follow the route. In the foreground the little Seille River could be discerned; it marked the old frontier. Across this had come the defeated troops. They had swarmed down the low, bare hills; they had crossed and vanished in the woods just at my feet; these woods were the

Forest of Champenoux. Into this forest the Germans had followed by the thousand, they were astride the main road to Nancy, which rolled white and straight at my feet. But in the woods the French rallied. For days there was fought in this stretch of trees one of the most terrible of battles.

As I stood on the Grand Mont I faced almost due east. In front of me and to the south extended the forest. Exactly at my feet the forest reached up the hill and there was a little cluster of buildings about a fountain. All was in ruins, and here, exactly here, was the high-water mark of the German advance. They had occupied the ruins for a few moments and then had been driven out. Elsewhere they had never emerged from the woods; they had approached the western shore, but the French had met them with machine guns and "seventy-fives." The brown woods at my feet were nothing but a vast cemetery; thousands of French and German soldiers slept there.

In their turn the Germans had gone back. Now, in the same woods, a French battery was shelling the Germans on the other side of the Seille. Under the glass I studied the little villages unfolding as on a map; they were all destroyed, but it was impossible to recognize this. Some were French, some German; you could follow the line, but there were no trenches; behind them French shells were bursting occasionally and black smoke rose just above the ground. Thousands of men faced each other less than four miles from where I stood, but all that there was to be detected were the shell bursts; otherwise one saw a pleasant country, rolling hills, mostly without woods, bare in the spring which had not yet come to turn them green. In the foreground ran that arbitrary line Bismarck had drawn between Frenchmen forty-six years before—the frontier—but of natural separation there was none. He had cut off a part of France, that was all, and one looked upon what had been and was still a bleeding wound.

I asked the French commandant about the various descriptions made by those who have written about the war. They have described the German attack as mounting the slope of the Grand Mont where we stood. He took me to the edge and pointed down. It was a cliff almost as steep as the Palisades. "*C'est une blague*," he smiled. "Just a story." The Germans had not charged here, but in the forest below, where the Nancy road passed through and enters the valley of the Amezeule. They had not tried to carry but to turn the Grand Mont. More than 200,000 men had fought for days in the valley below. I asked him about the legend of the Kaiser sitting on a hill, waiting in white uniform with his famous escort, waiting until the road was clear for his triumphal entrance into the capital of Lorraine. He laughed. I might choose my hill; if the Emperor had done this thing the hill was "over there," but had he? They are hard on legends at the front, and the tales that delight Paris die easily on the frontiers of war.

But since I had asked so much about the fighting my commandant promised to take me in the afternoon to the point where the struggle had been fiercest, still farther to the south, where all the hills break down and there is a natural gateway from Germany into France, the beginning of the famous Charmes Gap, through which the German road to Paris from the east ran, and still runs. Leaving Nancy behind us, and ascending the Meurthe Valley on the eastern bank, turning out of it before Saint Nicholas du Port, we came presently to the most completely war-swept fields that I have ever seen. On a perfectly level plain the little town of Haraucourt stands in sombre ruins. Its houses are nothing but ashes and rubble. Go out of the village toward the east and you enter fields pockmarked by shell fire. For several miles you can walk from shell hole to shell hole. The whole country is a patchwork of these shell holes. At every few rods a new line of old trenches approaches the road and wanders away again. Barbed-wire entanglements run up and down the gently sloping hillsides.

Presently we came out upon a perfectly level field. It was simply torn by shell fire. Old half-filled trenches wandered aimlessly about, and beyond, under a gentle slope, the little village of Corbessaux stood in ruins. The commandant called my attention to a bit of woods in front.

"The Germans had their machine guns there," said he. "We didn't know it, and a French brigade charged across this field. It started at 8:15, and at 8:30 it had lost more than 3,000 out of 6,000. Then the Germans came out of the woods in their turn, and our artillery, back at Haraucourt, caught them and they lost 3,500 men in a quarter of an hour. Along the roadside were innumerable graves. We looked at one. It was marked: "Here 196 French." Twenty feet distant was another; it was marked: "Here 196 Germans." In the field where we stood I was told some 10,000 men are buried. They were buried hurriedly, and even now, when it rains, arms and legs are exposed.

Two years had passed, almost two years, since this field had been fought for. The Germans had taken it. They had approached Haraucourt, but had not passed it. This was the centre and the most vital point in the Lorraine battle. What Foch's troops had done about La Fère Champenoise, those of Castelnau had done here. The German wave had been broken, but at what cost? And now, after so many months, the desolation of war remained. But yet it was not to endure. Beside the very graves an old peasant was ploughing, guiding his plough and his horses carefully among the tombs. Four miles away more trenches faced each other and the battle went on audibly, but behind this line, in this very field where so many had died, life was beginning.

Later we drove south, passing within the lines the Germans had held in their great advance; we travelled through Lunéville, which they had taken and left unharmed, save as shell fire had wrecked an eastern suburb. We visited Gerbéviller, where in an excess of rage the Germans had burned every structure in the town. I have never seen such a headquarters of desolation. Everything that had a shape, that had a semblance of beauty or of use, lies in complete ruin, detached houses, a château, the blocks in the village, all in ashes. Save for Sermaize, Gerbéviller is the most completely wrecked town in France.

You enter the village over a little bridge across the tiny Mortagne. Here some French soldiers made a stand and held off the German advance for some hours. There was no other battle at Gerbéviller, but for this defence the town died. Never was death so complete. Incendiary material was placed in every house, and all that thoroughness could do to make the destruction complete was done. Gerbéviller is dead, a few women and children live amidst its ashes, there is a wooden barrack by the bridge with a post-office and the inevitable postcards, but only on postcards, picture postcards, does the town live. It will be a place of pilgrimage when peace comes.

From Gerbéviller we went by Bayon to the Plateau of Saffais, the ridge between the Meurthe and the Moselle, where the defeated army of Castelnau made its last and successful stand. The French line came south from St. Geneviève, where we had been in the morning, through the Grand Mont, across the plain by Haraucourt and Corbessaux, then crossed the Meurthe by Dombasle and stood on the heights from Rosières south. Having taken Lunéville, the Germans attempted to cross the Meurthe coming out of the Forest of Vitrimont.

Standing on the Plateau of Saffais and facing east, the whole country unfolded again, as it did at the Grand Mont. The face of the plateau is seamed with trenches. They follow the slopes, and the village of Saffais stands out like a promontory. On this ridge the French had massed three hundred cannon. Their army had come back in ruins, and to steady it they had been compelled to draw troops from Alsace. Mühlhausen was sacrificed to save Nancy. Behind these crests on which we stood, a beaten army, almost routed, had in three days found itself and returned to the charge.

In the shadow of the dusk I looked across the Meurthe into the brown mass of the Forest of Vitrimont. Through this had come the victorious Germans. They had debouched from the wood; they had approached the river, hidden under the slope, but, swept by the hell of this artillery storm, they had broken. But few had lived to pass the river, none had mounted the slopes. There were almost no graves along these trenches. Afterward the Germans had in turn yielded to pressure from the south and gone back. Before the Battle of the Marne began the German wave of invasion had been stopped here in the last days of August. A second terrific drive, coincident with the Marne, had likewise failed. Then the Germans had gone back to the frontier. The old boundary line of Bismarck is now in many instances an actual line of fire, and nowhere on this front are the Germans more than three or four miles within French territory.

If you should look at the map of the wholly imaginary Battle of Nancy, drawn by Colonel Boucher to illustrate his book, published before 1910, a book describing the problem of the defence of the eastern frontier, you will find the lines on which the French stood at Saffais indicated exactly. Colonel Boucher had not dreamed this battle, but for a generation the French General Staff had planned it. Here they had expected to meet the German thrust. When the Germans decided to go by Belgium they had in turn taken the offensive, but, having failed, they had fought their long-planned battle.

Out of all the region of war, of war to-day and war yesterday, one goes back to Nancy, to its busy streets, its crowds of people returning from their day's work. War is less than fifteen miles away, but Nancy is as calm as London is nervous. Its bakers still make macaroons; even Taube raids do not excuse the children from punctual attendance at school. Nancy is calm with the calmness of all France, but with just a touch of something more than calmness, which forty-six years of living by an open frontier brings. Twenty-one months ago it was the gauge of battle, and half a million men fought for it; a new German drive may approach it at any time. Out toward the old frontier there is still a German gun, hidden in the Forest of Bézange, which has turned one block to ashes and may fire again at any hour. Zeppelins have come and gone, leaving dead women and children behind them, but Nancy goes on with to-day.

And to-morrow? In the hearts of all the people of this beautiful city there is a single and a simple faith. Nancy turns her face toward the ancient frontier, she looks hopefully out upon the shell-swept Grand-Couronne and beyond to the Promised Land. And the people say to you if you ask them about war and about peace, as one of them said to me: "Peace will come, but not until we have our ancient frontier, not until we have Metz and Strasbourg. We have waited a long time, is it not so?"

END OF VOLUME ONE

THE COUNTRY LIFE PRESS
GARDEN CITY, N.Y.

Date Due
